T0235369

Lecture Notes in Computer Science   9564

Commenced Publication in 1973
Founding and Former Series Editors:
Gerhard Goos, Juris Hartmanis, and Jan van Leeuwen

Editorial Board

David Hutchison
  Lancaster University, Lancaster, UK
Takeo Kanade
  Carnegie Mellon University, Pittsburgh, PA, USA
Josef Kittler
  University of Surrey, Guildford, UK
Jon M. Kleinberg
  Cornell University, Ithaca, NY, USA
Friedemann Mattern
  ETH Zurich, Zürich, Switzerland
John C. Mitchell
  Stanford University, Stanford, CA, USA
Moni Naor
  Weizmann Institute of Science, Rehovot, Israel
C. Pandu Rangan
  Indian Institute of Technology, Madras, India
Bernhard Steffen
  TU Dortmund University, Dortmund, Germany
Demetri Terzopoulos
  University of California, Los Angeles, CA, USA
Doug Tygar
  University of California, Berkeley, CA, USA
Gerhard Weikum
  Max Planck Institute for Informatics, Saarbrücken, Germany

More information about this series at http://www.springer.com/series/7409

Adam Wierzbicki · Ulrik Brandes
Frank Schweitzer · Dino Pedreschi (Eds.)

Advances in Network Science

12th International Conference and School, NetSci-X 2016
Wroclaw, Poland, January 11–13, 2016
Proceedings

 Springer

Editors
Adam Wierzbicki
Polish-Japanese Academy
Warzaw
Poland

Frank Schweitzer
ETH Zürich
Zürich
Switzerland

Ulrik Brandes
Universität Konstanz
Konstanz, Baden-Württemberg
Germany

Dino Pedreschi
University of Pisa
Pisa
Italy

ISSN 0302-9743   ISSN 1611-3349   (electronic)
Lecture Notes in Computer Science
ISBN 978-3-319-28360-9   ISBN 978-3-319-28361-6   (eBook)
DOI 10.1007/978-3-319-28361-6

Library of Congress Control Number: 2015958855

LNCS Sublibrary: SL3 – Information Systems and Applications, incl. Internet/Web, and HCI

© Springer International Publishing Switzerland 2016
This work is subject to copyright. All rights are reserved by the Publisher, whether the whole or part of the material is concerned, specifically the rights of translation, reprinting, reuse of illustrations, recitation, broadcasting, reproduction on microfilms or in any other physical way, and transmission or information storage and retrieval, electronic adaptation, computer software, or by similar or dissimilar methodology now known or hereafter developed.
The use of general descriptive names, registered names, trademarks, service marks, etc. in this publication does not imply, even in the absence of a specific statement, that such names are exempt from the relevant protective laws and regulations and therefore free for general use.
The publisher, the authors and the editors are safe to assume that the advice and information in this book are believed to be true and accurate at the date of publication. Neither the publisher nor the authors or the editors give a warranty, express or implied, with respect to the material contained herein or for any errors or omissions that may have been made.

Printed on acid-free paper

This Springer imprint is published by SpringerNature
The registered company is Springer International Publishing AG Switzerland

Preface

Network science is an emerging discipline concerned with the study of network models in domains ranging from biology and physics to computer science, from financial markets to cultural integration, and from social media to infectious diseases. It is also an essential tool in the understanding of many kinds of big data, leading to numerous practical applications. Network models help researchers and practitioners make sense of an increasingly complex world, especially regarding social phenomena mediated through information technology. This volume contains several contributions to research in the area of network science, selected from the best submissions to the NetSci-X 2016 conference. The conference acceptance rate for full papers was 20 %. The International Conference and School of Network Science (NetSci) is an interdisciplinary event, gathering all researchers interested in network science. After 11 editions, the conference is the largest and best known event in the area. Published for the first time in the *Lecture Notes in Computer Science* series, the volume preserves the interdisciplinary character of network science, while emphasizing its connection to computer science. Works of researchers of various backgrounds, such as the social sciences, biology, economics, and computer science, unite in the aim for a better understanding of complex networks. The development of better models of complex phenomena, such as complex networks, is in itself an important contribution to computer science. The use of such computational models can enhance existing information technology, as well as expand the scope of applications of information technology into new areas. For this reason, the study of network science can be beneficial to computer scientists, and advances in network science can be considered as advances in computer science.

November 2016

Adam Wierzbicki
Ulrik Brandes
Frank Schweitzer
Dino Pedreschi

Organization

NetSci-X 2016 was organized by the Department of Computational Intelligence, Faculty of Computer Science and Management, Wrocław University of Technology.

Executive Committee

General Chairs

Przemysław Kazienko	Wrocław University of Technology, Poland
Bolesław Szymański	Rensselaer Polytechnic Institute, USA

Steering Committee

Albert-László Barabási	Northeastern University, USA
Raissa D'Souza	University of California, USA
Ronaldo Menezes	Florida Institute of Technology, USA

Program Chairs

János Kertész	Central European University, Hungary
Renaud Lambiotte	University of Namur, Belgium
Maxi San Miguel	University of the Balearic Islands, Spain
Ulrik Brandes	University of Konstanz, Germany
Dino Pedreschi	University of Pisa, Italy
Frank Schweitzer	ETH Zurich, Switzerland
Adam Wierzbicki	Polish-Japanese Institute for Information Technology, Poland
Tao Jia	Southwest University, China
Michael Mäs	University of Groningen, The Netherlands
Radosław Michalski	Wrocław University of Technology, Poland

School and Tools Chair

Mikołaj Morzy	Poznań University of Technology, Poland

Exhibition Chair

Ronaldo Menezes	Florida Institute of Technology, USA

Executive Chair

Piotr Bródka	Wrocław University of Technology, Poland

Publicity Chair

Radosław Nielek	Polish-Japanese Institute of Information Technology, Poland

Publication Chair

Paulina Adamska   Polish-Japanese Institute of Information Technology,
                            Poland

Organizing Committee

Tomasz Kajdanowicz   Wrocław University of Technology, Poland
Radosław Michalski   Wrocław University of Technology, Poland

Program Committee

Maria Bielikova   Slovak University of Technology in Bratislava,
                            Slovakia
Mingming Chen   Rensselaer Polytechnic Institute, RPI, USA
Freddy Chong Tat Chua   HP Labs
Michele Coscia   National Research Council, Pisa, Italy
Ernesto Damiani   University of Milan, Italy
Pasquale De Meo   VU University, Amsterdam, The Netherlands
Schahram Dustdar   TU Wien, Austria
Elena Ferrari   University of Insubria, Italy
David Garcia   ETH Zurich, Switzerland
Jarosław Jankowski   West Pomeranian University of Technology, Poland
Mark Jelasity   University of Szeged, Hungary
Jarosław Kozlak   AGH University of Science and Technology, Poland
Konstantin Kuzmin   Rensselaer Polytechnic Institute, RPI, USA
Cheng-Te Li   Research Center for IT Innovation, Academia Sinica,
                            Taiwan
Gang Li   School of Information Technology, Deakin University
Matteo Magnani   Uppsala University, Sweden
Konstantinos Mersinas   Royal Holloway University of London, UK
Katarzyna Musial   King's College London, UK
Stanisław Saganowski   Wrocław University of Technology, Poland
Arun Sen   Arizona State University, USA
Rajesh Sharma   University of Bologna, Italy
Vaclav Snasel   VSB-Technical University of Ostrava, Czech Republic
Toyohide Watanabe   Nagoya Industrial Science Research Institute, Japan
Katarzyna Wegrzyn-Wolska   ESIGETEL
Katharina Anna Zweig   University of Technology and Science Kaiserslautern,
                            Germany
Anna Zygmunt   AGH
Sen Wu   Stanford University, USA
Michael Szell   Northeastern University, USA
Jeff Johnson   Open University, UK
Chenliang Li   Wuhan University, China
Jari Saramäki   Aalto University, Finland

Sven Kosub	Universität Konstanz, Germany
Tim Evans	Imperial College London, UK
Bettina Berendt	K.U. Leuven, Belgium
Kristian Kersting	TU Dortmund University, Germany
Ingo Scholtes	ETH Zurich, Switzerland
John Yen	The Pennsylvania State University, USA
Sergio Gomez	Universitat Rovira i Virgili, Spain
Matthieu Latapy	CNRS, France
Derek Greene	University College Dublin, Ireland
Marton Karsai	ENS de Lyon, France
Ginestra Bianconi	Queen Mary University, UK
Yamir Moreno	Universidad de Zaragoza, Spain
Javier Borge-Holthoefer	QCRI - Qatar Computing Research Institute, Qatar
Bernie Hogan	University of Oxford, UK
Szymon Jaroszewicz	Polish Academy of Sciences, Poland
Marek Kopel	Wrocław University of Technology, Poland

Additional Reviewers

M. Ortmann	M. Bockholt	J. Lerner
S. Tavassoli	S. Liu	M. Abufouda
M. Kleinbauer	E. De Panafieu	

Sponsoring Institutions

This conference was organized within the European Union's Seventh Framework Programme for research, technological development and demonstration under grant agreement no. 316097 [ENGINE].

Contents

Quad Census Computation: Simple, Efficient, and Orbit-Aware

Mark Ortmann[(⊠)] and Ulrik Brandes[(⊠)]

Department of Computer and Information Science,
University of Konstanz, Konstanz, Germany
{Mark.Ortmann,Ulrik.Brandes}@uni-konstanz.de

Abstract. The prevalence of select substructures is an indicator of network effects in applications such as social network analysis and systems biology. Moreover, subgraph statistics are pervasive in stochastic network models, and they need to be assessed repeatedly in MCMC sampling and estimation algorithms. We present a new approach to count all induced and non-induced 4-node subgraphs (the quad census) on a per-node and per-edge basis, complete with a separation into their non-automorphic roles in these subgraphs. It is the first approach to do so in a unified manner, and is based on only a clique-listing subroutine. Computational experiments indicate that, despite its simplicity, the approach outperforms previous, less general approaches.

1 Introduction

The $\mathcal{F}$-census of a graph is the frequency distribution of subgraphs from a family $\mathcal{F}$ of non-isomorphic graphs in an input graph. In this work we focus on four node subgraphs, i.e. *quads*.

Discrimination of graphs by a subgraph census was proposed already by Holland and Leinhardt [7,8] in the context of social networks and it is of utmost importance for the effects of exponential random graph models [20]. While there is extensive work on determining the subgraph census for varying subgraph sizes [9,10,12] and also for directed graphs [4], the focus is almost always on the global distribution, i.e., say, the number of triangles a graph contains but not how often a given node is part of a triangle. However, for many properties describing nodes and edges, respectively, it is necessary to know the subgraph census on a node or edge level basis. For example to calculate a node's *clustering coefficient* we need to know in how many triangles it is contained. The same holds for the *Jaccard index* computed with respect to an edge. Although, for these two examples it is not necessary to calculate the frequencies of all non-isomorphic induced 3-node subgraphs, the triad census, there exist edge weights that take different subgraph configurations into account [1] and the running time for most edge metrics [14] is dominated by calculating the frequencies of particular subgraphs.

We gratefully acknowledge financial support from Deutsche Forschungsgemeinschaft under grant Br 2158/11-1.

© Springer International Publishing Switzerland 2016
A. Wierzbicki et al. (Eds.): NetSci-X 2016, LNCS 9564, pp. 1–13, 2016.
DOI: 10.1007/978-3-319-28361-6_1

While k-subgraph censuses specific for nodes and edges are not used widely in social network analysis, this is different already for bioinformatics. So far, however, even here the use is restricted to connected k-node subgraphs, so called *graphlets* [19] or *motifs* [17].

A further differentiation of subgraph censuses consist in the distinction of node and edge automorphism classes (orbits) in each graphlet. For example, in a diamond (i.e. a complete 4-node graph with one missing edge), there are two node and edge orbits, see Fig. 1. The node orbits are defined by the nodes with degree 2, and those with degree 3, respectively. The edge orbits are determined by the edge connecting the nodes with degree 3, and all remaining edges, respectively. Milenković and Pržulj [16] and Solova et al. [21] utilize the characterization of each node and edge respectively by it's orbit-aware connected subgraph census, which they call graphlet degree vector, for clustering purposes.

Due to the importance of subgraph enumeration and censuses in bioinformatics, various computational methods [6,13,15,23] were proposed.

The general approach to determine a subgraph census on the global level is to solve a system of equations that relates the non-induced subgraph frequency of each non-isomorphic k-node subgraph with the number of occurrences in other k-node subgraphs [4,5,9,10,12]. It is known that the time needed to solve the system of equations for the 4-node subgraph census, which we refer to as the *quad census*, on a global level is $\mathcal{O}(a(G)m + i(G))$ [12], where $i(G)$ is the time needed to calculate the frequency of a given 4-node induced subgraph in G, and $a(G)$ is the *arboricity*, i.e., the minimum number of spanning forest needed to cover E. Following the idea of relating non-induced and induced subgraph counts, Marcus and Shavitt [13] present a system of equations for the orbit-aware connected quad census on a node level that runs in $\mathcal{O}(\Delta(G)m + m^2)$ time with $\Delta(G)$ denoting the maximum degree of G. Because of the larger number of algorithms invoked by Marcus and Shavitt's approach, Hočevar and Demšar [6] present a different system of equations, again restricted to connected quads, that requires fewer counting algorithms and runs in $\mathcal{O}(\Delta(G)^2 m)$ time, but does not determine the non-induced counts.

Contribution: We present the first algorithm to count both induced and non-induced occurrences of all 4-node subgraphs (quads). It is based on a fast algorithm for listing a single quad type and capable of distinguishing the various roles (orbits) of nodes and edges. While this simplifies and generalizes previous approaches, our experimental evaluation indicates that it is also more efficient.

In the following section we provide basic notation followed by an introduction of the system of equations and the algorithm utilized in Sect. 3. In Sect. 4 we present a running time comparison on real world and synthetic graphs showing that our approach is more efficient than related methods. We conclude in Sect. 5.

2   Preliminaries

We consider finite simple undirected graphs $G = (V, E)$ and denote the number of nodes by $n = n(G) = |V|$ and the number of edges by $m = m(G) = |E|$. The *neighborhood* of a node $v \in V$ is the set $N(v) = \{w : \{v, w\} \in E\}$ of all adjacent nodes, its cardinality $d(v) = |N(v)|$ is called the *degree* of v, and $\Delta(G) = \max_{v \in V}\{d(v)\}$ denotes the maximum degree of G.

For finite simple directed graphs $G = (V, E)$ we denote the *outgoing neighborhood* of a node $v \in V$ by $N^+(v) = \{w : (v, w) \in E\}$. The *incoming neighborhood* $N^-(v)$ is defined analogously.

A complete graph with k nodes is called K_k and K_3 is also called a *triangle*. We use $T(u) = \{\binom{N(u)}{2}\} \cap E\}$ to refer to the set of node pairs completing a triangle with u and $T(\{u, v\}) = N(u) \cap N(v)$ for the set of nodes completing a triangle with the edge $e = \{u, v\}$. For the cardinality of these sets we write $t(u) = |T(u)|$ and $t(e) = |T(e)|$. A *triad* or a *quad* are any graphs on exactly three or four nodes, respectively.

A subgraph $G' = (V', E')$ of $G = (V, E)$, $V' \subseteq V$, is called (node-)*induced*, if $E' = \binom{V'}{2} \cap E$, and it is called *non-induced*, if $E' \subseteq \binom{V'}{2} \cap E$.

Two undirected graphs G and G' are said to be *isomorphic*, if and only if there exists a bijection $\pi : V(G) \rightarrow V(G')$ such that $\{v, w\} \in E(G) \iff \{\pi(v), \pi(w)\} \in E(G')$. Each permutation, including identity, of the node set V, such that the resulting graph is isomorphic to G is called an *automorphism* and the groups formed by the set of automorphisms is denoted *automorphism class* or *orbit*.

3   Determining the Orbit-Aware Quad Census

The k-node subgraph census is usually computed via a system of linear equations relating the non-induced and induced k-subgraph frequencies, as the non-induced frequencies are easier to compute. Lin et al. [12] show that for $k = 4$ all non-induced frequencies, except for K_4, can be computed in $\mathcal{O}(a(G)m)$ time. This implies that the total running time to calculate the quad census at the level of the entire graph is in $\mathcal{O}(a(G)m + i(G))$, where $i(G)$ is the time needed to compute the induced frequencies for any induced quad.

The approach of Lin et al., however, is not suitable to answer questions such as how often a node or an edge is contained in a K_4. Furthermore, the automorphism class of the node/edge in the quad is sometimes of interest. All non-isomorphic graphs with four nodes are shown in Fig. 1 and the node/edge labels refer to their automorphism classes (orbits). For example in a diamond all edges of the C_4 belong to the same orbit while the diagonal edge belongs to another. Analogously the orbits of the nodes can be distinguished.

As our approach also relies on relating non-induced and induced frequencies we will start by presenting how the non-induced frequencies for a node/edge in a given orbit relate to the induced counts. Thereafter, we will present formulas to compute the respective non-induced frequencies and prove that our approach

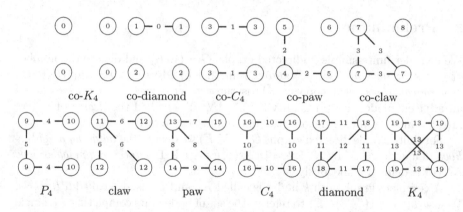

Fig. 1. All non-isomorphic subgraphs with four nodes (quads). Node and edge labels refer to the orbits and were enumerated such that each orbit is identified with a single quad

matches the running time of Lin et al., implying that it is asymptotically as fast as the fastest algorithm to compute the frequencies on a node and edge level for any induced quad. Note that in the following when we talk about non-induced frequencies we exclude those of the K_4, as it equals the induced frequency.

3.1 Relation of Induced and Non-induced Frequencies

To establish the relation between induced and non-induced frequencies, the number of times G' is non-induced in some other graph G with the same number of nodes has to be known. For instance, let us assume that G' is a P_3 and G a K_3 (co-paw and -claw without isolated node cf. Fig. 1). Having the definition of the edge set for non-induced subgraphs in mind we see that G contains three non-induced P_3, as each edge can be removed from a K_3 to create a P_3. Consequently, if we know the total number of non-induced P_3 and we subtract three times the number of K_3 we obtain the number of induced P_3 of the input graph.

Similarly, we can establish systems of equations relating induced and non-induced frequencies on a node and edge level distinguishing the orbits for quads, see Figs. 3 and 4. Note that both systems of equations are needed since we cannot compute the node from the edge frequencies and vice versa, but from both we can compute the global distribution. In the following we show the correctness for $ei_{10}(e)$.

Induced Orbit 10 Edge Census. Let us assume we want to know how often edge e is in orbit 10 or in other words part of a C_4. We know that a C_4 is a non-induced subgraph of a diamond, K_4 and of itself, cf. Fig. 2, and that there is no other quad containing a non-induced C_4. Let us first concentrate on the diamond. In a diamond we have two different edge orbits; orbit 11, i.e. the edges on the C_4, and orbit 12, i.e. the diagonal edge. Figure 2 shows that for every diamond where e is in orbit 12 there is no way to remove an edge, such that this graph becomes a C_4, but for each diamond where e is in orbit 11 we can remove the diagonal

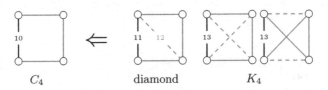

Fig. 2. The three quads containing a non-induced C_4. Dashed lines indicate that their removal creates an C_4. Edge label correspond to orbits

edge and end up with a C_4. Therefore, the non-induced number of subgraphs where e is in orbit 10 contains once the number of induced subgraphs where e is in orbit 11, but not those in orbit 12. As for the case of the C_4 in a K_4 all edges are in the same orbit. From a K_4 we can construct a C_4 in two ways. The first is to remove both diagonal edges, cf. Fig. 2; and the second to delete the two horizontal edges. As a consequence the induced number of e being in orbit 10 is given by $ei_{10}(e) = en_{10}(e) - ei_{11}(e) - 2ei_{13}(e)$.

Following this concept all other equations can be derived.

3.2 Calculating Non-induced Frequencies

The calculation of the non-induced frequencies is (computationally) easier than for the corresponding induced counts, except for K_4s. This is due to the fact that the non-induced frequencies can be constructed from smaller, with respect to the number of nodes, subgraphs. In the following we show the correctness of $nn_{14}(u)$ and $en_4(u, v)$.

Non-induced Orbit 14 Node Census. To determine $nn_{14}(u)$ we start by enumerating all triangles containing u. Let v and w form a triangle together with u. As u is in orbit 14 we know that each neighbor of v and w that is not u, v or w definitely creates a non-induced paw with u in orbit 14. While this does not necessarily hold for neighbors of u as they might not be connected to v or w (and, if they are, we already gave credit to this). Note that if x is a neighbor of u and v but not w we can only create one non-induced paw with u in orbit 14 and therefore $nn_{14}(u) = \sum_{\{v,w\} \in T(u)} (d(u) - d(v) - 4)$.

Non-induced Orbit 4 Edge Census. Edge $e = \{u, v\}$ is non-induced in orbit 4 for each path of length 2 starting at u or v that does not contain e. The number of P_3s starting at u equals $\sum_{w \in N(u) \setminus v} d(w) - 1$. However, the node v might be a neighbor of w and therefore, there is a path of length two connecting u and v. Since this creates a 3-node subgraph, more precisely a triangle, and not a quad we have to adjust for this by subtracting twice the number of triangles containing e. Consequently, $en_4(u, v) = \sum_{w \in N(u)} d(w) + \sum_{w \in N(v)} d(w) - 2(d(u) + d(v)) + 2 - 2t(u, v)$.

In the following, we focus on the algorithm calculating all required frequencies to solve the systems of equations.

$$
\begin{bmatrix}
1&1&1&1&1&1&1&1&1&1&1&1&1&1\\
0&1&0&0&1&0&0&1&0&1&1&1&0&1\\
0&0&1&2&1&2&2&2&3&2&2&3&4&4\\
0&0&0&1&0&0&0&0&1&1&0&1&2&2\\
0&0&0&0&1&0&0&2&0&2&2&3&0&4\\
0&0&0&0&0&1&0&0&1&0&1&1&2&2\\
0&0&0&0&0&0&1&1&1&0&0&1&2&2\\
0&0&0&0&0&0&0&1&0&0&0&1&0&2\\
0&0&0&0&0&0&0&0&1&0&0&1&4&4\\
0&0&0&0&0&0&0&0&0&1&0&1&0&2\\
0&0&0&0&0&0&0&0&0&0&1&1&0&2\\
0&0&0&0&0&0&0&0&0&0&0&1&0&4\\
0&0&0&0&0&0&0&0&0&0&0&0&1&1\\
0&0&0&0&0&0&0&0&0&0&0&0&0&1
\end{bmatrix}
\begin{bmatrix}
ei_0(u,v)\\
ei_1(u,v)\\
ei_2(u,v)\\
ei_3(u,v)\\
ei_4(u,v)\\
ei_5(u,v)\\
ei_6(u,v)\\
ei_7(u,v)\\
ei_8(u,v)\\
ei_9(u,v)\\
ei_{10}(u,v)\\
ei_{11}(u,v)\\
ei_{12}(u,v)\\
ei_{13}(u,v)
\end{bmatrix}
=
\begin{bmatrix}
en_0(u,v) = \binom{n-2}{2}\\
en_1(u,v) = m - d(u) - d(v) + 1\\
en_2(u,v) = (d(u)+d(v)-2)(n-3))\\
en_3(u,v) = t(u,v)(n-3)\\
en_4(u,v) = \sum_{w\in N(u)} d(w) + \sum_{w\in N(v)} d(w) - 2(d(u)+d(v)) + 2 - 2t(u,v)\\
en_5(u,v) = (d(u)-1)(d(v)-1) - t(u,v)\\
en_6(u,v) = \binom{d(u)-1}{2} + \binom{d(v)-1}{2}\\
en_7(u,v) = t(u) + t(v) - 2t(u,v)\\
en_8(u,v) = t(u,v)\cdot(d(u)+d(v)-4)\\
en_9(u,v) = \sum_{w\in T(u,v)} d(w) - 2t(u,v)\\
en_{10}(u,v) = |(N(u)\setminus v \times N(v)\setminus u) \cap E|\\
en_{11}(u,v) = \sum_{w\in T(u,v)} t(u,w) + t(v,w) - 2t(u,v)\\
en_{12}(u,v) = \binom{t(u,v)}{2}\\
en_{13}(u,v) = \text{Alg. K4}
\end{bmatrix}
$$

Fig. 3. System of equations for orbit aware quad census on a edge level. ei refers to the induced and en non-induced counts

$$
\begin{bmatrix}
1&1&1&1&1&1&1&1&1&1&1&1&1&1&1&1&1&1&1&1\\
0&1&0&1&2&1&0&2&0&2&1&3&1&3&2&1&2&2&3&3\\
0&0&1&1&2&1&0&2&0&2&1&3&1&1&2&3&2&3&2&3\\
0&0&0&1&0&0&0&0&1&1&0&0&1&1&1&2&2&2&3\\
0&0&0&1&0&0&1&0&1&0&3&0&3&1&0&1&1&3&3\\
0&0&0&0&0&1&0&2&0&1&1&0&2&2&3&2&2&4&4&6\\
0&0&0&0&0&0&1&0&3&0&1&0&1&0&1&3&1&3&1&3\\
0&0&0&0&0&0&0&1&0&0&0&0&1&1&0&0&1&2&3\\
0&0&0&0&0&0&0&1&0&0&0&0&0&1&0&1&0&1\\
0&0&0&0&0&0&0&0&1&0&0&0&2&1&0&2&2&4&6\\
0&0&0&0&0&0&0&0&0&1&0&0&0&1&2&2&4&2&6\\
0&0&0&0&0&0&0&0&0&0&1&0&1&0&0&0&0&1&1\\
0&0&0&0&0&0&0&0&0&0&0&1&0&1&1&0&2&1&3\\
0&0&0&0&0&0&0&0&0&0&0&0&1&0&0&0&0&2&3\\
0&0&0&0&0&0&0&0&0&0&0&0&0&1&0&0&2&2&6\\
0&0&0&0&0&0&0&0&0&0&0&0&0&0&1&0&2&0&3\\
0&0&0&0&0&0&0&0&0&0&0&0&0&0&0&1&1&1&3\\
0&0&0&0&0&0&0&0&0&0&0&0&0&0&0&0&1&0&3\\
0&0&0&0&0&0&0&0&0&0&0&0&0&0&0&0&0&1&3\\
0&0&0&0&0&0&0&0&0&0&0&0&0&0&0&0&0&0&1
\end{bmatrix}
\begin{bmatrix}
ni_0(u)\\
ni_1(u)\\
ni_2(u)\\
ni_3(u)\\
ni_4(u)\\
ni_5(u)\\
ni_6(u)\\
ni_7(u)\\
ni_8(u)\\
ni_9(u)\\
ni_{10}(u)\\
ni_{11}(u)\\
ni_{12}(u)\\
ni_{13}(u)\\
ni_{14}(u)\\
ni_{15}(u)\\
ni_{16}(u)\\
ni_{17}(u)\\
ni_{18}(u)\\
ni_{19}(u)
\end{bmatrix}
=
\begin{bmatrix}
nn_0(u) = \binom{n-1}{3}\\
nn_1(u) = \binom{n-2}{2}d(u)\\
nn_2(u) = (m - d(u))\cdot(n-3)\\
nn_3(u) = (\sum_{v\in N(u)} m - d(u)) - d(u)\cdot(d(u)-1)\\
nn_4(u) = \binom{d(u)}{2}(n-3)\\
nn_5(u) = ((\sum_{v\in N(u)} d(v)) - d(u))\cdot(n-3)\\
nn_6(u) = \sum_{v\in V} \binom{d(v)}{2} - ((\sum_{v\in N(u)} d(v)) - d(u)) - \binom{d(u)}{2}\\
nn_7(u) = t(u)\cdot(n-3)\\
nn_8(u) = \tfrac{1}{3}\sum_{v\in V} t(v) - t(u)\\
nn_9(u) = \sum_{v\in N(u)}(d(u)-1)\cdot(d(v)-1) - t(u,v)\\
nn_{10}(u) = (\sum_{v\in N(u)}(\sum_{w\in N(v)} d(w)) - d(v)) - d(u)\cdot(d(u)-1)\\
nn_{11}(u) = \binom{d(u)}{3}\\
nn_{12}(u) = \sum_{v\in N(u)} \binom{d(v)-1}{2}\\
nn_{13}(u) = t(u)\cdot(d(u)-2)\\
nn_{14}(u) = \sum_{\{v,w\}\in T(u)}(d(v)+d(w)-4)\\
nn_{15}(u) = \sum_{v\in N(u)} t(v) - t(u,v)\\
nn_{16}(u) = \sum_{\{v,w\}\in\binom{N(u)}{2}} |N(v)\cap N(w)| - 1\\
nn_{17}(u) = \sum_{\{v,w\}\in T(u)} t(v,w) - t(u)\\
nn_{18}(u) = \sum_{v\in N(u)} \binom{t(u,v)}{2}\\
nn_{19}(u) = \text{Alg. K4}
\end{bmatrix}
$$

Fig. 4. System of equations for orbit aware quad census on a node level. ni refers to the induced and nn non-induced counts

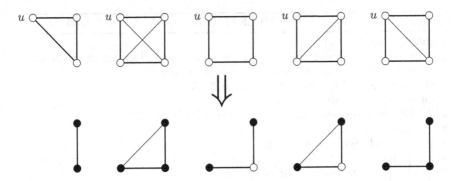

Fig. 5. Top: Configurations that have to be found by our algorithm. Bottom: Resulting patterns to be detected when processing node u. Filled nodes are marked as neighbors of u

3.3 Listing Complete Quads

In order to be able to solve the systems of equations we need to compute the non-induced quad counts as well as any of the induced frequencies. This requires an algorithm that is capable of solving the following tasks on a node and edge level:

1. Counting and listing all K_3.
2. Calculating non-induced C_4 frequencies.
3. Determine induced counts of any quad.

We chose to calculate the induced counts for K_4 to fulfill requirement 3. The reasons are (a) to our knowledge there are no algorithms calculating induced counts on a node and edge level for any other quad more efficiently than the algorithm we are presenting here; (b) a K_4 has the property that all nodes and edges lie in the same orbit; (c) all non-induced C_4 can be counted during the execution of our algorithm. Since listing, also known as enumerating, all K_4 has to solve the subproblem of listing all K_3 we will start explaining our algorithm by presenting how K_3s can be listed efficiently. Note that this algorithm satisfies requirement 1.

Listing all triangles in a graph is a well studied topic [18]. We show in our previous work [18] that one of the oldest triangle listing algorithms, namely K3 by Chiba and Nishizeki [3] is in practice the fastest. This algorithm is based on neighborhood intersection computations. To achieve the running time of $\mathcal{O}(a(G)m)$ Chiba and Nishizeki process the graph in a way, such that for each intersection only the neighborhood of the smaller degree node has to be scanned. This is done by processing the nodes sequentially in decreasing order of their degree. The currently processed node marks all its neighbors and is removed from the graph. Then the number of marked neighbors of a marked node is calculated.

Let us think of this algorithm differently. When we process node u and remove it from the graph then every triangle that contains u is an edge where both endpoints are marked, cf. Fig. 5. This perception of the algorithm directly points

---

Algorithm 1. K3 / C4 / COMPLETE (Chiba and Nishizeki 1985 [3])

---

1 initialize $mark$ with 0;
2 order nodes by successively removing the node of min. degree from the graph;
3 orient G and sort adjacencies according node ordering;
4 calculate $t(u)$ and $t(e)$ using K3; // line 5-15
5 **for** $u = v_2, \ldots, v_n$ **do**
6 $\quad$ **for** $v \in N^-(u)$ **do** $mark(v) \leftarrow mark(v) + 1$;
7 $\quad$ **for** $v \in N^-(u)$ **do**
8 $\quad\quad$ $mark(v) \leftarrow mark(v) - 1$;
9 $\quad\quad$ **for** $w \in \{w \in N(v) : w < u\}$ **do**
10 $\quad\quad\quad$ $visited(w) \leftarrow visited(w) + 1$;
11 $\quad\quad\quad$ $processed(w) \leftarrow processed(w) + 1$;
12 $\quad\quad$ **for** $w \in \{w \in N^+(v) : w < u\}$ **do** $mark(w) \leftarrow mark(w) + 2$;
13 $\quad\quad$ **for** $w \in \{w \in N^+(v) : w < u\}$ **do**
14 $\quad\quad\quad$ $mark(w) \leftarrow mark(w) - 2$;
15 $\quad\quad\quad$ **if** $mark(w) \neq 0$ **then**
16 $\quad\quad\quad\quad$ increment K_3 related non-induced counts;
17 $\quad\quad\quad\quad$ **for** $x \in \{x \in N^+(w) : x < u\}$ **do**
18 $\quad\quad\quad\quad\quad$ **if** $mark(x) = 3$ **then**
19 $\quad\quad\quad\quad\quad\quad$ increment induced K_4 count;

20 $\quad$ **for** $v \in N^-(u)$ **do**
21 $\quad\quad$ **for** $w \in \{w \in N(v) : w < u\}$ **do**
22 $\quad\quad\quad$ $processed(w) \leftarrow processed(w) - 1$;
23 $\quad\quad\quad$ **if** $processed(w) = 0$ **then**
24 $\quad\quad\quad\quad$ increment non-induced C_4 of u and w by $\binom{visited(w)}{2}$;
25 $\quad\quad\quad\quad$ $visited(w) \leftarrow 0$;
26 $\quad\quad\quad$ increment non-induced C_4 of $\{u, v\}, \{v, w\}$ and v by $visited(w) - 1$;

27 solve system of equations;

---

us to a solution for the second and third requirement. As shown in Fig. 5, when node u is removed from the graph, every K_4 that contains u becomes a K_3 where all nodes are marked, implying that K3 can be easily adapted to list all K_4s. Chiba and Nishizeki call this extension COMPLETE. Furthermore, only nodes that are connected to a neighbor of u can create a non-induced C_4 and each C_4 contains at least two marked nodes. Since all these nodes are processed already during the execution of algorithm K3 counting non-induced C_4 on a node and edge level can be also done in $\mathcal{O}(a(G)m)$ time. The corresponding algorithm is called C4 in [3] and the combination of these different algorithms is presented in Algorithm 1. It runs in $\mathcal{O}(a(G)^2 m)$ [3], and its novelty is that it follows the idea of directing the graph acyclic as we already proposed in the context of triangle listing [18]. Furthermore, this acyclic orientation allows omitting node removals, and given the proper node ordering, it has the property that the maximum outdegree is bounded by $\mathcal{O}(a(G))$. Therefore, unlike for algorithm COMPLETE and C4 [3], no amortized running time analysis is of need to prove that the running time is in $\mathcal{O}(a(G)^2m)$ and $\mathcal{O}(a(G)m)$, respectively, as we will show next.

Runtime. We will first show that the running time bound of our variant implementation of algorithm C4 is in $\mathcal{O}(a(G)m)$, therefore we ignore lines 4, 6, 8, 12 – 19 and 27 of Algorithm 1 for now.

The running time of the remaining algorithm is given by the following equation:

$$t(\mathtt{C4}) \leq \sum_{u \in V} d^-(u) + 2 \sum_{v \in N^-(u)} d^-(v) + d^+(v)$$

$$= m + 2 \sum_{v \in V} d^+(v)(d^-(v) + d^+(v))$$

$$\leq m + 4m\Delta^+(G)$$

As we order the nodes by successively removing the node of minimum degree from the graph, which can be computed in $\mathcal{O}(m)$ using a slightly modified version of the algorithm presented in [2], it holds that $\Delta^+(G) < 2a(G)$ [24]. The time required to initialize all marks is in $\mathcal{O}(n)$, orienting the graph is in $\mathcal{O}(n + m)$, and consequently the total running time is in $\mathcal{O}(a(G)m)$.

Let us now focus on the time required for calculating all K_4s and therefore ignore lines 9 – 11 and 20–27 of Algorithm 1 that is given by the following equation:

$$t(\mathtt{COMPLETE}) \leq \sum_{u \in V} d^-(u) + \sum_{v \in N^-(u)} 2d^+(v) + \sum_{w \in N^+(v)} d^+(w)$$

$$\leq m + \Delta^+(G) \sum_{v \in V} 2d^+(v) + \sum_{w \in N^+(v)} d^+(w)$$

$$\leq m + 2m\Delta^+(G) + \Delta^+(G) \sum_{v \in V} d^-(v)\Delta^+(G)$$

$$= m + 2m\Delta^+(G) + m\Delta^+(G)^2$$

By the same arguments it follows that our variant implementation of COMPLETE runs in $\mathcal{O}(a(G)^2m)$. Since, line 4 is in $\mathcal{O}(a(G)m)$ [18] and solving the system of equations requires $\mathcal{O}(n + m)$ time, the overall complexity of Algorithm 1 is in $\mathcal{O}(a(G)^2m)$.

4   Runtime Experiments

We provide experimental evidence that our approach is not only asymptotically faster but also more efficient in practice than the currently fastest orbit-aware quad census algorithm. Comparison is restricted to the *orca software* implementing the approach of Hočevar and Demšar [6], as the authors show that it is superior to other software tools in the context of quad census computation.

Additionally, it is the only software we are aware of that can compute the orbit-aware quad census on an edge level, even if only for connected quads. To the best of our knowledge, except in the orca code, there is no other documentation of their approach.

4.1 Setup and Data

We implemented our approach in C++ using the *Standard Template Library* and compiled the code with the g++ compiler version 4.9.1 set to the highest optimization level. The *orca software* is freely available as an R package. To avoid measuring error due to the R and C++ interface communication we extracted the C++ code and cleaned it from all R dependencies.

The tests were carried out on a single 64-bit machine with an 3.60 GHz quad-core Intel Core i7-4790 CPU, 32 GB RAM, running Ubuntu 14.10. The times were measured via the gettimeofday command with a resolution up to 10^{-6} s. We ran the executable in a single thread and forced it to one single core, which was dedicated only to this process. Times were averaged over 5 repetitions.

Data. We compared both approaches on a number of real world networks. The *Facebook100 dataset* [22] comprises 100 Facebook friendship networks of higher educational institutes in the US with network sizes of $762 \leq n < 41K$ nodes and $16K < m < 1.6M$ edges. Although these networks are rather sparse they feature a small diameter, thereby implying a high concentration of connected quads. Apart from this we tested the algorithms on a variety of networks from the *Stanford Large Network Set Collection* [11]. The downloaded data were taken from different areas to have realistic examples that encompass diverse network structures.

Additionally, we generated synthetic networks from two different models. The one class of generated graphs are small-worlds, which were created by arranging nodes on a ring, connecting each one with its r nearest neighbors, and then switching each dyad with probability p. The other class of graphs are drawn from a preferential attachment like model. Here we added n nodes over time to the initially empty network and each new node connects to r existing nodes, each of which either chosen by preferential attachment or with probability p by random. We generated graphs with fixed $n = 20000$ and varying average degree as well as graphs with $n \in \{50000, 140000, \ldots, 500000\}$ and gradually increasing average degree. Four graphs were generated for each parameter combination.

We refer the reader to [18] for a more detailed description of the utilized graph models, the tested Stanford graphs, the chosen average degree, and parameters r and p.

4.2 Results

In Fig. 6 we present the results of our experiments. In the top subfigure we plotted the avg. time needed by our approach against the avg. running time of *orca* for all but the largest Standford graphs. Each point that lies below the

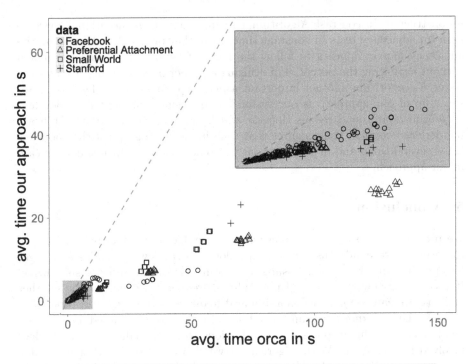

Graph	$|V|$	$|E|$	Alg. 1	orca	speedup
wiki-Talk	2 394 385	4 659 565	1m33s	7m41s	4.95
com-LiveJournal	3 997 962	34 681 189	2m47s	14m00s	5.00
soc-LiveJournal1	4 847 571	42 851 237	5m09s	24m33s	4.77
com-orkut	3 072 441	117 185 083	22m06s	109m52s	4.97

Fig. 6. Top: Avg. running time of *orca* vs. avg. running time of our approach in seconds for all but the largest SNAP graphs. Dots below the main diagonal indicate that the algorithm on the y-axis is faster. Embedded plot displays gray area in higher resolution. Bottom: Time comparison for the largest SNAP graphs

main diagonal indicates that our approach is faster than orca. Consequently, the picture makes it clear that our algorithm is faster than the *orca software* for each tested network, even though we compute the whole node and edge orbit aware quad census. The same findings are obtained for the larger graphs taken from SNAP.

The speed-up we achieve lies between 1.6 and 10 for the tested graphs. In general, however, the speed-up should be in $\Theta(\log \Delta(G))$ for larger graphs. The reason is that, once n exceeds $30K$, the algorithm implemented in the orca software runs in $\mathcal{O}(\Delta(G)^2 m \log \Delta(G))$, instead of $\mathcal{O}(\Delta(G)^2 m)$. The logarithmic factor originates from the time required for adjacency testing. While the orca software uses an adjacency matrix for these queries for graphs with $n \leq 30K$, it takes $\mathcal{O}(\log \Delta(G))$ for larger graphs (binary search) since no adjacency matrix is constructed. In contrast Algorithm 1 requires only $\mathcal{O}(n)$ additional space to perform adjacency tests in constant time. Note that orca's algorithm using the adjacency matrix appears to follow the ideas of Chiba and Nishizeki, though without exploiting the potential of utilizing a proper node ordering. Besides the faster K_4 algorithm another important aspect explaining the at least constant speed-up of our approach is our system of equations. For both the node and edge orbit-aware quad census Hočevar and Demšar do not calculate the exact non-induced counts. This requires that each induced subgraph with 3 nodes is listed several times and more importantly also non-cliques, which is not the case in our approach.

5 Conclusion

We presented two systems of equations that enable us to efficiently determine the orbit-aware quad census of a graph down to the level of nodes and edges by applying an efficient single-subgraph listing algorithm and it's subroutine. It was shown how induced and non-induced frequencies relate to one another and that we can compute the non-induced frequencies in $\mathcal{O}(a(G)m)$ time. This matches the best known running time bound for the more restricted non-induced quad census on the graph level, i.e., oblivious to the specific nodes and edges involved in each quad. With Algorithm 1 we showed a routine that is capable of computing all non-induced frequencies and listing all K_4 while running in $\mathcal{O}(a(G)^2 m)$ time, which is the asymptotically best known running time bound for listing any induced quad. This implies that the total running time of our approach matches the best known running time for quad census computation on a graph level in sparse graphs [12]. In experiments we were able to show that the simplicity of our system of equations in combination with this efficient algorithm outperforms the currently best software to calculate the quad census. We point out that Algorithm 1 can be parallelized with little effort and by following the same technique our orbit aware quad census can be extended to directed graphs.

References

1. Auber, D., Chiricota, Y., Jourdan, F., Melançon, G.: Multiscale visualization of small world networks. In: 9th IEEE Symposium on Information Visualization (Info-Vis 2003), 20–21 October 2003, Seattle, WA, USA (2003)
2. Batagelj, V., Mrvar, A.: A subquadratic triad census algorithm for large sparse networks with small maximum degree. Soc. Netw. **23**(3), 237–243 (2001)
3. Chiba, N., Nishizeki, T.: Arboricity and subgraph listing algorithms. SIAM J. Comput. **14**(1), 210–223 (1985)
4. Eppstein, D., Goodrich, M.T., Strash, D., Trott, L.: Extended dynamic subgraph statistics using h-index parameterized data structures. Theoret. Comput. Sci. **447**, 44–52 (2012). doi:10.1016/j.tcs.2011.11.034
5. Eppstein, D., Spiro, E.S.: The h-index of a graph and its application to dynamic subgraph statistics. In: Dehne, F., Gavrilova, M., Sack, J.-R., Tóth, C.D. (eds.) WADS 2009. LNCS, vol. 5664, pp. 278–289. Springer, Heidelberg (2009)

6. Hočevar, T., Demšar, J.: A combinatorial approach to graphlet counting. Bioinformatics **30**(4), 559–565 (2014)
7. Holland, P.W., Leinhardt, S.: A method for detecting structure in sociometric data. Am. J. Sociol. **76**(3), 492–513 (1970)
8. Holland, P.W., Leinhardt, S.: Local structure in social networks. Sociol. Methodol. **7**, 1–45 (1976)
9. Kloks, T., Kratsch, D., Müller, H.: Finding and counting small induced subgraphs efficiently. Inf. Process. Lett. **74**(3–4), 115–121 (2000)
10. Kowaluk, M., Lingas, A., Lundell, E.: Counting and detecting small subgraphs via equations and matrix multiplication. In: Proceedings of the Twenty-Second Annual ACM-SIAM Symposium on Discrete Algorithms, SODA 2011, San Francisco, California, USA, 23–25 January 2011, pp. 1468–1476 (2011)
11. Leskovec, J., Krevl, A.: SNAP Datasets: stanford large network dataset collection, June 2014. http://snap.stanford.edu/data
12. Lin, M.C., Soulignac, F.J., Szwarcfiter, J.L.: Arboricity, h-index, and dynamic algorithms. Theor. Comput. Sci. **426**, 75–90 (2012)
13. Marcus, D., Shavitt, Y.: RAGE - A rapid graphlet enumerator for large networks. Comput. Netw. **56**(2), 810–819 (2012)
14. Melançon, G., Sallaberry, A.: Edge metrics for visual graph analytics: a comparative study. In: 12th International Conference on Information Visualisation, IV 2008, 8–11 July 2008, London, UK, pp. 610–615 (2008)
15. Milenković, T., Lai, J., Pržulj, N.: GraphCrunch: a tool for large network analyses. BMC Bioinformatics **9**(70), 1–11 (2008)
16. Milenković, T., Pržulj, N.: Uncovering biological network function via graphlet degree signatures. Cancer Inf. **6**, 257–273 (2008)
17. Milo, R., Shen-Orr, S., Itzkovitz, S., Kashtan, N., Chklovskii, D., Alon, U.: Network motifs: simple building blocks of complex networks. Science **298**(5594), 824–827 (2002)
18. Ortmann, M., Brandes, U.: Triangle listing algorithms: back from the diversion. In: 2014 Proceedings of the Sixteenth Workshop on Algorithm Engineering and Experiments, ALENEX 2014, Portland, Oregon, USA, 5 January 2014, pp. 1–8 (2014)
19. Pržulj, N., Corneil, D.G., Jurisica, I.: Modeling interactome: scale-free or geometric? Bioinformatics **20**(18), 3508–3515 (2004)
20. Robins, G., Pattison, P., Kalish, Y., Lusher, D.: An introduction to exponential random graph (p^*) models for social networks. Soc. Netw. **29**(2), 173–191 (2007)
21. Solava, R.W., Michaels, R.P., Milenković, T.: Graphlet-based edge clustering reveals pathogen-interacting proteins. Bioinformatics **28**(18), 480–486 (2012)
22. Traud, A.L., Kelsic, E.D., Mucha, P.J., Porter, M.A.: Comparing community structure to characteristics in online collegiate social networks. SIAM Rev. **53**(3), 526–543 (2011)
23. Wernicke, S., Rasche, F.: FANMOD: a tool for fast network motif detection. Bioinformatics **22**(9), 1152–1153 (2006)
24. Zhou, X., Nishizeki, T.: Edge-coloring and f-coloring for various classes of graphs. In: Du, D.Z., Zhang, X.S. (eds.) Algorithms and Computation. LNCS, vol. 834, pp. 199–207. Springer, Heidelberg (1994)

Posting Topics ≠ Reading Topics:
On Discovering Posting and Reading Topics in Social Media

Wei Gong[✉], Ee-Peng Lim, and Feida Zhu

School of Information Systems, Singapore Management University,
Singapore, Singapore
{wei.gong.2011,eplim,fdzhu}@smu.edu.sg

Abstract. Social media users make decisions about what content to post and read. As posted content is often visible to others, users are likely to impose self-censorship when deciding what content to post. On the other hand, such a concern may not apply to reading social media content. As a result, the topics of content that a user posted and read can be different and this has major implications to the applications that require personalization. To better determine and profile social media users' topic interests, we conduct a user survey in Twitter. In this survey, participants chose the topics they like to post (posting topics) and the topics they like to read (reading topics). We observe that users' posting topics differ from their reading topics significantly. We find that some topics such as "Religion", "Business" and "Politics" attract much more users to read than to post. With the ground truth data obtained from the survey, we further explore the discovery of users' posting and reading topics separately using features derived from their posted content, received content and social networks.

1 Introduction

Social media platforms such as Facebook and Twitter connect millions of users with very large social networks where they create, share and consume content. With regards to content generation and consumption, social media users perform essentially two main types of actions: *posting* and *reading*. Posting is a user action that generates content. For example, tweeting, retweeting and replying are the posting actions in Twitter. Reading, on the other hand, refers to content consumption which often does not generate any public data trace. In social media, some users post often. They are *active users*. Some other users prefer to read content only. When users demonstrate reading as their only actions, they are known as *lurkers* or *silent users* [9,20,24].

Users, active or silent, are individuals with topic interests. We call the topics a user likes to post the *posting topics* and the topics a user likes to read the *reading topics*. We postulate that posting topics are not the same as reading topics. This is because, when posting content in social media, users select what

© Springer International Publishing Switzerland 2016
A. Wierzbicki et al. (Eds.): NetSci-X 2016, LNCS 9564, pp. 14–28, 2016.
DOI: 10.1007/978-3-319-28361-6_2

content to post, to whom the content is shared [1,10], and may practise self-censorship when selecting and crafting the content [5,22]. In contrast, reading is typically invisible to others. Users therefore have less worries about how other people perceive them when reading online content. For example, a user interested in politics is likely to read political news and discussions, but may choose not to post political content to avoid unwanted disputes on some controversial issues. In the extreme case, some users may become lurkers who only read but not post.

As discovering user topic interests is important in many applications such as viral marketing, recommendation systems and targeted advertising [6,17,18], a number of studies have focused on predicting users' topic interests [7,19,23,26, 28]. While these studies contribute to the discovery of *general* topic interests of users, they do not distinguish between the posting and reading topics. We believe that differentiating user posting and reading topics is important to the above personalization applications. An application (viral marketing, for example) that requires users sharing information (e.g., news, products) with others should focus on the posting topics. A targeted advertising, on the other hand, needs to discover reading topics so as to select the ads that users are likely to pay attention to. To the best of our knowledge, the state of the art research has left out the posting and reading topic consideration, which in turn motivates this work.

Research Objectives. Our research aims to answer the following research questions: (a) how different are posting and reading topics? (b) are there topics that are more likely to be reading topics but not posting topics, and vice versa? (c) can we predict posting and reading topics accurately, and finally (d) can we predict lurkers' reading topics accurately?

This paper seeks to answer the above questions by focusing on Twitter platform and formulating two research goals. The first goal is to empirically study the posting and reading topics of Twitter users. In particular, we invest significant efforts in conducting a user survey involving 95 participants who are requested to declare their posting and reading topics. Our analysis of the survey data shows that the topics users like to post can be significantly different from the topics they like to read. We also find that "Politics", "Religion" and "Business" are some topics many users who like to read but not to post.

The second goal of this work seeks to discover user posting and reading topics. This task has two main challenges. First, social media companies may record user browsing history, but often do not make such data available to researchers. The lack of reading behavior data is thus a major challenge for reading topic discovery. Second, lurkers have very little posting behavior, and their reading behavior is also not available. Discovering reading topics for lurkers – who are potential customers and constitute a significant proportion of online users [9] – then becomes another big challenge. To achieve our goal with the limited user behavior data, we make use of users' historical content and following networks so as to develop different ranking strategies to rank user interested topics in posting and reading. We evaluate them using the ground truth data obtained from our survey. We find that predicting user reading topics can be as accurate as predicting user posting topics. We also demonstrate that although predicting lurkers' reading topics is harder than that of active users', we can still predict lurkers' reading topics with reasonable accuracy.

2   Related Work

Posting behavior is a direct way for a user to express herself. Previous studies have shown that social media users *select* what content to post and to whom [1,5,10,22]. For example, Hampton et al. [10] found that people are less willing to discuss a political issue in social media than in person, and people are less likely to express their views online if they believe they have views different from others. Some studies [5,22] showed that when selecting and crafting the content, users may practise self-censorship. Das and Kramer [5] examined 3.9 million Facebook users and found that 71 % of users exercised self-censorship to decide what content to share. Similarly, Sleeper et al. [22] found that Facebook users "thought about sharing but decided not to share". These studies suggest that users may not disclose their activities, emotions, opinions and topic interests when posting in social media.

Reading behavior refers to user actions that consume content. Previous studies on user behavior have showed that social media users spend much more time reading than posting [2,25]. Despite its prevalence, reading behavior has not been studied extensively like posting behavior [12]. It is partly due to a lack of publicly available data traces of user browsing history. Compared with posting content, users enjoy a higher level of privacy when reading online content. They can read content and choose not to share or discuss about it [20]. Thus, social media users may show different opinions, personal values, personalities and topic interests when come to posting and reading behaviors. However, earlier studies often analyze social media users by considering their posting behavior only [4,7,13,21,26], which may yield a biased understanding of the users. For these reasons, we analyze and discover social media users' topics interests by considering both their posting and reading behaviors.

The closest work of ours is probably [15], which studied the difference between user posting topics and the topics of user received content in Twitter. However, as point out in [11], Twitter users typically receive large number of tweets and are not likely to read them all. Thus in our case, we study the difference between user posting topics and reading topics which are the topics that users actually like to read.

3   Posting and Reading Topics

To assess the difference between Twitter user posting and reading topics, and obtain the ground truth for evaluating the methods of discovering user posting and reading topics, we conduct a user survey. In this section, we first describe the procedure of this survey. Next, we analyze the survey data and present the findings.

3.1 Survey Procedure

Participants in the survey should have used Twitter for some time and have some social connections. We thus require that all participants have their accounts for at least 3 months and each participant at the point of survey follows at least 10 other accounts and is followed by at least 5 other accounts. We sent a recruitment email to all undergraduate students of a Singapore's public university. We allowed both lurkers and active users to participate in this survey. We finally obtained survey results from 95 Twitter users including 49 protected accounts and 46 public accounts. Each participant received 10 Singapore dollars incentive for completing the survey.

In the survey, participants provided their Twitter account information[1] and activity data including how often they post (i.e., tweet) and how many tweets they read per day. Participants also rated a set of 23 topics (See Table 1 in Sect. 3.3) based on how much they like to post and read these topics. The possible ratings are "Like", "Somewhat Like", and "Do Not Like". We will describe how this set of topics are derived at the end of this section (see Sect. 3.3).

We then crawled all participants' tweets from March 1st to March 30th, 2015, their followers and followees using Twitter API. For the participants with public accounts, we can crawl their information directly. To collect the protected accounts' information, we first created a special Twitter account following the protected accounts and then crawled the protected accounts' tweets and social networks using the special account.

3.2 Survey Results and Findings

Twitter Use. Figure 1 shows Twitter posting and reading frequency distribution among the participants. In general, these participants read much more than they tweet. To check the reliability of the survey data, we compared the user declared posting frequency with the actual tweet history data from March 1st to March 30th, 2015. Figure 1(a) shows very similar distributions between survey data and tweet history data. It suggests that most of the participants provided information that tally with their actual posting frequencies in Twitter.

Difference Between Posting and Reading Topics. Next, we examine the difference between user posting and reading topics using our survey results. For clarity, we organize this analysis around four questions. The first question is: *What are the popular posting and reading topics?* Fig. 2 plots the posting and reading topics' popularity among the participants. A posting (reading) topic's popularity is the number of participants who like to post (read) the topic. We observe that some topics are popular (or unpopular) for both posting and reading. For example, "TV & Films" and "Music" are among the popular topics,

---

[1] Twitter accounts are considered as personal identifiable information, so we can not use Amazon Mechanical Turk (AMT) for conducting this survey. The restrictions of using AMT: https://requester.mturk.com/help/faq#restrictions_use_mturk.

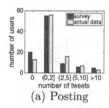
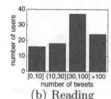

(a) Posting   (b) Reading

Fig. 1. Distribution of posting and reading frequency.

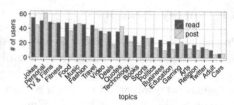

Fig. 2. Popularity of posting and reading topics.

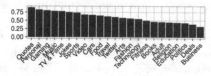

(a) Proportion of posting participants among reading participants. (P_y^p)

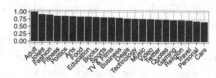

(b) Proportion of reading participants among posting participants. (P_y^r)

Fig. 3. Proportion of users who like to post/read a topic out of those who like to read/post the same topic.

and "Cars" and "Gaming" are among the unpopular topics for both posting and reading. Some topics have significant popularity difference between posting and reading. For example, 48 participants like to read "Fitness" and only 28 participants like to post it. On the other hand, 43 participants like to post "Quotes" and 36 participants like to read it.

The second and third questions are: *Do Twitter users like to post a topic if they like to read it? And do Twitter users like to read a topic if they like to post it?* To answer them, we define the proportion of participants who like to post a topic y given that they like to read it as $P_y^p = \frac{|U_y^p \cap U_y^r|}{|U_y^r|}$, where U_y^p is the set of participants who like to post topic y, and U_y^r is the set of participants who like to read topic y. Similarly, the proportion of participants who like to read a topic y given that they like to post it is calculated as $P_y^r = \frac{|U_y^p \cap U_y^r|}{|U_y^p|}$. Figure 3(a) and (b) show P_y^p and P_y^r respectively for the set of 23 topics.

Figure 3(a) shows that if a user likes to read a topic, on average, she would post it with 0.6 probability as $avg_y(P_y^p) = 0.6$. In contrast, the average probability of users liking to read topics which they like to post is significantly higher, with $avg_y(P_y^r) = 0.8$ (see Fig. 3(b)). In addition, P_y^p varies largely between topics compared to P_y^r, as the standard deviations of P_y^p and P_y^r are 0.16 and 0.08 respectively. Particularly, only 32% of users who like to read "Business" also like to post it. Similarly, topics such as "Politics" and "Religion" also have low P_y^p (0.43 and 0.44). Topics such as "Gaming" and "Music" have much higher P_y^p (0.8 and 0.78). Such topics are more likely to be shared if users like to read them.

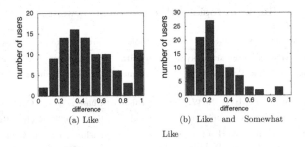

Fig. 4. Distribution of the differences between user posting and reading topics.

Our fourth question asks: *how different are individual Twitter users' posting and reading topics?* Suppose a user declares a set of posting topics π^p and a set of reading topics π^r. We compute user posting and reading topic difference as $d = 1 - \frac{|\pi^p \cap \pi^r|}{|\pi^p \cup \pi^r|}$, where $\frac{|\pi^p \cap \pi^r|}{|\pi^p \cup \pi^r|}$ is the Jaccard coefficient of π^p and π^r. Jaccard coefficient is commonly used to measure the similarity of two sets. Hence d measures the difference between π^p and π^r. Both π^p and π^r can be defined by either topics that are liked with at least the "Like" or "Somewhat Like" rating.

Figure 4(a) shows the distribution of the differences between user's "Like" posting topics and reading topics. Figure 4(b) shows the distribution of the differences between user's "Like" and "Somewhat Like" posting topics and reading topics. As the mean differences of 0.5 and 0.28 are significantly larger than 0, we conclude that users have different topic interests in posting and reading.

In summary, we demonstrate that topics are different in attracting users to post and read and that for some topics such as "Business" and "Politics", only a small proportion of users who like to read them choose to post. We also show that Twitter users' posting topics are significantly different from their reading topics.

3.3   Topics in Tweets

Now, we describe how we obtained the 23 topics to cover all or most of the topics for our participants. We first crawled the tweets generated by a large number of users. We started our crawling process by randomly selecting 434 seed users from Singapore. We then crawled all their followees, who can be based anywhere. In this way, we obtained 93,312 users. Among them, 81,171 users have public accounts. We crawled the latest 200 tweets or whatever available from each public user using Twitter API. Next, we selected the tweets that are posted between Aug 25, 2014 and Nov 25, 2014, discarding tweets that are not written in English, stop words in tweets, and users with less than 10 tweets. Finally, we were left with 50,266 users and their more than 6.2 million tweets.

Next, we adopt T-LDA [28] to learn topics from these tweets. Zhao et al. [28] showed that T-LDA can uncover topics in tweets better than several other

Table 1. Topics and some related keywords.

Topics	Some related keywords	Topics	Some related keywords
Arts	Art, Artwork, @fineartamerica	Adult	Adult, Porn, Sex, Pornography
Books	Journal, Book, Poet, Writer, Author	Business	Business, Economy, Finance, Oil
Cars	F1, Formula, Driver, BMW, Car	Deals	Chance, Deals, Contest, Cashback
Education	Education, Library, Publish	Food	Food, Cook, Recipe, Restaurant
Fitness, Health	Fitness, Health, Workout, Gym, Muscle, Weight, Training, Treatment	Fashion	Fashion, #ootd, #nyfw, Carpet, Dress, Collection, Beauty, Style
Gaming	Game, Xbox, PS4, Gaming, Dota, League	Jokes, Funny	Funny, Joke, Humor, LOL, Humour, Fun
Music	Music, #mtvstars, Concert, kpop	Quotes	Quote, Happiness, Positive
Personal activity	Eating, Super, God, Hell, Moment, Feeling, Asleep, Weather	Politics	Politics, Obama, War, Immigration, Election, Congress, Minister, Military
Religion	Religion, Lord, Buddhism, Christain	Sports	Sports, Basketball, NBA, Football, Goal
Technology, Science	Technology, Tech, Google, Apple, Mobile, NASA, Science, Solar, Comet, Earth	Twitter	Twitter, Followers, Unfollowers, Fustunfollow, Unfollowed
TV & Films	TV, Movie, Trailer, Plot, IMDb	Travel	Travel, Tour, Vacation, Hotel, Island
Video	Video, Youtuber, Youbube, Viewer		

LDA based methods. We call the topics generated by T-LDA the L-topics. In T-LDA, each L-topic is represented as a word distribution. We manually read the word distribution and then assigned a topic name to it. For example, a L-topic with top words: *collection, fashion, dress, wearing,* and *makeup* was assigned the topic name "Fashion". We manually checked all the L-topics generated with the number of L-topics $K' = 20, 30, 40, 50$ and 60. Note that multiple L-topics may be assigned with the same topic name and L-topics without clear topic may not be assigned with topic names. We finally obtained the 23 topics used in our survey, i.e., $Y = \{y_1, y_2, \ldots, y_T\}$ where $T = 23$. For each topic $y_t \in Y$, we manually selected a set of keywords γ_{y_t} from the top words in each of the L-topics that are assigned as y_t. Table 1 shows the 23 topics and some related keywords.

4   Posting and Reading Topic Discovery

Another goal of this work is to discover user posting and reading topics. We consider this problem as a form of ranking problem: we use ranking strategies to rank topics and aim to give user interested topics higher ranks and uninterested topics lower ranks. A ranking strategy takes certain information (e.g., content and following networks) of a user as input and outputs a topic ranking for her. We define some notations first for easy reading. Let $Y = \{y_1, y_2, \ldots, y_T\}$ be a set of topics to be ranked. A ranking σ is a bijection from $\{y_1, y_2, \ldots, y_T\}$ to itself. We use $\sigma(y_t)$ to denote the rank or position given to topic y_t, $\sigma^{-1}(k)$ to denote the topic at the k-th position, $\sigma^{-1}(1...k)$ to denote the set of topics in the top k positions, and π to represent a set of ground truth posting or reading topics according to which type of topic interests we want to discover.

To evaluate a ranking strategy on a set of testing users U_{test}, we use measurer *mean average precision at position n* (MAP@n) which is a common way to measure rankings. In our case, n represents the number of top ranking topics chosen as the predicted topics. For example, if $n = 5$, then we will use $\sigma^{-1}(1...5)$ as the predicted topics. To calculate MAP@n for U_{test}, we first calculate *average precision at position n* (ap@n) for each user in U_{test}: $ap@n = \frac{\sum_{k=1}^{n} P(k)}{n}$ where $P(k)$ represents the precision at the cut-off k topics in the ranking, i.e., $P(k) = \frac{|\sigma^{-1}(1..k) \cap \pi|}{k}$ if $\sigma^{-1}(k) \in \pi$, otherwise, $P(k) = 0$. The MAP@n for U_{test} is the average of the average precision of each user, i.e., $\text{MAP@}n = \frac{\sum_{u \in U_{test}} ap_u@n}{|U_{test}|}$.

The rest of this section is organized as follows. First, we present three different ranking strategies: Popularity, Content, and Followee-Expertise. Each ranking strategy takes different information of a user for posting or reading topic discovery. Next, we propose a model that learns to combine rankings determined from different strategies. Finally, we show the performance of discovering user posting and reading topics.

4.1   Ranking Strategies

Popularity. Popularity strategy ranks posting and reading topics according to their popularity. We call the Popularity strategy *Post-Popularity* (*Read-Popularity*) if we aim to discover posting topics (reading topics). The intuition of Popularity strategy is that users are likely to be interested in popular topics. The popularity of each posting or reading topic is obtained from a set of training users U_{train}. Let $\pi^{(u)}$ be the set of ground truth posting or reading topics for user u. For each topic $y \in Y$, we obtain its popularity measured by the number of training users interested in y, i.e., $|\{u|y \in \pi^{(u)}, u \in U_{train}\}|$. We then rank the topics by their popularity.

Content. A user related content can be tweets posted by herself or received from her followees. The posted tweets are the content she likes to share. The received tweets include the content she likes to read. We therefore have two ranking strategies based on posted content and received content to predict user posting and reading topics respectively. They are *Posted-Content* and *Received-Content* strategies respectively. User posted and received content is commonly used for topic discovery [23, 26, 27]. The intuition of the Content strategies is that users are likely to be interested in the topics that their posted and received content is associated with.

The Content strategies rank topics as follows. We first obtain tweets from a set of users including the users whose topic interests we aim to infer and their followees. We then use T-LDA to generate all users' L-topic distributions from their content. Recall that to differentiate the topics learned by T-LDA from the topics to be ranked (Y), we call the former the L-topics $X = \{x_1, x_2, \ldots, x_K\}$.

Next, we map L-topics in X to topics in Y. For each topic $y_t \in Y$, we have defined a set of related keywords, i.e., γ_{y_t}. Each L-topic $x_k \in X$ is represented as a word distribution. We empirically use the top 30 words in the distribution as x_k's keywords, i.e., γ_{x_k}. We then find a topic y_{t_k} for x_k such that they share the most common keywords, i.e., $y_{t_k} = \arg \max_{y_t} |\gamma_{x_k} \cap \gamma_{y_t}|$. In this way, we can map every L-topic x_k to a topic y_{t_k}. It is possible to have multiple L-topics mapped to one topic in Y.

Finally, with the mapping from X to Y, we determine user topic distribution as follows. From T-LDA, each user is assigned a L-topic distribution, i.e., $\langle l_1, l_2, \ldots, l_K \rangle$ where l_k represents how likely the user is interested in x_k. For each $y_t \in Y$, we obtain the likelihood that the user is interested in y_t by summing up l_k for x_k's that are mapped to y_t, i.e., $z_t = \sum_{t_k=t} l_k$. Thus we obtain a topic distribution $\langle z_1, z_2, \ldots, z_T \rangle$ for this user. The Content ranking strategy returns the topics according to their topic ordering in $\langle z_1, z_2, \ldots, z_T \rangle$.

Followee-Expertise. A user's choice of following other users can reveal her reading topic interests. We particularly focus on followees who are well known to be associated with topics. These users are known as *topic experts* [8]. For example, if a Twitter account is well known to post content related to sports events, then this account is an expert in topic "Sports". The topic a user is well known to be associated with is her *topic expertise* or *expertise*. When a user has an expertise, it is likely to be followed by other users interested in that expertise. For example, if a user likes sports, she may follow sports news accounts or stars whose expertise is "Sports". Thus, the intuition behind *Followee-Expertise* strategy is that a user is likely to be interested in reading a topic if many of her followees have expertise in that topic [3].

We adopt a method proposed in [8] to obtain followees with expertise. This method exploits the *List* feature of Twitter. In Twitter, users can create lists to organize their followees. Each list has a name given by the user who created this list. Some list names do not carry any meaning (e.g., "list #2"). Some list names show the social relationships of the members (e.g., "family"). There are also many list names that reveal the members' expertise (e.g., "music").

We therefore make use of list names to obtain followees with expertise. First, we crawled the number of lists each followee is member of and the names of the lists. The users who are member of only very few lists are usually not well known and these lists are usually for social purpose. We therefore only included those followees who appear in at least 10 lists. For our survey participants, we obtained 15,395 followees. 8,601 of them are public users. Among the 8,601 followees, 43 percent of them appear in at least 10 lists. As Twitter API has rate limits, we collected at most 1000 lists per followee. Next, for each followee, we removed the stop words from the names of the lists she is member of and chose at most 20 top frequent words that appear in the names. We use $\beta^{(f)}$ to denote the chosen words for followee f. Finally, to know f's expertise, we again utilize the keywords from each topic in Y: f's expertise is $y^{(f)} \in Y$ if $\beta^{(f)}$ and $y^{(f)}$'s related keyword set $\gamma_{y^{(f)}}$ share the most number of words, i.e., $y^{(f)} = \arg\max_y |\beta^{(f)} \cap \gamma_y|$. For example, for account @latimessports, we obtained $\beta^{(@latimessports)} = \{sports, news, media, lakers, nfl, baseball, \ldots\}$, and the topic expertise is "Sports".

For a user whose reading topics are to be predicted, we use the above way to derive a set of her followees with expertise, i.e., F^e. Each followee $f \in F^e$ has an expertise $y^{(f)}$. Followee-Expertise ranks topic $y \in Y$ in higher position than $y' \in Y$, if the number of followees with expertise y is larger than the number of followees with expertise y', i.e., $|\{f|y^{(f)} = y, f \in F^e\}| > |\{f|y^{(f)} = y', f \in F^e\}|$. For example, if a user follows 8 accounts with expertise "Sports", 4 accounts with "Politics" and 10 accounts with "Music", then the user's reading topic ranking is "Music", "Sports" and "Politics".

4.2   Learning to Combine Rankings

The above three ranking strategies utilize different information to infer users' posting or reading topic rankings. It is possible that different ranking strategies can complement each other so as to achieve better performance [16]. We therefore propose a model that learns to combine rankings generated from different ranking strategies.

We are given a set of training users U_{train} that we wish to uncover their posting or reading topics. For each user, we have a collection of rankings which are generated by different ranking strategies. We use $\sigma_i^{(u)}$ to represent the i-th ranking for user u. Remember that we use $\pi^{(u)}$ to denote the set of ground truth topics for user u. We have Posted-Content and Post-Popularity strategies for predicting posting topics, and Received-Content, Read-Popularity, and Followee-Expertise strategies for predicting reading topics.

For the i-th ranking strategy, we define a set of parameters $w_i = \{w_{i1}, w_{i2}, \ldots, w_{iT}\}$ where w_{it} represents how important the topic at position t is in the i-th ranking strategy and $0 < w_{it} < 1$. We then combine user u's rankings as follows: for each topic $y \in Y$, we obtain its overall (or combined) importance by summing up the topic y's importance in all ranking strategies, i.e., $\sum_i w_{i\sigma_i^{(u)}(y)}$ where $\sigma_i^{(u)}(y)$ represents the rank assigned to y by the i-th ranking for user u. We then can re-rank all the topics based on their overall importance, and get a combined ranking $\phi^{(u)}$ for user u.

A good combined ranking $\phi^{(u)}$ should rank the topics from ground truth topics $\pi^{(u)}$ in front positions. Thus the topics in $\pi^{(u)}$ should be much more important than the other topics. This means we need $\dfrac{\sum_{y \in \pi^{(u)}} \sum_i w_{i\sigma_i^{(u)}(y)}}{\sum_{y \in Y} \sum_i w_{i\sigma_i^{(u)}(y)}}$ to be close to 1. In other words, we want the total importance of the user interested topics (the numerator) to be close to the total importance of all topics (the denominator).

We then can write our model as follows. We minimize the following function:

$$F(w) = \frac{1}{2|U_{train}|} \sum_{u \in U_{train}} (1 - \frac{\sum_{y \in \pi^{(u)}} \sum_i w_{i\sigma_i^{(u)}(y)}}{\sum_{y \in Y} \sum_i w_{i\sigma_i^{(u)}(y)}})^2 \tag{1}$$

To simplify the representation, we can rewrite $F(w)$ as $F(w) = \frac{1}{2|U_{train}|}$ $\sum_{u \in U_{train}} (1 - \frac{\sum_i \sum_t a_{it}^{(u)} w_{it}}{\sum_i \sum_t w_{it}})^2$ where $a_{it}^{(u)}$ equals to 1 if there exists a topic $y \in \pi^{(u)}$ such that $\sigma_i^{(u)}(y) = t$. Otherwise, $a_{it}^{(u)}$ equals to 0.

In order to ensure w_{it} falls within $(0, 1)$, we transform it using logistic function: $w_{it} = \frac{1}{1+e^{-\theta_{it}}}$. Thus, instead of learning w, we learn θ. To avoid overfitting, we add a regularization term to our objective function.

$$F(\theta) = \frac{1}{2|U_{train}|} \sum_{u \in U_{train}} (1 - \frac{\sum_i \sum_t a_{it}^{(u)} w_{it}}{\sum_i \sum_t w_{it}})^2 + \frac{\lambda}{2|U_{train}|} \sum_i \sum_t \theta_{it}^2 \tag{2}$$

where $w_{it} = \frac{1}{1+e^{-\theta_{it}}}$ and λ is a control of the fitting parameters θ. As F is not convex, in order to improve the chances of finding a global minimum, a common strategy is to use gradient descent with random restart, which performs gradient descent many times (e.g., 100 times) with randomly chosen initial points, and selects the locally optimized point with the lowest F value. We write the derivative of F of θ_{jv}:

$$\frac{\partial}{\partial \theta_{jv}} F(\theta) = -\frac{1}{|U_{train}|} \sum_{u \in U_{train}} ((1 - \frac{\sum_i \sum_t a_{it}^{(u)} w_{it}}{\sum_i \sum_t w_{it}})$$

$$\frac{a_{jv}^{(u)} \sum_i \sum_t w_{it} - \sum_i \sum_t a_{it}^{(u)} w_{it}}{(\sum_i \sum_t w_{it})^2} \frac{e^{-\theta_{jv}}}{(1 + e^{-\theta_{jv}})^2}) + \frac{\lambda}{|U_{train}|} \theta_{jv} \tag{3}$$

The update rule is $\theta_{jv} := \theta_{jv} - \alpha \frac{\partial}{\partial \theta_{jv}} F(\theta)$, where α is the learning rate. After we learn θ and then obtain parameter w_i for each ranking strategy i, we can get the combined ranking for user u by computing the overall importance for each topic y using $\sum_i w_{i\sigma_i^{(u)}(y)}$.

4.3 Results of Posting and Reading Topic Discovery

We use the ground truth topics obtained from our survey to evaluate the ranking strategies. All the following results are the average MAP by repeating 5-fold cross-validation 10 times. We empirically set $\lambda = 0.1$ and $\alpha = 20$.

Posting Topic Discovery. We use 69 participants who posted no less than 5 tweets from March 1st to March 30th, 2015 for this part of evaluation, and the remaining users are considered as lurkers who mainly focus on reading. We apply Posted-Content and Post-Popularity to predict user posting topics. Table 2 shows the performance of these two ranking strategies and the performance of the combined rankings. To determine the significance of results, we use the randomly shuffled topics (i.e., the Random predictor) as baseline. In the Table, n represents

Table 2. Performance (MAP@n) of posting topic discovery.

		Random	Posted-content	Post-popularity	Combined
Like	n = 3	0.22	0.38	0.55	**0.58**
	n = 5	0.2	0.31	0.48	**0.51**
	n = 7	0.18	0.31	0.50	**0.52**
Like and	n = 3	0.49	0.65	0.85	**0.86**
somewhat like	n = 5	0.46	0.57	0.79	**0.80**
	n = 7	0.44	0.55	**0.76**	**0.76**

the number of topics that are chosen as the predicted topics. "Like" means that we use the topics that a user likes to post as the ground truth topics, and "Like and Somewhat Like" means that we use the topics that a user rates "Like" or "Somewhat Like" as the ground truth topics.

We observe firstly that all our ranking strategies yield performance significantly better than Random. Secondly, Post-Popularity performs much better than Posted-Content. One possible reason is that inferring topics from tweets is still a challenging problem as tweets are short and people use many informal and idiosyncratic words in tweets [14]. The performance of Post-Popularity shows that there are some "universal" posting topics such as "TV & Films" and "Music". Finally, the combined ranking method achieves the best performance.

Reading Topic Discovery. We use all the survey participants in reading topic discovery evaluation. Table 3 shows the performance of Received-Content, Read-Popularity and Followee-Expertise and their combined rankings. We summarize our observations as follows. First, all our ranking strategies perform significantly better than Random. Secondly, compared with Read-Popularity and Followee-Expertise, Received-Content does not predict user reading topics well. One possible reason is the difficulty of inferring topics in tweets. Another possible reason is that Twitter users are only interested in a subset of tweets they received. Thirdly, Followee-Expertise, an unsupervised method, mostly performs better than Read-Popularity. Fourthly, again, the combined ranking can achieve the best performance. Lastly, comparing Tables 2 and 3, we notice that reading topic discovery can achieve comparable performance as posting topic discovery, which suggests that although we do not have user reading behavior data traces, we can still predict user reading topics with reasonable accuracy.

Reading Topic Discovery for Lurkers. In order to see how well we can predict lurkers' reading topics, we divide the testing users into lurker group and active user group. The lurker group consists of the users who post less than 5 tweets from March 1st to March 30th, 2015 and the remaining users belong to the active user group. Figure 5 shows the performance of predicting reading topics for lurkers and active users. We set $n = 5$ and the ground truth topics are the "Like" topics. Other settings have consistent findings. We first observe that all our methods perform much better than Random for both lurker and active user

Table 3. Performance (MAP@n) of reading topic discovery.

		Random	Received-content	Read-popularity	Followee-expertise	Combined
Like	n = 3	0.29	0.39	0.50	0.52	**0.56**
	n = 5	0.25	0.34	0.41	0.43	**0.48**
	n = 7	0.22	0.33	0.41	0.42	**0.46**
Like and somewhat like	n = 3	0.61	0.71	0.82	0.86	**0.87**
	n = 5	0.60	0.66	0.78	0.79	**0.80**
	n = 7	0.57	0.65	0.78	0.77	**0.80**

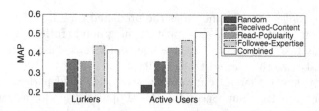

Fig. 5. Performance of predicting lurkers and active users' reading topics.

groups. Secondly, overall, predicting active users' reading topics is easier than predicting lurkers'. Thirdly, Read-Popularity does not perform well for lurkers. It shows that compared with active users, lurkers are less likely to pay attention to the popular reading topics. Lastly, we find that Followee-Expertise performs best for the lurker group. Thus, using only this unsupervised method, we can achieve promising prediction results for lurkers.

5   Discussion and Conclusion

One of the main contributions of this work is to show that social media users' posting topics are different from their reading topics. We also observe that topics are different in attracting people to post and to read. For example, users seem to have less concerns when posting topics such as "TV & Films" and "Music". However, for topics such as "Adult", "Religion", "Politics" and "Business", many users who are interested in reading them do not share them in Twitter. Our findings imply that to measure the popularity of a tweet or an event, we need to consider its topic. For example, if a tweet is about "Politics", then the number of users sharing it could possibly underestimate its popularity or influence.

Our work also contributes to the prediction of users' posting and reading topics. We have evaluated the prediction performance using different ranking strategies. We demonstrated that predicting reading topics can achieve similar performance as predicting posting topics, although the reading content is not observed. We also showed that we can predict lurkers' reading topics using the topic experts among the lurkers' followees. Posting and reading topics can be useful in different practical scenarios. For example, posting topics can be used to predict if users will share an event or product. Users' reading topics can be used to predict if they will pay attention to an advertisement.

In the future work, we could examine and compare the differences between posting and reading topics for a much larger user community and in other social media platforms such as Facebook. Another future direction is to study users' views and opinions when they are interested in certain topics but do not share them, and the context which encourages people to speak up.

Acknowledgments. The authors gratefully thank Ingmar Weber for the inspiring discussion. This research is supported by the Singapore National Research Foundation under its International Research Centre @ Singapore Funding Initiative and administered by the IDM Programme Office, Media Development Authority (MDA).

References

1. Balasubramanian, S., Mahajan, V.: The economic leverage of the virtual community. Int. J. Electron. Commer. **5**(3), 103–138 (2001)
2. Benevenuto, F., Rodrigues, T., Cha, M., Almeida, V.: Characterizing user behavior in online social networks. In: IMC (2009)
3. Bhattacharya, P., Zafar, M.B., Ganguly, N., Ghosh, S., Gummadi, K.P.: Inferring user interests in the twitter social network. In: RecSys (2014)
4. Chen, J., Hsieh, G., Mahmud, J.U., Nichols, J.: Understanding individuals' personal values from social media word use. In: CSCW (2014)
5. Das, S., Kramer, A.: Self-censorship on Facebook. In: ICWSM (2013)
6. Davidson, J., Liebald, B., Liu, J., Nandy, P., Van Vleet, T., Gargi, U., Gupta, S., He, Y., Lambert, M., Livingston, B., Sampath, D.: The youtube video recommendation system. In: RecSys (2010)
7. Diao, Q., Jiang, J.: A unified model for topics, events and users on Twitter. In: EMNLP (2013)
8. Ghosh, S., Sharma, N., Benevenuto, F., Ganguly, N., Gummadi, K.: Cognos: crowdsourcing search for topic experts in microblogs. In: SIGIR (2012)
9. Gong, W., Lim, E.P., Zhu, F.: Characterizing silent users in social media communities. In: ICWSM (2015)
10. Hampton, K., Rainie, L., Lu, W., Dwyer, M., Shin, I., Purcell, K.: Social media and the "spiral of silence". Pew Research Internet Project (2014). http://www.pewinternet.org/2014/08/26/social-media-and-the-spiral-of-silence/
11. Hong, L., Bekkerman, R., Adler, J., Davison, B.D.: Learning to rank social update streams. In: SIGIR (2012)
12. Hsieh, G., Chen, J., Mahmud, J.U., Nichols, J.: You read what you value: understanding personal values and reading interests. In: CHI (2014)
13. Kosinski, M., Stillwell, D., Graepel, T.: Private traits and attributes are predictable from digital records of human behavior. PNAS **110**(15), 5802–5850 (2013)
14. Kouloumpis, E., Wilson, T., Moore, J.: Twitter sentiment analysis: the good the bad and the OMG! In: ICWSM (2011)
15. Kulshrestha, J., Zafar, M.B., Noboa, L.E., Gummadi, K.P., Ghosh, S.: Characterizing information diets of social media users. In: ICWSM (2015)

16. Lebanon, G., Lafferty, J.D.: Cranking: combining rankings using conditional probability models on permutations. In: ICML (2002)
17. Li, X., Guo, L., Zhao, Y.E.: Tag-based social interest discovery. In: WWW (2008)
18. Linden, G., Smith, B., York, J.: Amazon. com recommendations: item-to-item collaborative filtering. IEEE Internet Comput. **7**(1), 76–80 (2003)
19. Michelson, M., Macskassy, S.A.: Discovering users' topics of interest on twitter: a first look. In: AND (2010)
20. Nonnecke, B., Preece, J.: Lurker demographics: counting the silent. In: CHI (2000)
21. Pak, A., Paroubek, P.: Twitter as a corpus for sentiment analysis and opinion mining. In: LREC (2010)
22. Sleeper, M., Balebako, R., Das, S., McConahy, A.L., Wiese, J., Cranor, L.F.: The post that wasn't: exploring self-censorship on facebook. In: CSCW (2013)
23. Spasojevic, N., Yan, J., Rao, A., Bhattacharyya, P.: Lasta: large scale topic assignment on multiple social networks. In: KDD (2014)
24. Tagarelli, A., Interdonato, R.: "Who's out there?": identifying and ranking lurkers in social networks. In: ASONAM (2013)
25. Wang, G., Konolige, T., Wilson, C., Wang, X., Zheng, H., Zhao, B.Y.: You are how you click: clickstream analysis for Sybil detection. In: SEC (2013)
26. Xu, Z., Ru, L., Xiang, L., Yang, Q.: Discovering user interest on twitter with a modified author-topic model. In: WI-IAT (2011)
27. Yang, Z., Xu, J., Li, X.: Data selection for user topic model in twitter-like service. In: ICPADS (2011)
28. Zhao, W.X., Jiang, J., Weng, J., He, J., Lim, E.-P., Yan, H., Li, X.: Comparing Twitter and traditional media using topic models. In: Clough, P., Foley, C., Gurrin, C., Jones, G.J.F., Kraaij, W., Lee, H., Mudoch, V. (eds.) ECIR 2011. LNCS, vol. 6611, pp. 338–349. Springer, Heidelberg (2011)

Going Beyond GDP to Nowcast Well-Being Using Retail Market Data

Riccardo Guidotti[1,2]([⊠]), Michele Coscia[3], Dino Pedreschi[2],
and Diego Pennacchioli[1]

[1] KDDLab ISTI CNR, Via G. Moruzzi, 1, Pisa, Italy
{riccardo.guidotti,diego.pennacchioli}@isti.cnr.it
[2] KDDLab, CS Department, University of Pisa, L. B. Pontecorvo, 3, Pisa, Italy
dino.pedreschi@di.unipi.it
[3] CID - HKS, 79 JFK Street, Cambridge, MA, USA
michele_coscia@hks.harvard.edu

Abstract. One of the most used measures of the economic health of a nation is the Gross Domestic Product (GDP): the market value of all officially recognized final goods and services produced within a country in a given period of time. GDP, prosperity and well-being of the citizens of a country have been shown to be highly correlated. However, GDP is an imperfect measure in many respects. GDP usually takes a lot of time to be estimated and arguably the well-being of the people is not quantifiable simply by the market value of the products available to them. In this paper we use a quantification of the average sophistication of satisfied needs of a population as an alternative to GDP. We show that this quantification can be calculated more easily than GDP and it is a very promising predictor of the GDP value, anticipating its estimation by six months. The measure is arguably a more multifaceted evaluation of the well-being of the population, as it tells us more about how people are satisfying their needs. Our study is based on a large dataset of retail micro transactions happening across the Italian territory.

1 Introduction

Objectively estimating a country's prosperity is a fundamental task for modern society. We need to have a test to understand which socio-economic and political solutions are working well for society and which ones are not. One such test is the estimation of the Gross Domestic Product, or GDP. GDP is defined as the market value of all officially recognized final goods and services produced within a country in a given period of time. The idea of GDP is to capture the average prosperity that is accessible to people living in a specific region.

No prosperity test is perfect, so it comes as no surprise to reveal that GDP is not perfect either. GDP has been harshly criticised for several reasons [1]. We focus on two of these reasons. First: GDP is not an easy measure to estimate. It takes time to evaluate the values of produced goods and services, as to evaluate them they first have to be produced and consumed. Second: GDP does

© Springer International Publishing Switzerland 2016
A. Wierzbicki et al. (Eds.): NetSci-X 2016, LNCS 9564, pp. 29–42, 2016.
DOI: 10.1007/978-3-319-28361-6_3

not accurately capture the well-being of the people. For instance income inequality skews the richness distribution, making the per capita GDP uninteresting, because it does not describe the majority of the population any more. Moreover, arguably it is not possible to quantify well-being just with the number of dollars in someone's pocket: she might have dreams, aspirations and sophisticated needs that bear little to no correlation with the status of her wallet.

In this paper we propose a solution to both shortcomings of GDP. We introduce a new measure to test the well-being of a country. The proposed measure is the average sophistication of the satisfiable needs of a population. We are able to estimate such measure by connecting products sold in the country to the customers buying them in significant quantities, generating a customer-product bipartite network. The sophistication measure is created by recursively correcting the degree of each customer in the network. Customers are sophisticated if they purchase sophisticated products, and products are sophisticated if they are bought by sophisticated customers. Once this recursive correction converges, the aggregated sophistication level of the network is our well-being estimation.

The average sophistication of the satisfiable needs of a population is a good test of a country's prosperity as it addresses the two issues of GDP we discussed. First, it shows a high correlation with the GDP of the country, when shifting the GDP by two quarters. The average sophistication of the bipartite network is an effective nowcasting of the GDP, making it a promising predictor of the GDP value the statistical office will release after six months. Second, our measure is by design an estimation of the sophistication of the needs satisfied by the population. It is more in line with a real well-being measure, because it detaches itself from the mere quantity of money circulating in the country and focuses closely on the real dynamics of the population's everyday life.

The analysis we present is based on a dataset coming from a large retail company in Italy. The company operates $\sim$ 120 shops in the West Coast in Italy. It serves millions of customers every year, of which a large majority is identifiable through fidelity cards. We analyze all items sold from January 2007 to June 2014. We connect each customer to all items she purchased during the observation period, reconstructing 30 quarterly bipartite customer-product networks. For each network, we quantify the average sophistication of the customers and we test its correlation with GDP, for different temporal shift values.

2   Related Work

Nowcasting is a promising field of research to resolve the delay issues of GDP. Nowcasting has been successfully combined with the analysis of large datasets of human activities. Two famous examples are Google Flu trends [2] and the prediction of automobile sales [3]. Social media data has been used to nowcast employment status and shocks [4,5]. Such studies are not exempt from criticisms: [6] proved that nowcasting with Google queries alone is not enough and the data must be integrated with other models. Nowcasting has been already applied to GDP too [7], however the developed model uses a statistical approach that is intractable for a high number of variables, thus affecting the quality of results. Other examples can be found focusing on the Eurozone [8], or on different targets such as poverty risk [9] and income distribution [10].

Our proposal of doing GDP nowcasting using retail data is based on the recent branch of research that considers markets as self-organizing complex systems. In [11], authors model the global export market as a bipartite network, connecting the countries with the products they export. Such structure is able to predict long-term GDP growth of a country. This usage of complex networks has been replicated both at the macro economy level [12] and at the micro level of retail [13]. At this level, in previous work we showed that the complex system perspective still yields an interesting description of the retail dynamics [14]. We defined a measure of product and customer sophistication and we showed its power to explain the distance travelled by customers to buy the products they need [15], and even their profitability for the shop [16]. In this work, we borrow these indicators and we use them to tackle the problem of nowcasting GDP. An alternative methodology uses electronic payment data [17]. However in this case the only issue addressed is the timing issue, but no attempt is made into making the measure more representative of the satisfaction of people's needs.

The critiques to GDP we mentioned have resulted in the proliferation of alternative well-being indicators. We mention the Index of Sustainable Economic Welfare (ISEW), the Genuine Progress Indicator (GPI) [18] and the Human Development Index (HDI)[1]. A more in depth review about well-being alternatives is provided in [19]. These indicators are designed to correct some shortcomings of GDP, namely incorporating sustainability and social cost. However, they are still affected by long delays between measurements and evaluation. They are also affected by other criticisms: for instance, GPI includes a list of adjustment items that is considered inconsistent and somewhat arbitrary. Corrections have been developed [20], but so far there is no final reason to prefer them to GDP and thus we decide to adhere to the standard and we consider only the GDP measure, and we remark that no alternative has addressed the two mentioned issues of GDP in a universally recognized satisfactory way.

3   Data

Our analysis is based on real world data about customer behaviour. The dataset we used is the retail market data of one of the largest Italian retail distribution companies. The dataset has been already presented in previous works [15, 16] and we refer to those publications for an in-depth description of our cleaning strategy. We report here when we perform different operations.

The dataset contains retail market data in a time window spanning from Jan 1st, 2007 to June, 30th 2014. The active and recognizable customers are $\sim 1\,\mathrm{M}$. The stores of the company cover the West Coast of Italy. We aggregated the items sold using the Segment classification in the supermarket's marketing hierarchy. We end up with $\sim 4,500$ segments, to which we refer as products.

---

[1] http://hdr.undp.org/en/statistics/hdi.

At this point we need to define the time granularity of our observation period. We choose to use a quarterly aggregation mainly because we want to compare our results with GDP, and GDP assumes a better relevance in a quarterly aggregation. For each quarter, we have ∼ 500 k active customers.

Since our objective is to establish a correlation between the supermarket data and the Gross Domestic Product of Italy, we need a reliable data source for GDP. We rely on the Italian National Bureau of Statistic ISTAT. ISTAT publishes quarterly reports about the status of the Italian country under several aspects, including the official GDP estimation. ISTAT is a public organization and its estimates are the official data used by the Italian central government. We downloaded the GDP data from the ISTAT website[2].

Fig. 1. The geographical distribution of observed customers (yellow dots) and shops (blue dots) in the territory of Italy (Color figure online).

Figure 1 shows that the observed customers cover the entire territory of Italy. However, the shop distribution is not homogeneous. Shops are located in a few Italian regions. Therefore, the coverage of these regions is much more significant, while customers from other regions usually shop only during vacation periods in these regions. Our analysis is performed on national GDP data, because regional GDP data is disclosed only with a yearly aggregation. However, the correlation between national GDP and the aggregated GDP of our observed regions (Tuscany, Lazio and Campania) during our observation period is 0.95 ($p < 0.001$). This is because Italy has a high variation on the North-South axis, which we cover, while the West-East variation, which we cannot cover, is very low.

---

[2] http://dati.istat.it/Index.aspx?lang=en&themetreeid=91, date of last access: September 23rd, 2015.

4   Methodology

In this section we present the methodology implemented for the paper. First, we present the algorithm we use to estimate the measure of sophistication (Sect. 4.1). Second, we discuss the seasonality issues (Sect. 4.2).

4.1   Sophistication

The sophistication index is used to objectively quantify the sophistication level of the needs of the customers buying products. We introduced the sophistication index in [15], which is an adaptation from [11], necessary to scale up to large datasets. We briefly report here how to compute the customer sophistication index, and we refer to the cited papers for a more in-depth explanation.

The starting point is a matrix with customers on rows and products on the columns. This matrix is generated for each quarter of each year of observation. Each cell contains the number of items purchased by the customer of the product in a given quarter (e.g. Q1 of 2007, Q2 of 2007 and so on). We then have 30 of such matrices. The matrices are already very sparse, with an average fill of 1.4 % (ranging from 33 to 37 million non zero values). Our aim is to increase the robustness of these structures, by constructing a bipartite network connecting customers exclusively to the subset of products they purchase in significant quantities. Figure 2 provides a simple depiction of the output bipartite network.

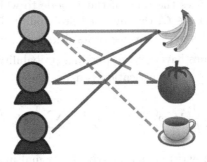

Fig. 2. The resulting bipartite network connecting customers to the products they buy in significant quantities.

To filter the edges, we calculate the Revealed Comparative Advantage (RCA, known as Lift in data mining [21]) of each product-customer cell [22], following [11]. Given a product p_i and a customer c_j, the RCA of the couple is defined as follows:

$$RCA(p_i, c_j) = \frac{X(p_i, c_j)}{X(p_*, c_j)} \left(\frac{X(p_i, c_*)}{X(p_*, c_*)} \right)^{-1},$$

where $X(p_i, c_j)$ is the number of p_i bought by c_j, $X(p_*, c_j)$ is the number of products bought by c_j, $X(p_i, c_*)$ is the total number of times p_i has been sold and $X(p_*, c_*)$ is the total number of products sold. RCA takes values from 0 (when $X(p_i, c_j) = 0$, i.e. customer c_j never bought a single instance of product p_i) to $+\infty$. When $RCA(p_i, c_j) = 1$, it means that $X(p_i, c_j)$ is exactly the expected value under the assumption of statistical independence, i.e. the connection between customer c_j and product p_i has the expected weight. If $RCA(p_i, c_j) < 1$ it means that the customer c_j purchased the product p_i less than expected, and vice-versa. Therefore, we keep an edge in the bipartite network iff its corresponding RCA is larger than 1. Note that most edges were already robust. When filtering out the edges, we keep 93 % of the original connections.

The customer sophistication is directly proportional to the customer's degree in the bipartite network, i.e. with the number of different products she buys. Differently from previous works [15] that used the traditional economic complexity algorithm [11], in this work we use the Cristelli formulation of economic complexity [23]. Note that the two measures are highly correlated. Therefore, in the context of this paper, there is no reason to prefer one measure over the other, and we make the choice of using only one for clarity and readability.

Consider our bipartite network $G = (C, P, E)$ described by the adjacency matrix $M^{|C| \times |P|}$, where C are customers and P are products. Let c and p be two ranking vectors to indicate how much a C-node is linked to the most linked P-nodes and, similarly, P-nodes to C-nodes. It is expected that the most linked C-nodes connected to nodes with high p_j score have an high value of c_i, while the most linked P-nodes connected to nodes with high c_i score have an high value of p_j. This corresponds to a flow among nodes of the bipartite graph where the rank of a C-node enhances the rank of the P-node to which is connected and vice-versa. Starting from $i \in C$, the unbiased probability of transition from i to any of its linked P-nodes is the inverse of its degree $c_i^{(0)} = \frac{1}{k_i}$, where k_i is the degree of node i. P-nodes have a corresponding probability of $p_j^{(0)} = \frac{1}{k_j}$. Let n be the iteration index. The sophistication is defined as:

$$c_i^{(n)} = \sum_{j=1}^{|P|} \frac{1}{k_j} M_{ij} p_j^{(n-1)} \forall i \quad p_j^{(n)} = \sum_{i=1}^{|C|} \frac{1}{k_i} M_{ij} c_i^{(n-1)} \forall j$$

These rules can be rewritten as a matrix-vector multiplication

$$c = \bar{M} p \quad p = \bar{M}^T c \qquad (1)$$

where $\bar{M}$ is the weighted adjacency matrix. So, like previously we have

$$c^{(n)} = \bar{M} \bar{M}^T c^{(n-1)} \quad p^{(n)} = \bar{M}^T \bar{M} p^{(n-1)}$$

$$c^{(n)} = \mathcal{C} c^{(n-1)} \quad p^{(n)} = \mathcal{P} p^{(n-1)}$$

where $\mathcal{C}^{(|C| \times |C|)} = \bar{M} \bar{M}^T$ and $\mathcal{P}^{(|P| \times |P|)} = \bar{M}^T \bar{M}$ are related to $x^{(n)} = A x^{(n-1)}$. This makes sophistication solvable using the power iteration method (and it is proof of convergence). Note that this procedure is equivalent to the HITS ranking algorithm, as proved in [24].

At the end of our procedure, we have a value of customer and product sophistication for each customer for each quarter. For the rest of the section we focus

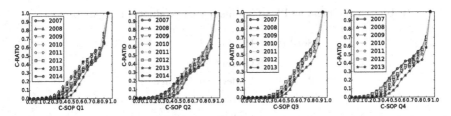

Fig. 3. The customer sophistication distributions per quarter and per year. Each plot reports the probability (y axis) of a customer to have a given sophistication value (x axis), from quarter 1 to quarter 4 (left to right) for each year.

on customer sophistication for space reasons. Each customer is associated with a timeline of 30 different sophistications. The overall sophistication is normalized to take values between 0 and 1. Figure 3 shows the distribution of the customer sophistication per quarter and per year. We chose to aggregate the visualization by quarter because the same quarters are similar across years but different within years, due to seasonal effects.

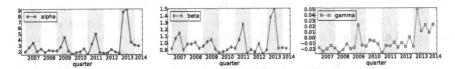

Fig. 4. The different values taken by the fit parameters across the observation period for the sophistication distribution.

Figure 3 shows that the sophistication distribution is highly skewed. We expect it to be an exponential function: by definition the vast majority of the population is unsophisticated and highly sophisticated individuals are an elite. The fit function cannot be a power-law because the different levels of sophistication for least to most sophisticated do not span a sufficiently high number of orders of magnitude. We fitted a function of the form $f(x) = \gamma + \beta \times \alpha^x$ for each quarterly snapshot of our bipartite networks. Figure 4 reports the evolution of the fit parameters α, β and γ. The figure shows that the fit function is mostly stable over time. The fits have been performed using ordinary least squares regression.

To prove the quality of our sophistication measure in capturing need sophistication, we report in Table 1 a list of the top and bottom sophisticated products, calculated aggregating data from all customers. Top sophisticated products are non daily needed products and are usually non-food. The least complex products are food items. Being Italian data, pasta is the most basic product.

Table 1. The most and least sophisticated products in our dataset.

SOP rank	Product
1	Cosmetics
2	Underwear for men
3	Furniture
4	Multimedia services
5	Toys
...	...
−5	Fresh Cheese
−4	Red Meat
−3	Spaghetti
−2	Bananas
−1	Short Pasta

4.2 Seasonality

Both GDP and the behavior of customers in the retail market are affected by seasonality. Different periods of the year are associated with different economic activities. This is particularly true for Italy in some instances: during the month of August, Italian productive activities come to an almost complete halt, and the country hosts its peak tourist population. The number and variety of products available in the supermarket fluctuates too, with more fruit and vegetables available in different months, or with Christmas season and subsequent sale shocks.

A number of techniques have been developed to deal with seasonal changes in GDP. One of the most popular seasonal adjustments is done through the X-13-Arima method, developed by the U.S. Census Bureau [25]. However, we are unable to use this methodology for two reasons. First, it requires an observation period longer than the one we are able to provide in this paper. Second, the methodologies present in literature are all fine-tuned to specific phenomena that are not comparable to the shopping patterns we are observing. Thus we cannot apply them to our sophistication timelines. Given that we are not able to make a seasonal adjustment for the sophistication, we chose to not seasonally adjust GDP too. We acknowledge this as a limitation of our study and we leave the development of a seasonal adjustment for sophistication as a future work.

5 Experiments

In this section we test the relation between the statistical properties of the bipartite networks generated with our methodology and the GDP values of the country. We first show the evolution of aggregated measures of expenditure, number of items, degree and sophistication along our observation period. We then test the correlation with GDP, with various temporal shifts to highlight the potential predictive power of some of these measures.

Before showing the timelines, we describe our approach for the aggregation of the properties of customers. The behavior of customers is highly differentiated. We already shown that the sophistication distribution is highly skewed and best represented as an exponential function. The expenditure and the number of items purchased present a skewed distribution among customers: few customers spend high quantities of money and buy many items, many customers spend little quantities of money and buy few items. For this reason, we cannot aggregate these measures using the average over the entire distribution, as it is not well-behaved for skewed values. To select the data we use the inter-quantile range, the measure of spread from the first to the third quantile. In practice, we trim the outliers out of the aggregation and then we compute the average, the Inter-Quartile Mean, or "IQM". The IQM is calculated as follows:

$$x_{\text{IQM}} = \frac{2}{n} \sum_{i=\frac{n}{4}+1}^{\frac{3n}{4}} x_i$$

assuming n sorted values.

Also note that all the timelines we present have been normalized. All variables take values between zero and one, where zero represents the minimum value observed and one the maximum. As for the notation used, in the text and in the captions of the figures we use the abbreviations reported in Table 2.

Table 2. The abbreviations for the measures used in the experiment section.

Abbreviation	Description
IQM	Inter-Quartile Mean
GDP	Gross Domestic Product
EXP	IQM of the total expenditure per customer
PUR	IQM of the total number of items purchased per customer
C-DEG	IQM of the number of products purchased in significant quantities (i.e. the bipartite network degree) per customer
P-DEG	IQM of the number of customers purchasing the product in significant quantities (i.e. the bipartite network degree)
C-SOP	IQM of the sophistication per customer
P-SOP	IQM of the sophistication per product

The first relation we discuss is between GDP and the most basic customer variables. Figure 5 depicts the relation between GDP and the IQM expenditure (left), and GDP and IQM of number of items purchased (right). Besides the obvious seasonal fluctuation, we can see that the two measures are failing to capture the overall GDP dynamics. GDP has an obvious downward trend, due to the fact that our observation window spans across the global financial crisis,

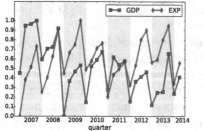 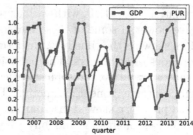

Fig. 5. The relation between GDP and IQM customer expenditure (left) and IQM number of items purchased (right).

which hit Italy particularly hard starting from the first quarter of 2009. However, the average expenditure in the observed supermarket has not been affected at all. Also the number of items has not been affected. If we calculate the corresponding correlations, we notice a negative relationship which, however, fails to pass a stringent null hypothesis test ($p > 0.01$).

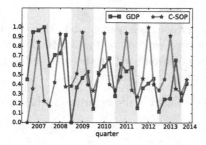 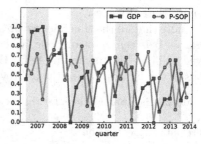

Fig. 6. The relation between GDP and IQM customer (left) and product (right) sophistication.

Turning to our sophistication measure, Fig. 6 depicts the relation between GDP and our complex measures of sophistication. On the left we have the measure of customer sophistication we discussed so far. We can see that the alignment is indeed not perfect. However, averaging out the seasonal fluctuation, customer sophistication captures the overall downward trend of GDP. The financial crisis effect was not only a macroeconomic problem, it also affected the sophistication of the satisfiable needs of the population. Note that, again, we have a negative correlation. This means that, as GDP shrinks, customers become more sophisticated. This is because the needs that once were classified as basic are not basic any more, hence the rise in sophistication of the population. Differently from before, the correlation is actually statistically significant ($p < 0.01$).

We also report on the left the companion sophistication measure: since we can define the customer sophistication as the average sophistication of the products they purchase, we can also define a product sophistication as the average sophistication of the customers purchasing them. Figure 6 (right) shows the reason why we do not focus on product sophistication: the overall trend for product sophistication tends to be the opposite of the customer sophistication. This anti-correlation seems to imply that, as the customers struggle in satisfying their needs, the once top-sophisticated products are not purchased any more, lowering the overall product sophistication index. However, this is only one of many possible interpretations and we need further investigation in future works.

Table 3. The correlations of all the used measures with GDP at different shift values. We highlight the statistically significant correlations.

Measure \ Shift	-3	-2	-1	0	1	2
EXP	-0.29302	-0.49830	-0.53078*	0.23976	-0.27619	-0.37073
PUR	-0.27091	-0.49836*	-0.53046**	0.18638	-0.30909	-0.32432
C-DEG	0.24624	0.39808	-0.55479*	0.13727	0.08191	0.36001
P-DEG	-0.12409	-0.26289	-0.57657**	0.30255	-0.22198	-0.28325
C-SOP	-0.32728	**-0.67007*****	0.23261	0.09251	-0.15844	-0.58773**
P-SOP	-0.02675	-0.12916	0.60974**	-0.18587	0.15342	-0.03843

$^*p < 0.1$, $^{**}p < 0.05$, $^{***}p < 0.01$

We sum up the correlation tests performed in Table 3. In the Table, we report the correlation values for all variables. We test different shift values, where the GDP timeline is shifted of a given number of quarters with respect to the tested measure. When shift $= -1$, it means that we align the GDP with the previous quarter of the measure (e.g. GDP Q4-08 aligned with measure's Q3-08).

We also report the significance levels of all correlations. Note that all p-values are being corrected for the multiple hypothesis test. When considering several hypotheses, as we are doing here, the problem of multiplicity arises: the more hypotheses we check, the higher the probability of a false positive. To correct for this issue, we apply a Holm-Bonferroni correction. The Holm-Bonferroni method is an approach that controls the family-wise error rate (the probability of witnessing one or more false positive) by adjusting the rejection criteria of each of the individual hypotheses [26]. Once we adjust the p-values, we obtain the significance levels reported in the table. Only one correlation passes the Holm-Bonferroni test for significance at $p < 0.01$ and it is exactly the one involving the customer sophistication with shift equal to -2. This correlation is highlighted in bold in Table 3, and it represents the main result of the paper.

Note that in the table we also report the correlation values using the IQM for the customer and product degree measures, of which we have not shown the timelines, due to space constraints. We include them because, as we discussed previously, our sophistication measures are corrected degree measures. If the degree measures were able to capture the same correlation with GDP there would be no need for our more complex measures. Since the degree measures do not pass the Holm-Bonferroni test we can conclude that the sophistication measures are necessary to achieve our results.

We finally provide a visual representation of the customer and product sophistication correlations with GDP at different shift levels in Fig. 7. The figure

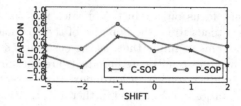

Fig. 7. The correlation between average customer sophistication and GDP with different shifting values.

highlights the different time frames in which the two measures show their predictive power over GDP. The customer sophistication has its peak at shift equal to -2. The cyclic nature of the data implies also a strong, albeit not significant, correlation when the shift is equal to 2. Instead, the product sophistication obtains its highest correlation with GDP with shift equal to -1. This might still be useful in some cases, as the GDP for a quarter is usually released by the statistical office with some weeks of delay.

6   Conclusion

In this paper we tackled the problem of having a fast and reliable test for estimating the well-being of a population. Traditionally, this is achieved with many measures, and one of the most used is the Gross Domestic Product, or GDP, which roughly indicates the average prosperity of the citizens of a country. GDP is affected by several issues, and here we tackle two of them: it is a hard measure to quantify rapidly and it does not take into account all the non-tangible aspects of well-being, e.g. the satisfied needs of a population. By using retail information, we are able to estimate the overall sophistication of the needs satisfied by a population. This is achieved by constructing and analyzing a customer-product bipartite network. In the paper we show that our customer sophistication measure is a promising predictor of the future GDP value, anticipating it by six months. It is also a measure less linked with the amount of richness around a person, and it focuses more on the needs this person is able to satisfy.

This paper opens the way for several future research tracks. Firstly, in the paper we were unable to define a proper seasonal adjustment for our sophistication measure. The seasonality of the measure is evident, but it is not trivial how to deal with it. A longer observation period and a new seasonal adjustment measure is needed and our results show that this is an worthwhile research track. Secondly, we showed that there is an interesting anti-correlation between the aggregated sophistication measures calculated for customers and products. This seems to imply that, in harsh economic times, needs that once were basic become sophisticated (increasing the overall customer sophistication) and needs that were sophisticated are likely to be dropped (decreasing the overall product sophistication). More research is needed to fully understand this dynamic.

Finally, in this paper we made use of a quarterly aggregation to build our bipartite networks. We made this choice because the quarterly aggregation is the most fine-grained one we can obtain for GDP estimations. However, now that we showed the correlation, we might investigate if the quarterly aggregation is the most appropriate for our analysis. If we can obtain comparable results with a lower level of aggregation (say monthly or weekly) our well-being estimation can come closer to be calculated almost in real-time.

Acknowledgements. We gratefully thank Luigi Vetturini for the preliminary analysis that made this paper possible. We thank the supermarket company Coop and Walter Fabbri for sharing the data with us and allowing us to analyse and to publish the results. This work is partially supported by the European Community's H2020 Program under the funding scheme FETPROACT-1-2014: 641191 CIMPLEX, and INFRAIA-1-2014-2015: 654024 SoBigData.

References

1. Costanza, R., Kubiszewski, I., Giovannini, E., Lovins, H., McGlade, J., Pickett, K.E., Ragnarsdóttir, K.V., Roberts, D., De Vogli, R., Wilkinson, R.: Time to leave gdp behind. Nat. Comment **505**, 283–285 (2014)
2. Wilson, N., Mason, K., Tobias, M., Peacey, M., Huang, Q., Baker, M.: Interpreting google flu trends data for pandemic h1n1 influenza: the new zealand experience. Euro surveillance: bulletin européen sur les maladies transmissibles = European communicable disease bulletin **14**(44), 429–433 (2008)
3. Choi, H., Varian, H.: Predicting the present with google trends. Econ. Rec. **88**(s1), 2–9 (2012)
4. Toole, J.L., Lin, Y.R., Muehlegger, E., Shoag, D., Gonzalez, M.C., Lazer, D.: Tracking employment shocks using mobile phone data. arXiv preprint arXiv:1505.06791 (2015)
5. Llorente, A., Cebrian, M., Moro, E., et al.: Social media fingerprints of unemployment. arXiv preprint arXiv:1411.3140 (2014)
6. Lazer, D., Kennedy, R., King, G., Vespignani, A.: The parable of google flu: traps in big data analysis. Science **343**, 1203–1205 (2014)
7. Giannone, D., Reichlin, L., Small, D.: Nowcasting: the real-time informational content of macroeconomic data. J. Monetary Econ. **55**(4), 665–676 (2008)
8. Foroni, C., Marcellino, M.: A comparison of mixed frequency approaches for nowcasting euro area macroeconomic aggregates. Int. J. Forecast. **30**(3), 554–568 (2014)
9. Navicke, J., Rastrigina, O., Sutherland, H.: Nowcasting indicators of poverty risk in the european union: a microsimulation approach. Soc. Indic. Res. **119**(1), 101–119 (2014)
10. Leventi, C., Navicke, J., Rastrigina, O., Sutherland, H.: Nowcasting the income distribution in europe (2014)
11. Hausmann, R., Hidalgo, C., Bustos, S., Coscia, M., Chung, S., Jimenez, J., Simoes, A., Yildirim, M.: The Atlas of Economic Complexity. Puritan Press, Boston (2011)
12. Caldarelli, G., Cristelli, M., Gabrielli, A., Pietronero, L., Scala, A., Tacchella, A.: A network analysis of countries export flows: firm grounds for the building blocks of the economy. PLoS ONE **7**(10), e47278 (2012)

13. Chawla, S.: Feature selection, association rules network and theory building. J. Mach. Learn. Res. Proc. Track **10**, 14–21 (2010)
14. Pennacchioli, D., Coscia, M., Rinzivillo, S., Giannotti, F., Pedreschi, D.: The retail market as a complex system. EPJ. Data Sci. **3**(1), 1–27 (2014)
15. Pennacchioli, D., Coscia, M., Rinzivillo, S., Pedreschi, D., Giannotti, F.: Explaining the product range effect in purchase data. In: 2013 IEEE International Conference on Big Data, pp. 648–656. IEEE (2013)
16. Guidotti, R., Coscia, M., Pedreschi, D., Pennacchioli, D.: Behavioral entropy and profitability in retail. In: DSAA (2015)
17. Galbraith, J.W., Tkacz, G.: Nowcasting gdp with electronic payments data (2015)
18. Lawn, P.A.: A theoretical foundation to support the index of sustainable economic welfare (isew), genuine progress indicator (gpi), and other related indexes. Ecol. Econ. **44**(1), 105–118 (2003)
19. Helbing, D., Balietti, S.: How to create an innovation accelerator. Eur. Phys. J. Spec. Top. **195**(1), 101–136 (2011)
20. Lawn, P.A.: An assessment of the valuation methods used to calculate the index of sustainable economic welfare (isew), genuine progress indicator (gpi), and sustainable net benefit index (snbi). Environ. Dev. Sustain. **7**(2), 185–208 (2005)
21. Geng, L., Hamilton, H.J.: Interestingness measures for data mining: a survey. ACM Comput. Surv. **38**(3), 1–32 (2006)
22. Balassa, B.: Trade liberalization and 'revealed' comparative advantage. Manchester Sch. **33**, 99–123 (1965)
23. Cristelli, M., Gabrielli, A., Tacchella, A., Caldarelli, G., Pietronero, L.: Measuring the intangibles: a metrics for the economic complexity of countries and products. PloS One **8**(8), e70726 (2013)
24. Guidotti, R.: Mobility Ranking-Human Mobility Analysis Using Ranking Measures. University of Pisa, Pisa (2013)
25. Monsell, B.C.: Update on the development of x-13arima-seats. In: Proceedings of the Joint Statistical Meetings: American Statistical Association (2009)
26. Holm, S.: A simple sequentially rejective multiple test procedure. Scand. J. Stat. **6**, 65–70 (1979)

To Trust or Not to Trust Lurkers?: Evaluation of Lurking and Trustworthiness in Ranking Problems

Roberto Interdonato and Andrea Tagarelli[✉]

DIMES, University of Calabria, Rende, Italy
{rinterdonato,tagarelli}@dimes.unical.it

Abstract. Research on social trust analysis has traditionally focused on the trustworthy/untrustworthy behaviors that are exhibited by active users. By contrast, due to their inherent reticence to regularly contribute to the online community life, the silent users in a social network, a.k.a. *lurkers*, have been taken out of consideration so far. Nevertheless, analysis and mining of lurkers in social networks has been recently recognized as an important problem. Determining trust/distrust relationships that involve lurkers can provide a unique opportunity to understand whether and to what extent such users can be trusted or distrusted from the other users. This is important from both the perspective of protecting the active users from untrustworthy or undesired interactions, and the perspective of encouraging lurkers to more actively participate in the community life through the guidance of active users. In this paper we aim at understanding and quantifying relations between lurkers and trustworthy/untrustworthy users in ranking problems. We evaluate lurker ranking methods against classic approaches to trust/distrust ranking, in scenarios of *who-trusts-whom* networks and *followship* networks. Results obtained on Advogato, Epinions, Flickr and FriendFeed networks indicate that lurkers should not be a-priori flagged as untrustworthy users, and that trustworthy users can indeed be found among lurkers.

1 Introduction

Measuring trust behaviors has long been an important topic in psychology and social science [1]. Trust is a complex relationship: deciding the trustworthiness of a user relies on a host of factors, such as personal relationship and past experiences of that user with her/his friends, and opinions about actions that the user has made in the past. In social network analysis from a computer science perspective, most existing studies have mainly focused on behavioral aspects discriminating between users who play "good" roles (e.g., reliable or influential users) and users who play "bad" roles (e.g., spammers) [4,7,12]. In any case, regardless of the specific task being addressed (e.g., trust prediction [10,16,17], trust/distrust ranking [9,22,28]), research on trust computing has normally depended on the variety of *active* behaviors shown by the users in

© Springer International Publishing Switzerland 2016
A. Wierzbicki et al. (Eds.): NetSci-X 2016, LNCS 9564, pp. 43–56, 2016.
DOI: 10.1007/978-3-319-28361-6_4

an online community. These behaviors are generally expressed at different levels and intentions of information production, that is, trustworthy users typically produce useful contents, whereas untrustworthy users produce undesired or even malicious contents and links.

By contrast, poor attention has been paid to the fact that all large-scale online communities are characterized by a *participation inequality principle*. This principle essentially states only a small portion of users creates the vast majority of social content, while the crowd just observes ongoing discussions, reads posts, watches videos and so on. In other words, the real audience of an online social network (OSN) does not actively contribute; rather, it *lurks*. A *lurker* is hence someone who gains benefit from others' information and services without giving back to the OSN [6,21,23]. Lurking behaviors are often explained by a subjective reticence (rather than malicious motivations) of users to contribute to the community wisdom; a lurker often simply feels that gathering information by browsing is enough without the need of being further involved in the community [23]. Lurking can be expected or even encouraged because it allows users (especially newcomers) to learn or improve their understanding of the etiquette of an online community [6]. In this respect, a major goal is to *de-lurk* such users, i.e., to develop a mix of strategies aimed at encouraging lurkers to return their acquired social capital, through a more active participation to the community life. This has the important long-term effect of helping sustain the OSN over time with fresh ideas and perspectives.

It is worth emphasizing that *lurkers are not to be trivially regarded as totally inactive users*, i.e., registered users who do not use their account to join the OC. Recently, the study in [27] has indeed shown that the overlap between lurkers and inactive users is relatively small when "one-click" interactions (e.g., likes, favorite-markings) are taken into account, confirming that lurkers enjoy the contents produced by the other users while maintaining a low profile in terms of visible activity.

The study of lurking behaviors in SNs is per se difficult, and in fact we have witnessed little research in computer science, until recently. The pioneering work in [25,26] has filled a lack of knowledge on the opportunity of analyzing lurkers in OSNs. It provides a solution to the identification and ranking of lurkers in an OSN, based on new eigenvector-centrality methods that are unsupervised and domain-independent. Notably, while exploiting information on the network structure solely, it was shown that the methods present the unique ability of detecting non-trivial lurking cases in an effective way. This was also confirmed by a qualitative manual inspection of results conducted through the evaluation OSN websites. We shall provide technical details on lurker ranking in Sect. 2.

Challenge: Trustworthiness in Lurking Contexts. A common scenario in question-answering systems (where timeliness is crucial) as well as in microblogging services is that active users tend to avoid wasting their time with people that are very likely to not reply or show slow responsiveness, or who have few feedbacks. Since these behavioral traits are part of lurking behaviors (as it was shown from both social and computer science perspectives, e.g., [6,27]), the above can be generalized to users who are reticent to contribute to the production and active sharing of information in the OSN. Therefore, one might conclude that *lurkers could in principle be perceived as "untrustworthy" users.*

On the other hand, it has been shown in many studies (cf. [24] for a recent overview) that one of the most effective delurking actions correspond to the guidance and encouragement information from elders/master users to help lurkers become familiar with the online social environment as quickly as possible. Therefore, *active users play a central role to contribute turning lurkers into participants/contributors* in the community life, which is important to capitalize on the returned social capital.

In any case, because of the lack of user-generated content and of the limited activity in the community life that characterize lurkers, determining trust or distrust relationships that involve lurkers appears to be challenging. In this respect, our study finds major motivations in the struggle between the opportunity of bringing lurkers to social life and the need to protect the active users from untrustworthy/unwanted contacts.

Contributions. In this paper we aim at understanding and quantifying relations between lurkers and trustworthy/untrustworthy users in ranking problems. Our contributions are summarized as follows:

- We push forward research on lurking analysis and mining by investigating how and to what extent lurkers are related to trustworthy and untrustworthy users. The notion of trust/distrust we consider refers to two different scenarios. The first scenario is the classic one in trust computing, which concerns *who-trusts-whom* networks (e.g., Advogato) where explicit trust statements are available for every pair of users; in this case, our assumption relies on an intuitive analogy between lurkers and users that take the role of "observer", or at most "apprentice". The second scenario refers instead to social media networks, in which trust statements are not available but can still be inferred from user interactions [2]. In particular, we focus on *followship* networks (i.e., social graphs) for which one-click interaction data are also available.
- We also advance research on trust computing by introducing a new perspective in social trust analysis, which is built on the awareness that most people are lurkers in social networks and, as such, they should be encouraged to more actively participate in the OSN life. Moreover, we propose to use in social networks that lack any explicit trust indicators, an entropy-based oracle function that infers the likelihood of a user to be trustworthy. This is essential for trust/distrust ranking algorithms, which require trust assessment in terms of an oracle function to decide about the trustworthiness of a user.
- We provide a comparative evaluation of lurker ranking methods [25] with a de-facto standard in global trust ranking, namely *TrustRank* [11], and its counterpart for distrust ranking, called *Anti-TrustRank* [15]. Both algorithms are scalable and involve a biased PageRank algorithm in their computation core, where the bias depends either on trust information or distrust information. Results obtained on Advogato, Epinions, Flickr and FriendFeed networks

indicate that lurkers should not be a-priori flagged as untrustworthy users, and that trustworthy users can indeed be found among lurkers.

2 Background

2.1 LurkerRank

We provide here a short overview of earlier work on ranking lurkers in social networks [25]. The authors provide a quantitative definition of lurking which is based solely on the network structure. This is modeled as a directed graph where any edge (v, u) means that u is "consuming" or "receiving" information from v. Upon the assumption that lurking behaviors build on the *amount of information a node receives*, the key intuition is that the strength of a user's lurking status can be determined based on three basic principles, which are informally reported as follows:

- *Overconsumption:* The excess of information-consumption over information-production. The strength of a node's lurking status is proportional to its in/out-degree ratio.
- *Authoritativeness of the information received:* The valuable amount of information received from its in-neighbors. The strength of a node's lurking status is proportional to the influential (non-lurking) status of its in-neighbors.
- *Non-authoritativeness of the information produced:* The non-valuable amount of information sent to its out-neighbors. The strength of a node's lurking status is proportional to the lurking status of its out-neighbors.

The above principles form the basis for three ranking models that differently account for the contributions of a node's in-neighborhood and out-neighborhood. A complete specification of the lurker ranking models is provided in terms of PageRank and AlphaCentrality based formulations.

Given a node u, let B_u and R_u be the sets of in-neighbors and out-neighbors of u, respectively, and with $in(u) = |B_u|$ and $out(u) = |R_u|$ the in-degree and out-degree of u, respectively. The PageRank-style iterative equations for the computation of the LurkerRank r_u of a node u are given as follows [25]:

- LRin (i.e., in-neighbors-driven LurkerRank):

$$r_u = d \left(\frac{1}{out(u)} \sum_{v \in B_u} \frac{out(v)}{in(v)} r_v \right) + \frac{1-d}{N}$$

- LRout (i.e., out-neighbors-driven LurkerRank):

$$r_u = d \left(\frac{in(u)}{\sum_{v \in R_u} in(v)} \sum_{v \in R_u} \frac{in(v)}{out(v)} r_v \right) + \frac{1-d}{N}$$

- LRin-out (i.e., in-out-neighbors-driven LurkerRank):

$$r_u = d\left[\left(\frac{1}{out(u)}\sum_{v\in B_u}\frac{out(v)}{in(v)}r_v\right)\left(1+\left(\frac{in(u)}{\sum_{v\in R_u}in(v)}\sum_{v\in R_u}\frac{in(v)}{out(v)}r_v\right)\right)\right]+\frac{1-d}{N}$$

where d is a damping factor in $[0,1]$, usually set to 0.85, and N is the set of nodes in the network graph. The AlphaCentrality-style methods are defined similarly, e.g., acLRin for the Alpha-centrality-based in-neighbors-driven LurkerRank computes the rank r_u as:

$$r_u = d\left(\frac{1}{out(u)}\sum_{v\in B_u}\frac{out(v)}{in(v)}r_v\right)+1$$

and analogously acLRout and acLRin-out. Note that the values of $in(\cdot)$ and $out(\cdot)$ are Laplace add-one smoothed (to prevent zero or infinite ratios) [25].

2.2   TrustRank and Anti-TrustRank

Many solutions for trust ranking have been developed in the past years by resorting to PageRank-style methods [9,14,22,28]. However, PageRank is vulnerable to adversarial information retrieval, i.e., link spamming techniques can enable web pages to achieve higher score than what they actually deserve.

A well-known method that was introduced to combat web spam and detect trustworthy pages is *TrustRank* [11]. The key assumption of this method is the approximate isolation principle, i.e., high-quality pages are unlikely to point to spam or low-quality pages. The TrustRank algorithm consists of three steps:

1. Compute a *seed set* of pages labeled by an *oracle function*, obtained by a ranking based on the *inverse-PageRank*.
2. Run the biased PageRank algorithm on the normalized graph matrix using the "good part" of the seed set as the teleportation set, with uniform probability of teleportation.
3. Rank the pages in decreasing order of TrustRank score.

Note that pages in the seed set should be well-connected to other pages in order to propagate trust to many pages quickly. Therefore, they are chosen among those that have a large out-degree. For this purpose, inverse-PageRank is computed by reversing the in-links and out-links in the graph, i.e., by running PageRank on the transpose of the graph matrix; a high inverse pagerank indicates that trust can flow with a small number of hops along out-links.

Anti-TrustRank [15] follows an intuition similar to TrustRank, however it is designed to detect untrustworthy pages. It starts with a seed set of spam pages and propagates distrust in the reverse direction. Like TrustRank, Anti-Trust-Rank consists of three steps:

1. Compute a *seed set* of spam pages labeled by an *oracle function*, obtained by a ranking based on the PageRank.

2. Run the biased PageRank algorithm on the normalized transposed graph matrix using the seed set as the teleport set, with uniform probability of teleportation.
3. Rank the pages in decreasing order of Anti-TrustRank score.

For TrustRank (resp. Anti-TrustRank) we devised an alternative to step (1) which uses a ranking based on the add-one smoothed *in-degree/out-degree* (resp. *out-degree/in-degree*) ratio of the nodes instead of inverse-PageRank (resp. PageRank) to perform the preliminary ordering of the nodes for the seed set selection. To distinguish between the two alternatives we will indicate with TR_InvPR and ATR_PR the original TrustRank and Anti-TrustRank algorithms, respectively, and with TR_IO and ATR_OI the alternative ones.

Motivations for Using TrustRank and Anti-TrustRank in this Study. TrustRank and Anti-TrustRank are *global trust* ranking methods, as they produce a ranking of the nodes in a network according to some notion of trust/distrust. By contrast, *local trust* ranking methods (e.g., [8,12,13,28]) compute a trust score for a target node given a source node. Our selection of such methods to compare with LurkerRank methods, is explained by several motivations. First, TrustRank is a de-facto standard in global trust ranking, and Anti-TrustRank represents the counterpart of TrustRank for distrust ranking. Moreover, both methods involve a biased PageRank algorithm in their computation core, where the bias depends either on trust or distrust information. Besides the damping factor required for the PageRank computation, the only parametric aspect of both methods is related to the seed set selection, whose outcome is much more easily understandable than other parameters typically used in local trust ranking approaches (e.g., maximum length of path in the trust graph or minimum trust threshold). TrustRank and Anti-TrustRank allow us to focus the evaluation on trust and distrust analysis separately; by contrast, methods such as PageTrust [14] and PolarityTrust [22] jointly computes trust and distrust scores but with increased storage and indexing costs. Finally, TrustRank and Anti-TrustRank are scalable, since their computation is linear in the size of the trust graph; this in general represents an advantage with respect to local trust ranking, which by definition requires a cost at least quadratic in the size of the trust graph.

3   Evaluation Methodology

3.1   Data

Our experimental evaluation was performed on four datasets, two of which are *who-trusts-whom* networks and the other two are *followship* networks. Table 1(a) summarizes structural characteristics of the datasets.

We used the trust networks of Advogato.org and Epinions.com, which are de-facto benchmarks for trust analysis tasks. We built our *Advogato* network dataset by aggregating the daily-snapshot graph files available at the www.trustlet.org site, which cover the period Jan 1, 2008 - Apr 2, 2014. Edges in

Table 1. Main structural characteristics of the evaluation network datasets (a) and different edge orientation in TrustRank and LurkerRank graph models (b).

data	# nodes	# links	avg in-degree	avg path length	cluster. coef.	assortativ.
Advogato	7,422	56,508	7.61	3.79	0.093	-0.069
Epinions	131,828	841,372	6.38	4.53	0.081	-0.064
Flickr	2,302,925	33,140,018	14.39	4.36	0.107	0.015
FriendFeed	94,779	3,269,303	34.49	3.30	0.019	-0.144

(a)

description	$u \rightarrow v$	$u \leftarrow v$
u's certificate to v	TrustRank	LurkerRank
u likes v's post	TrustRank	LurkerRank

(b)

the *Advogato* network graph are labeled according to three different levels of certifications (trust links), namely *master, journeyer, apprentice*; a user without any trust certificate is called an *observer*. For each link from user u to user v, in the final aggregated graph we kept the last certification given by u to v. *Epinions* is the trust/distrust network studied in [19]. This network consists of about 132K users who issued above 841K statements (links).

We also used the followship graphs of two social media networks, Flickr and FriendFeed. We used the entire *Flickr* data studied in [20], originally collected in 2006–2007. For evaluation purposes, we also retrieved information originally stored in the dataset about the number of favorite markings every user's photos had. Our *FriendFeed* dataset refers to [5]. In order to fairly exploit information on the "likes" every user received in the network, we used the maximal strongly connected component of the subgraph containing all users that received a "like" and their neighborhoods.

Graph Models. The different characteristics of TrustRank and LurkerRank algorithms require the use of two different graph models, which have opposite edge orientation, as summarized in Table 1(b). Note that the Anti-TrustRank algorithm runs on the same graph as TrustRank, since it starts upon the transposition of the adjacency matrix.

3.2 Setup of Trust/Distrust Ranking Methods

In TrustRank the notion of human-checking for a page to be spam is formalized by a binary function called *oracle*. However, a human-based oracle may not always be available, and hence relying on it could limit the applicability and scalability of TrustRank and similar algorithms (like Anti-TrustRank). To deal with this issue, in this work we follow different approaches to the definition of oracle function and of "goodness/badness" of a user, depending on whether the data provide trust indicators that are *explicit* or *implicit*. We elaborate on the two cases next.

Explicit Trust Indicators. *Advogato* and *Epinions* provide annotations on the trustworthiness/untrustworthiness of links between users, as previously discussed. We exploit such annotations to define the following oracle functions:

- *majority voting* (henceforth denoted as MV) over the set of trust/distrust statements that each user receives.
- *advogato-trust-metric* (henceforth denoted as AT), which exploits information on the user certifications available from the Advogato site.[1] This of course applies to *Advogato* only.
- *controversial scoring* (henceforth denoted as CS), which applies to *Epinions* only. Similarly to [18], CS is calculated for each user u as

$$CS(u) = \frac{trust(u) - distrust(u)}{trust(u) + distrust(u)}$$

where $trust(u)$ (resp. $distrust(u)$) is the number of $+1$s (resp. -1s) received by u from her/his neighbors. A user with CS equal to 1 (resp. -1) is trusted (resp. distrusted) by all her/his neighbors.

To decide if a user is to be regarded as "good" or "bad", we again distinguish between *Advogato* and *Epinions*. For each of the oracle functions in *Advogato*, we defined two variants of *goodness*: (i) users that are certified as *master* are considered good (henceforth denoted as M), or (ii) users that are certified as *master* or as *journeyer* are considered good (henceforth $M|J$). Dually, we defined two variants of *badness*: (i) users that are certified as *observer* are considered bad (henceforth denoted as O), or (ii) users that are certified as *observer* or as *apprentice* are considered bad (henceforth $O|A$). For *Epinions*, we defined goodness/badness for the CS function based on numerical thresholds at 0.5, 0.75; here, we aimed to resemble a mapping to ordinal scale of the Advogato certification levels. Notions of goodness/badness are straightforward for the MV function (henceforth $MV+$ to denote majority of trust certificates, whereas $MV-$ stands for the opposite).

Implicit Trust Indicators. Unlike trust network data, online social networks (OSNs) do not contain explicit trust assessments among users. Nevertheless, behavioral trust information can be inferred from some forms of user interaction that would provide an intuitive way of indicating trust in another user. Adali et al. [2] have in fact demonstrated that retweet data are a valid mechanism to infer trust in OSNs like Twitter. Accordingly, we leverage information on the number of *favorite markings* received by a user's photographs in *Flickr*, and on the number of *likes* received by a user's posts in *FriendFeed*, as empirical indicators of trust.

In order to define an oracle function based on the above indicators of trust, we postulate that the higher the number of users that indicate trust in a user u (by means of implicit trust statements), the more likely is the trustworthiness of user u. We formalize this intuition as an *entropy-based oracle* function H, in such a way that for any user u

$$H(u) = -\frac{1}{\log N(u)} \sum_{v \in N(u)} p_v \log p_v$$

---

[1] www.advogato.org/trust-metric.html.

with $p_v = ET(v, u)/(\sum_{z \in N(u)} ET(z, u))$, where $N(u)$ is the set of neighbors of node u, and $ET(v, u)$ is the empirical trust function measuring the number of implicit trust statements (i.e., likes or favorites) assigned by node v to node u. Analogously to the trust networks case, we defined goodness/badness for the H function based on numerical thresholds equal to the median (Q_2) and third quartile (Q_3) of the distribution of H values over all users.

3.3   Assessment Criteria

We assessed the ranking methods in terms of *Kendall tau rank correlation* coefficient and *Bpref* measure.

Kendall tau correlation evaluates the similarity between two rankings, expressed as sets of ordered pairs, based on the number of inversions of node pairs which would be needed to transform one ranking into the other. Given two rankings $\mathcal{L}', \mathcal{L}''$, it is computed as: $Kendall(\mathcal{L}', \mathcal{L}'') = 1 - (2\Delta(\mathcal{P}(\mathcal{L}'), \mathcal{P}(\mathcal{L}'')))/(N(N-1))$, where $N = |\mathcal{L}'| = |\mathcal{L}''|$ and $\Delta(\mathcal{P}(\mathcal{L}'), \mathcal{P}(\mathcal{L}''))$ is the symmetric difference distance between the two rankings, calculated as number of unshared node pairs between the two lists.

Binary preference (Bpref) [3] evaluates the performance from a different view, i.e., the number of non-relevant candidates. It computes a preference relation of whether judged relevant candidates R of a list $\mathcal{L}'$ are retrieved, i.e., occur in a second list $\mathcal{L}''$, ahead of judged irrelevant candidates N, and is formulated as $Bpref(R, N) = (1/|R|) \sum_r (1 - (\#of\ n\ ranked\ higher\ than\ r)/|R|)$, where r is a relevant retrieved candidate, and n is a member of the first $|R|$ irrelevant retrieved candidates. In our setting, we considered as relevant the *good*-certificated (resp. *bad*-certificated) nodes, as computed by the TrustRank (resp. Anti-TrustRank) oracle function, and as irrelevant all the remaining nodes.

4   Results

We organize the presentation of our results as follows. We begin with an evaluation of each of the ranking methods to assess their ability of ranking trustworthy and untrustworthy users. Then we provide a comparative evaluation of the ranking methods in terms of correlation of their ranking results.

Notations: We recall main notations that will be used throughout this section. The prefixes TR_ and ATR_ will be used to denote TrustRank and Anti-TrustRank methods, respectively. MV stands for majority voting criterion (further, $MV+$ and $MV-$ are used to denote majority of trusts and distrusts, in *Epinions*. $M, M|J, O, O|A$ refer to the four goodness/badness notions used for *Advogato* (i.e., master, journeyer, etc.) and AT stands for Advogato trust metric. CS refers to the controversial scoring function used for *Epinions*. H refers to the entropy-based oracle function used for *Flickr* and *FriendFeed* networks.

In the result tables reported in the following (Tables 2, 3, 4 and 5), we will show in bold the best-performing values per method, and in underlined bold the absolute best-performing values for the specific dataset.

Table 2. Trustworthiness evaluation (left table) and untrustworthiness evaluation (right table) of Bpref performance on trust networks.

dataset relevant set	Advogato M	M|J	Epinions CS ≥ 0.5	CS ≥ 0.75	MV+	dataset relevant set	Advogato O	O|A	Epinions CS < 0.5	CS < 0.75	MV−
LRin	.135	.598	.290	.240	.336	LRin	.228	.243	.640	.650	**.637**
LRin-out	.142	.604	.299	.247	.345	LRin-out	.300	.294	.631	.645	.627
LRout	*.486*	*.673*	.789	.731	.825	LRout	.050	.086	.188	.220	.167
acLRin	.124	.596	.304	.253	.351	acLRin	.279	.282	.627	.640	.622
acLRin-out	.173	.609	.288	.235	.336	acLRin-out	*.364*	*.347*	**.641**	**.654**	.636
acLRout	*.486*	*.673*	**.837**	**.780**	**.872**	acLRout	.050	.086	.144	.175	.123
TR_InvPR	.659	.718	.791	.737	.826	ATR_PR	.287	.303	.422	.453	.401
TR_IO	**.733**	**.767**	*.809*	*.765*	*.838*	ATR_OI	**.375**	**.369**	*.470*	*.496*	*.456*

The *relevant* set corresponds to the *good*-certificated nodes (resp. *bad*-certificated nodes) in the trustworthiness (resp. untrustworthiness) evaluation, as computed by the oracle function of each method.

Note that we tested TrustRank and Anti-TrustRank with different sizes of the seed set, varying from 5 % to 25 % of the total number of nodes. We observed no significant variations in the ranking, therefore for the sake of brevity of presentation we will present results obtained with seed set size equal to 10 %.

4.1 Trust and Distrust Evaluation

Table 2 reports Bpref results for the evaluation of trustworthiness and untrustworthiness, respectively. We focus here on *Advogato* and *Epinions*, since the explicit trust indicators such networks provide fit more closely to a ground-truth-like evaluation.

Looking at Table 2 (left side), TrustRank methods achieved higher Bpref than LurkerRank methods in detecting trustworthy users, under both settings of oracle's goodness (i.e., M and $M|J$), on *Advogato*. However, on *Epinions*, TrustRank performed better for trustworthy users only against the in-neighbors-driven and in-out-neighbors-driven variants of LurkerRank; by contrast, LRout performance was very close to that of TR_InvPR, and even acLRout was the absolute best-performing method.

Concerning the evaluation of untrustworthy users (Table 2 (right side)), on *Advogato*, Anti-TrustRank behaved better than LurkerRank, although the best-performing LurkerRank method (i.e., acLRin-out) was quite close to the best-performing Anti-TrustRank variant. Even more surprisingly, on *Epinions*, the in-neighbors- and in-out-neighbors-driven variants of LurkerRank achieved higher Bpref than Anti-TrustRank methods.

4.2 Ranking Correlation Analysis

LurkerRank vs. TrustRank. Tables 3 and 4 (left side) report the Kendall rank correlation obtained by comparing TrustRank and LurkerRank on the various datasets. Both in trust networks and OSNs, LRout and acLRout showed higher correlation with TrustRank than the other LurkerRank methods.

Table 3. Kendall correlation between LurkerRank and TrustRank methods on *Advogato* (left table) and *Epinions* (right table).

oracle, goodness	LRin	LRin-out	LRout	ac-LRin	ac-LRin-out	ac-LRout
TR_InvPR *AT, M*	.367	.276	**.741**	.305	.205	**.710**
TR_InvPR *AT, M|J*	.382	.293	.738	.323	.220	.707
TR_IO *AT, M*	.356	.262	.723	.290	.193	.691
TR_IO *AT, M|J*	.316	.217	.692	.244	.149	.661
TR_InvPR *MV, M*	.310	.238	.642	.264	.182	.613
TR_InvPR *MV, M|J*	.284	.228	.577	.254	.184	.551
TR_IO *MV, M*	.352	.257	.713	.284	.189	.682
TR_IO *MV, M|J*	.314	.212	.683	.238	.145	.652

oracle, goodness	LRin	LRin-out	LRout	ac-LRin	ac-LRin-out	ac-LRout
TR_InvPR $CS \geq 0.5$	-.091	-.044	**.717**	-.039	-.049	**.683**
TR_IO $CS \geq 0.5$	-.211	-.201	.676	-.197	-.206	.651
TR_InvPR $CS \geq 0.75$	-.093	-.047	.716	-.041	-.052	.682
TR_IO $CS \geq 0.75$	-.210	-.204	.675	-.200	-.208	.650
TR_InvPR *MV+*	**-.089**	**-.043**	**.717**	**-.037**	**-.047**	**.683**
TR_IO *MV+*	-.212	-.201	.676	-.197	-.204	.651

Table 4. Kendall correlation of LurkerRank with TrustRank methods (left table) and Anti-TrustRank methods (right table) on social media networks. Upper subtables show results on *Flickr*, and bottom subtables show results on *FriendFeed*.

oracle, goodness	LRin	LRin-out	LRout	ac-LRin	ac-LRin-out	ac-LRout
TR_InvPR $H \geq Q_2$	.282	.440	.553	.443	**.410**	.552
TR_IO $H \geq Q_2$	.292	.434	.615	.440	.385	.610
TR_InvPR $H \geq Q_3$	.293	**.441**	.562	.445	.402	.561
TR_IO $H \geq Q_3$	**.298**	.439	**.618**	**.446**	.386	**.614**
TR_InvPR $H \geq Q_2$	-.035	-.045	.334	-.035	-.018	.334
TR_IO $H \geq Q_2$	-.031	-.041	.335	-.031	-.017	.335
TR_InvPR $H \geq Q_3$	.024	.004	**.340**	.024	.010	**.340**
TR_IO $H \geq Q_3$	.021	.002	.339	.021	.008	.339

oracle, badness	LRin	LRin-out	LRout	ac-LRin	ac-LRin-out	ac-LRout
ATR_PR $H < Q_2$	.127	.368	.236	.356	.422	.244
ATR_OI $H < Q_2$	.182	.442	.296	.433	.468	.299
ATR_PR $H < Q_3$	.120	.371	.238	.359	.431	.247
ATR_OI $H < Q_3$	**.205**	**.459**	.306	**.450**	**.477**	**.308**
ATR_PR $H < Q_2$	.185	.138	.399	.185	.060	.399
ATR_OI $H < Q_2$	**.296**	**.242**	.356	**.296**	**.136**	.356
ATR_PR $H < Q_3$	.186	.139	**.402**	.186	.062	**.402**
ATR_OI $H < Q_3$	**.296**	**.242**	.356	**.296**	**.136**	.356

On the trust networks, the highest correlation corresponded to similar scores (i.e., 0.74 for *Advogato* and 0.72 for *Epinions*, both comparing LRout with TR_InvPR). The various LurkerRank methods performed quite differently from each other: the gap of both LRin/acLRin and LRin-out/acLRin-out w.r.t. LRout/acLRout was smaller on *Advogato* (0.4 on average), while on *Epinions* the difference in correlation among the same methods was about 0.8. More specifically, while on *Advogato* LRin/acLRin and LRin-out/acLRin-out showed some correlation with TrustRank (in the range of 0.14–0.38), on *Epinions* the correlation was always negative (in the order of −0.2 w.r.t. TR_IO and −0.09 w.r.t. TR_InvPR).

As concerns evaluation on OSNs, LRout and acLRout again obtained higher correlation scores w.r.t. the other LurkerRank methods, but lower than the scores observed for trust networks (up to 0.62 on *Flickr* and 0.34 on *FriendFeed*). LRin/acLRin and LRin-out/acLRin-out showed some significant correlation with TrustRank (0.38–0.44) on *Flickr*, but no correlation on *FriendFeed*.

LurkerRank vs. Anti-TrustRank. Ranking correlation results obtained by comparing LurkerRank with Anti-TrustRank are reported in Tables 4 (right side) and 5.

A first remark is that the highest correlation scores were lower than those obtained when comparing LurkerRank with TrustRank in both trust networks. Moreover, again in contrast to the previous analysis vs. TrustRank, on *Advogato* the relative differences in performance among the LurkerRank methods were much less larger. On both trust networks, LRin/acLRin and LRin-out/ acLRin-out generally showed higher correlation with Anti-TrustRank than LRout and acLRout. By contrast, the correlation between LRin and Anti-TrustRank

Table 5. Kendall correlation between LurkerRank and Anti-TrustRank methods on *Advogato* (left table) and *Epinions* (right table).

	oracle, badness	LRin	LRin-out	LRout	ac-LRin	ac-LRin-out	ac-LRout
ATR_PR	AT,O	.477	.428	.369	.472	.354	.349
ATR_PR	$AT,O\|A$	.454	.419	.349	.460	.351	.332
ATR_OI	AT,O	.300	.307	.234	.332	.270	.227
ATR_OI	$AT,O\|A$	.313	.316	.244	.343	.276	.235
ATR_PR	MV,O	**.550**	**.485**	**.439**	**.540**	**.394**	**.413**
ATR_PR	$MV,O\|A$	.465	.409	.347	.452	.337	.328
ATR_OI	MV,O	.469	.423	.430	.467	.346	.406
ATR_OI	$MV,O\|A$	.345	.337	.285	.366	.288	.273

	oracle, badness	LRin	LRin-out	LRout	ac-LRin	ac-LRin-out	ac-LRout
ATR_PR	$CS<0.5$	.310	.336	.183	.344	.301	.157
ATR_OI	$CS<0.5$	.411	.435	.125	.444	.376	.086
ATR_PR	$CS<0.75$	.314	.342	.178	.350	.303	.152
ATR_OI	$CS<0.75$	**.418**	**.443**	.122	**.452**	**.383**	.082
ATR_PR	$MV-$	.303	.328	**.194**	.335	.293	**.166**
ATR_OI	$MV-$	.407	.431	.126	.439	.372	.087

was very weak in both OSNs, where the highest scores were obtained by LRout/acLRout and acLRin-out (up to 0.48).

Remarks on Seed-Set Selection and Oracle Functions. The methods used to select the seed set impacted differently on the four datasets. On *Epinions* TR_IO showed higher correlation with LRin/acLRin and LRin-out/acLRin-out than TR_InvPR, while the latter showed higher correlation with LRout and acLRout than the former. The seed set selection methods did not lead to large variation in performance on *Advogato* when comparing TrustRank with LurkerRank, while ATR_PR always showed higher correlation with LurkerRank than Anti-TrustRank_OI. An opposite situation was observed on OSNs, where ATR_OI showed higher correlation with LurkerRank than ATR_PR, while no clear trend can be identified when comparing TR_IO and TR_InvPr with LurkerRank.

As concerns the oracle functions, on *Advogato* LurkerRank generally showed higher correlation with TrustRank (resp. Anti-TrustRank) when using AT (resp. MV). By contrast, on *Epinions*, no significantly different effect was observed when using CS or MV.

4.3   Summary of Findings and Discussion

"To trust or not to trust lurkers?" is the question we raised in this paper. In the attempt to give a first answer to it, we summarize main findings of our study.

The LurkerRank methods based on the out-neighbors-driven model (i) behaved as good as or even better than TrustRank methods in terms of Bpref, and (ii) they showed high Kendall correlation with TrustRank methods. These findings should be interpreted at the light of a major conclusion we had in [25] that LRout and acLRout are less effective in scoring lurkers than the other LurkerRank methods. This implies that LRout and acLRout are able to produce high ranking scores also for (relatively active) users that are likely to be trustworthy. In short: *Trustworthy users can be found among lurkers.*

Concerning untrustworthiness, the in-neighbors-driven and in-out-neighbors-driven variants of LurkerRank (iii) achieved higher Bpref than Anti-TrustRank methods, and (iv) they showed moderate Kendall correlation with Anti-TrustRank methods in trust networks, but also poor correlation in social media networks. Note that point (iii) refers only to trust networks, wherein we assumed that those rates of information-production to information-consumption that are peculiar of lurking behaviors may be hidden in explicit trust/distrust links. In effect, when considering social media networks, no LurkerRank methods showed significant correlation with a method like Anti-TrustRank specifically designed to detect untrustworthy/spam users. Therefore, we would tend to state that: *Lurkers are not necessarily untrustworthy users.*

5   Conclusion

In this paper we took a first step towards the understanding of relations between lurking and trust/distrust behaviors. We conducted our analysis upon a comparison between existing algorithms specifically designed for ranking lurkers and trustworthy/untrustworthy users.

As future work, we will incorporate content-sensitive information in our lurking-oriented trust/distrust analysis. Moreover, our results depend on trust or distrust ranking methods that only take into account global metrics: it would be important to investigate whether personalized or local trust metrics, used in combination with global trust ranking, can aid improving the understanding of such complex behavioral dynamics as those concerning trust and lurking.

References

1. Adali, S.: Modeling Trust Context in Networks. Springer Briefs in Computer Science. Springer, New York (2013)
2. Adali, S., Escriva, R., Goldberg, M.K., Hayvanovych, M., Magdon-Ismail, M., Szymanski, B.K., Wallace, W.A., Williams, G.T.: Measuring behavioral trust in social networks. In: Proceedings of IEEE International Conference on Intelligence and Security Informatics, pp. 150–152 (2010)
3. Buckley, C., Voorhees, E.M.: Retrieval evaluation with incomplete information. In: Proceedings of ACM SIGIR Conference on Research and Development in Information Retrieval (SIGIR), pp. 25–32 (2004)
4. Castillo, C., Mendoza, M., Poblete, B.: Information credibility on twitter. In: Proceedings of ACM Conference on World Wide Web (WWW), pp. 675–684 (2011)
5. Celli, F., Di Lascio, F.M.L., Magnani, M., Pacelli, B., Rossi, L.: Social network data and practices: the case of friendfeed. In: Chai, S.-K., Salerno, J.J., Mabry, P.L. (eds.) SBP 2010. LNCS, vol. 6007, pp. 346–353. Springer, Heidelberg (2010)
6. Edelmann, N.: Reviewing the definitions of "lurkers" and some implications for online research. Cyberpsychology Behav. Soc. Network. 16(9), 645–649 (2013)
7. Ghosh, S., Viswanath, B., Kooti, F., Sharma, N.K., Korlam, G., Benevenuto, F., Ganguly, N., Gummadi, P.K.: Understanding and combating link farming in the Twitter social network. In: Proceedings of ACM Conference on World Wide Web (WWW), pp. 61–70 (2012)
8. Golbeck, J.: Computing and Applying Trust in Web-based Social Networks. Ph.D. thesis, College Park, MD, USA (2005)
9. Graham, F.C., Tsiatas, A., Xu, W.: Dirichlet pagerank and ranking algorithms based on trust and distrust. Internet Math. 9(1), 113–134 (2013)
10. Guha, R.V., Kumar, R., Raghavan, P., Tomkins, A.: Propagation of trust and distrust. In: Proceedings of ACM Conference on World Wide Web (WWW), pp. 403–412 (2004)

11. Gyöngyi, Z., Garcia-Molina, H., Pedersen, J.O.: Combating web spam with trustrank. In: Proceedings of International Conference on Very Large Data Bases (VLDB), pp. 576–587 (2004)
12. Hamdi, S., Bouzeghoub, A., Gançarski, A.L., Yahia, S.B.: Trust inference computation for online social networks. In: Proceedings of International Conference on Trust, Security and Privacy in Computing and Communications (TrustCom), pp. 210–217 (2013)
13. Jiang, W., Wang, G., Wu, J.: Generating trusted graphs for trust evaluation in online social networks. Future Gener. Comp. Syst. **31**, 48–58 (2014)
14. de Kerchove, C., Dooren, P.V.: The pagetrust algorithm: how to rank web pages when negative links are allowed? In: Proceedings of SIAM International Conference on Data Mining (SDM), pp. 346–352 (2008)
15. Krishnan, V., Raj, R.: Web spam detection with anti-trust rank. In: Proceedings of International Workshop on Adversarial Information Retrieval on the Web (AIR-Web), pp. 37–40 (2006)
16. Leskovec, J., Huttenlocher, D.P., Kleinberg, J.M.: Predicting positive and negative links in online social networks. In: Proceedings of ACM Conference on World Wide Web (WWW), pp. 641–650 (2010)
17. Liu, H., Lim, E., Lauw, H.W., Le, M., Sun, A., Srivastava, J., Kim, Y.A.: Predicting trusts among users of online communities: an epinions case study. In: Proceedings of ACM Conference on Electronic Commerce (EC), pp. 310–319 (2008)
18. Massa, P., Avesani, P.: Controversial users demand local trust metrics: an experimental study on epinions.com community. In: Proceedings of AAAI Conference on Artificial Intelligence (AAAI), pp. 121–126 (2005)
19. Massa, P., Avesani, P.: Trust-aware bootstrapping of recommender systems. In: Proceedings of ECAI Workshop on Recommender Systems, pp. 29–33 (2006)
20. Mislove, A., Koppula, H.S., Gummadi, K.P., Druschel, P., Bhattacharjee, B.: Growth of the flickr social network. In: Proceedings of the 1st ACM SIGCOMM Workshop on Social Networks (WOSN 2008) (2008)
21. Nonnecke, B., Preece, J.J.: Lurker demographics: counting the silent. In: Proceedings of ACM Conference on Human Factors in Computing Systems (CHI), pp. 73–80 (2000)
22. Ortega, F.J., Troyano, J.A., Cruz, F.L., Vallejo, C.G., Enríquez, F.: Propagation of trust and distrust for the detection of trolls in a social network. Comput. Netw. **56**(12), 2884–2895 (2012)
23. Preece, J.J., Nonnecke, B., Andrews, D.: The top five reasons for lurking: improving community experiences for everyone. Comput. Hum. Behav. **20**(2), 201–223 (2004)
24. Sun, N., Rau, P.P.L., Ma, L.: Understanding lurkers in online communities: a literature review. Comput. Hum. Behav. **38**, 110–117 (2014)
25. Tagarelli, A., Interdonato, R.: "Who's out there?": identifying and ranking lurkers in social networks. In: Proceedings of International Conference on Advances in Social Networks Analysis and Mining (ASONAM), pp. 215–222 (2013)
26. Tagarelli, A., Interdonato, R.: Lurking in social networks: topology-based analysis and ranking methods. Soc. Netw. Anal. Min. **4**(230), 27 (2014)
27. Tagarelli, A., Interdonato, R.: Time-aware analysis and ranking of lurkers in social networks. Soc. Netw. Anal. Min. **5**(1), 23 (2015)
28. Walter, F.E., Battiston, S., Schweitzer, F.: Personalised and dynamic trust in social networks. In: Proceedings of ACM Conference on Recommender Systems (RecSys), pp. 197–204 (2009)

Modelling Trend Progression Through an Extension of the Polya Urn Process

Marijn ten Thij[(⊠)] and Sandjai Bhulai

Faculty of Sciences, Vrije Universiteit Amsterdam, Amsterdam, The Netherlands
{m.c.ten.thij,s.bhulai}@vu.nl

Abstract. Knowing how and when trends are formed is a frequently visited research goal. In our work, we focus on the progression of trends through (social) networks. We use a random graph (RG) model to mimic the progression of a trend through the network. The context of the trend is not included in our model. We show that every state of the RG model maps to a state of the Polya process. We find that the limit of the component size distribution of the RG model shows power-law behaviour. These results are also supported by simulations.

Keywords: Retweet graph · Twitter · Graph dynamics · Random graph model · Polya process

1   Introduction

How can we reach a large audience with our message? What is the best way to reach a large audience with an advertisement? These are questions that are asked many times in our modern day society. Not only for corporate interest, but also for public interest by governments and charities. Everyone wants to get their message across to a large audience. Finding out how to do this is a frequently visited research goal in many fields, e.g. economics [23], evolutionary biology [8,27] and physics [20].

In our work, we focus on the progression of trends through the network of users. Incident to our approach, we focus on the microscopic dynamics of user-to-user interaction to derive the overall behaviour, which is similar to the approach used in other works, e.g. [11,25]. Our work differs from these in that we model the spread of the messages in a step-by-step fashion, whereas [11,25] use a given degree distribution per user as a start of their analysis.

Our goal is to devise a model that mimics the progression of a trend through (social) networks. By doing this, we focus only on the pattern of progression of the trends and not their content. Based on observations from *Twitter* data, we have built a model that captures the different changes that occur in a network whilst a topic is spreading. In [24], we derived basic growth properties of the model and the speed of convergence of these properties. In this paper, we derive the component size distribution of the model.

© Springer International Publishing Switzerland 2016
A. Wierzbicki et al. (Eds.): NetSci-X 2016, LNCS 9564, pp. 57–67, 2016.
DOI: 10.1007/978-3-319-28361-6_5

In Sect. 2, we describe related fields of study, and in Sect. 3 we introduce the RG model and the Polya process. Here we show that the RG model can be easily mapped to the Polya process. Then, in Sect. 4, we derive the behaviour of the component size distribution. Finally, we state our conclusions and discuss the possibilities for further research in Sect. 5.

2   Related Work

There are many studies that focus on information diffusion in online social networks. In [12], Guille et al. provide a survey, in which they distinguish two approaches: a descriptive approach and a predictive approach. A few examples of these approaches are given below.

A large number of descriptive studies into information diffusion have added to the knowledge about how messages progress through online social networks. Lerman and Ghosh [17] find that diffusion of information in *Twitter* and *Digg* is very dependent on the network structure. Bhattacharya and Ram [4] study the diffusion of news items in *Twitter* for several well-known news media and find that these cascades follow a star-like structure. Friggeri et al. [10] study rumors in Facebook and find bursty spreading patterns. Sadikov and Martinez [22] find that on *Twitter*, tags tend to travel to distant parts of the network and URLs tend to travel shorter distances. Bhamidi et al. [3] propose and validate a so-called superstar random graph model for a giant component of a retweet graph. Hoang and Lim [13] propose a dynamic model that uses both user and item virality and user susceptability as descriptors to model information diffusion. Iwata et al. [14] use an inhomogeneous Poisson Process to model the diffusion of item adoption. Another angle to model information diffusion uses epidemic spreading: By a maximum entropy argument Bauckhage et al. [2] find a closed form expression for the path length distribution in a network. Finally, Carton et al. [5] propose to perform an audience analysis when analysing diffusion processes, thus including not only the diffusers in the analysis but also the receivers of the content.

Romero et al. [21] use the predicitive approach to analyse the spread mechanics of content through hashtag use and derive probabilities that users adopt a hashtag. Kupavskii et al. [15] predict the number of retweets based on several features. They find that the flow of a message is one of the most important features in the prediction. Altshuler et al. [1] use past information and diffusion models to derive a lower bound on the probability that a topic becomes trending. Zaman et al. [28] predict future retweets based on features at the user level. Wu and Raschid [26] define a user specific potential function which reflects the likelihood of a follower sharing the users content in the future.

Classification and clustering of trends on *Twitter* has also attracted considerable attention in the literature. Zubiaga et al. [29] derive four different types of trends, using fifteen features to make their distinction. They distinguish trends triggered by news, current events, memes or commemorative tweets. Lehmann et al. [16] study different patterns of hashtag trends in *Twitter*. They also observe four different classes of hashtag trends. Rattanaritnont et al. [19] propose to distinguish topics based on four factors, namely cascade ratio, tweet ratio, time of tweet and patterns in topic-sensitive hashtags. Ferrara et al. [9] cluster memes based on content and user, tweet and network similarity measures.

We use the analysis of urn processes in this paper, in contrast to other works in this area. Pemantle [18] presents a survey of different techniques that are used in this field of research. In this work, we focus on extensions of the Polya urn problem, which is thoroughly analysed by Chung et al. in [6]. Specifically, we are interested in the infinite generalized Polya urn model, as studied in Sect. 4 of [6].

3   Problem Formulation

In this section, we first describe the setup of the RG model. Then, the Polya process is introduced. Finally, we show that every state of the model maps to a state of the Polya process.

Our main object of study is the retweet graph $G = (V, E)$, which is a graph of users that have participated in the discussion of a specific topic. A directed edge $e = (u, v)$ indicates that user v has retweeted a tweet of u. We observe the retweet graph at the time instances $t = 0, 1, 2, \ldots$, where either a new node or a new edge is added to the graph, and we denote by $G_t = (V_t, E_t)$ the retweet graph at time t. As usual, the out- (in-) degree of node u is the number of directed edges with source (destination) in u. For every new message initiated by a new user u a tree H_u is formed. Then, T_t denotes the forest of message trees. Note that in the RG model, a new message from an already existing user u (that is, $u \in T_t$) does not initiate a new message tree. We define $|T_t|$ as the number of new users that have started a message tree up to time t. I.e. G_t can be seen as a simple representation of the union of message trees $\cup_{H_u \in T_t} H_u$.

The goal of the model is to capture the development of trending behaviour. We do this by combining the spread of several messages. As a result of this approach, we first need to model the progression of a single message in the network. To this end, we use the superstar model of Bhamidi et al. [3] for modelling distinct components of the retweet graph, to which we add the mechanism for new components to arrive and the existing components to merge. In this paper, our aim is to analyse the component size distribution of G_t. For the sake of simplicity of the model, we neglect the friend-follower network of *Twitter*. Note that in *Twitter* every user can retweet any message sent by any public user, which supports our simplification.

We consider the evolution of the retweet graph in time $(G_t)_{t \geq 0}$. We use a subscript t to indicate G_t and related notions at time t. We omit the index t when referring to the graph at $t \to \infty$. Let G_0 denote the graph at the start of the progression. In the analysis of this paper, we assume G_0 consists of a single node. Note that in reality, this does not need to be the case: any directed graph can be used as an input graph G_0.

Recall that G_t is a graph of *users*, and an edge (u, v) means that v has retweeted a tweet of u. We consider time instances $t = 1, 2, \ldots$ when either a new node or a new edge is added to the graph G_{t-1}. We distinguish three types of changes in the retweet graph:

- T_1: a new user u has posted a new message on the topic, so node u is added to G_{t-1};
- T_2: a new user v has retweeted an existing user u, so node v and edge (u, v) are added to G_{t-1};
- T_3: an existing user v has retweeted another existing user u, so edge (u, v) is added to G_{t-1}.

Note that the initial node in G_0 is equivalent to a T_1 arrival at time $t = 0$. Assume that each change in G_t at $t = 1, 2, \ldots$ is T_1 with probability $\lambda/(1 + \lambda)$, independently of the past. Also, assume that a new edge (retweet) is coming from a new user with probability p. Then, the probabilities of T_1, T_2 and T_3 arrivals are, $\frac{\lambda}{\lambda+1}$, $\frac{p}{\lambda+1}$, $\frac{1-p}{\lambda+1}$ respectively. The parameter p governs the process of components merging together, while λ governs the arrival of new components in the graph.

For both T_2 and T_3 arrivals we define the same mechanism to choose the source of the new edge (u, v) as follows.

Let $u_0, u_1, \ldots$ be the users that have been added to the graph as T_1 arrivals, where u_0 is the initial node. Denote by $H_{i,t}$ the subgraph of G_t that includes u_i and all users that have retweeted the message of u_i in the interval $(0, t]$. We call such a subgraph a message tree with root u_i. We assume that the probability that a T_2 or T_3 arrival at time t will attach an edge to one of the nodes in $H_{i,t-1}$ with probability $p_{H_{i,t-1}}$ is proportional to the size of the message tree:

$$p_{H_{i,t-1}} = \frac{|H_{i,t-1}|}{\sum_{H_{j,t-1} \subset \mathcal{T}_{t-1}} |H_{j,t-1}|}.$$

This creates a preferential attachment mechanism in the formation of the message trees.

For the selection of the source node, we use the superstar model, with parameter q chosen uniformly over all message trees. This model was suggested in [3] for modelling the largest connected component of the retweet graph on a given topic, in order to describe a progression mechanism for a single retweet tree. Our extensions compared to [3] are that we allow new message trees to appear (T_1 arrivals), and that different message trees may either remain disconnected or get connected by a T_3 arrival.

For a T_3 arrival, the target of the new edge (u, v) is chosen uniformly at random from V_{t-1}, with the exception of the earlier chosen source node u, to prevent self-loops. That is, any user is equally likely to retweet a message from another existing user. Thus, after a T_3 arrival a message tree can have cycles.

Note that we do not include tweets and retweets that do not result in new nodes or edges in the retweet graph. This could be done, for example, by introducing dynamic weights of vertices and edges, that increase with new tweets and retweets. Here, we consider only an unweighted model.

Polya Process. In our analysis of the previously stated model, we use the Polya process, which is defined in [6] as follows:

Given two parameters $\gamma \in \mathbb{R}, 0 \leq \bar{p} \leq 1$, we start with one bin, containing one ball. We then introduce balls one at a time. For each new ball, with probability $\bar{p}$, we create a new bin and place the ball in that bin; with probability $1 - \bar{p}$, we place the ball in an existing bin (of size m), such that the probability that the ball is placed in a bin is proportional to m^γ.

We only consider the case where $\gamma = 1$ in this paper.

Let $f_{i,t}$ denote the fraction of bins that contain i balls at time t. In [6], the authors find that under the following assumptions:

(i) for each i, there exists $f_i \in \mathbb{R}^+$ s.t. a.s. $\lim_{t\to\infty} f_{i,t}$ exists and is equal to f_i,

(ii) a.s. $\lim_{t\to\infty} \sum_{j=1}^{\infty} f_{j,t} j^\gamma$ exists, is finite, and is equal to $\sum_{j=1}^{\infty} f_j j^\gamma$.

The limit of the fraction of bins that contain i balls (denoted by f_i) satisfies

$$f_i \propto i^{-(1+1/(1-\bar{p}))}.$$

Mapping from Retweet Graph to Balls and Bins. In this section, we show that every retweet graph G_t can be mapped to a state of the Polya process, with $\gamma = 1$ and $\bar{p} = \frac{\lambda}{\lambda+1}$.

Lemma 1. *Every retweet graph G_t can be represented as a state S of the Polya process.*

Proof. Suppose we have a retweet graph G_t, that consists of k components of known sizes, moreover $G_t = \{C_1, C_2, \ldots, C_k \mid |C_1|, |C_2|, \ldots, |C_k|\}$. For instance, in Fig. 1a $G_t = \{C_{green}, C_{yellow}, C_{blue}, C_{red} \mid |C_{green}| = 5, |C_{yellow}| = 2, |C_{blue}| = 4, |C_{red}| = 2\}$. First, we take C_{green} that consists of five nodes and fill a bin with five green balls. Then, we take C_{yellow}, and fill a bin with $|C_{yellow}| = 2$ yellow balls. Next, we take C_{blue} and fill a bin with $|C_{blue}| = 4$ blue balls. Finally, we take C_{red} and fill a bin with $|C_{red} = 2|$ red balls. These four bins with their corresponding balls then form a state S of the Polya process, depicted in Fig. 1b. Note that by using this procedure for an arbitrary graph G_t, we can always construct a state S.

A Special Case: $p = 1$. In this subsection, we show that the RG model with parameter $p = 1$ is equivalent to the Polya process w.p. $\gamma = 1, \bar{p} = \frac{\lambda}{\lambda+1}$. We use this to find the limiting distribution of the component sizes of the RG model.

Theorem 2. *RG model w.p. $p = 1$ is equivalent to a Polya process w.p. $\gamma = 1$, $\bar{p} = \frac{\lambda}{\lambda+1}$.*

Proof. From Lemma 1 we know that a retweet graph G_t can be mapped to a state S of the Polya process. Next we show that the probability distribution of an arrival to G_t is identical to the probability distribution of an addition of a ball to the state S in the Polya process, given $p = 1$ in the RG model.

Since $p = 1$, we have two types of arivals, T_1 and T_2. First, we consider a T_1 arrival

$$\mathbb{P}(T_1 \text{ arrival}) = \frac{\lambda}{\lambda+1} = \bar{p} = \mathbb{P}(\text{new bin is created}). \qquad (1)$$

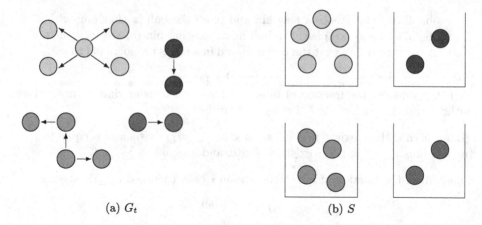

(a) G_t (b) S

Fig. 1. Mapping from retweet graph G_t (a) to Polya process state S (b).

Then, for a T_2 arrival, a new node is added to an existing component. The probability that a new node arrives to component i in G_t is

$$\mathbb{P}\,(\text{arrival to component } i \text{ in } G_t) = \frac{|C_i|}{|V_t|}. \tag{2}$$

For the Polya process, the probability that a new ball arrives in bin i in S is as follows

$$\mathbb{P}\,(\text{arrival to bin } i \text{ in } S) = \frac{X_i^{\gamma}}{\sum_{j=1}^{k} X_j^{\gamma}} = \frac{X_i}{\sum_{j=1}^{k} X_j}. \tag{3}$$

Using these equations and Lemma 1, we find that

$$\mathbb{P}\,(\text{arrival to component } i \text{ in } G_t) = \frac{|C_i|}{|V_t|} = \frac{|C_i|}{\sum_{j=1}^{k} |C_j|} = \frac{X_i}{\sum_{j=1}^{k} X_j},$$
$$= \mathbb{P}\,(\text{arrival to bin } i \text{ in } S).$$

Thus, the probability distribution of an arrival to the RG model w.p. $p = 1$ is identical to the probability distribution of the Polya process w.p. $\gamma = 1, \bar{p} = \frac{\lambda}{\lambda+1}$. In combination with Lemma 1, we conclude that the RG model is equivalent to a Polya process with parameters $\gamma = 1$ and $\bar{p} = \frac{\lambda}{\lambda+1}$.

From this equivalence, we immediately obtain the limiting component size distribution of the RG model from [6], given $p = 1$.

Corollary 3. *For f_i, the fraction of components of size i, it holds that*

$$f_i \propto i^{-(\lambda+2)},$$

for the RG model w.p. $p = 1$.

4   Component Size Distribution

Using the fact that the RG model can be mapped to a Polya process, we derive the limiting behaviour of the component size distribution for general p.

Theorem 4. *For the RG model, the limit f_i of the fraction of components of size i a.s. satisfies*

$$f_i \propto i^{-\left(1 + \frac{\lambda + 1}{p}\right)}.$$

Proof. Given the mapping from the retweet graph to the Polya process, we can derive f_i for the RG model similar to the derivation in [6]. In that paper, the authors define $p_{i,t}$ as follows

$$p_{i,t} := \mathbb{P}\left(\text{ball at time } t \text{ is placed in bin of size } i\right), \tag{4}$$

with the convention $p_{0,t} = \bar{p}$. Therefore, we can find an expression for f_i by finding an expression for $p_{i,t}$ in the RG model and then following a similar line of reasoning as in [6]. Note that (4) is equal to

$$p_{i,t} := \mathbb{P}\left(\text{ball at time } t \text{ increases a bins size to } i + 1\right).$$

Rewriting this equation to the RG model it holds that,

$$p_{i,t} = \mathbb{P}\left(\text{arrival at time } t \text{ results in a component of size } i + 1\right).$$

Then, let $T_x \to |C_n| = i+1$ denote a T_x arrival to component C_n augmenting its size to $i+1$ and let $T_3 + C_o$ denote that a T_3 arrival connects to component C_0. We find that for $i \geq 2$

$$p_{i,t} = \mathbb{P}\left(T_2 \to |C_n| = i+1\right) \cdot \mathbb{P}\left(T_2 \text{ arrival}\right) + \mathbb{P}\left(T_3 \to |C_n| = i+1\right) \cdot \mathbb{P}\left(T_3 \text{ arrival}\right),$$

$$= \mathbb{P}\left(T_2 \to |C_n| = i+1\right) \cdot \mathbb{P}\left(T_2 \text{ arrival}\right),$$

$$+ \sum_{k=1}^{i} \mathbb{P}\left(T_3 \to |C_n| = i+1 \mid T_3 + C_o, |C_o| = k\right) \cdot \mathbb{P}\left(T_3 \text{ arrival}\right) \cdot \mathbb{P}\left(T_3 + C_o \mid |C_o| = k\right),$$

$$= \frac{f_{i,t} \cdot i}{\sum_{j=1}^{\infty} f_{j,t} \cdot j} \cdot \frac{p}{\lambda + 1} + \sum_{k=1}^{i} \frac{f_{k,t} \cdot k}{\sum_{j=1}^{\infty} f_{j,t} \cdot j} \cdot \frac{1 - p}{\lambda + 1} \cdot \frac{2 \cdot k \cdot (i - k + 1)}{|V_t|^2 - |V_t|},$$

$$= \frac{f_{i,t} \cdot i}{\sum_{j=1}^{\infty} f_{j,t} \cdot j} \cdot \frac{p}{\lambda + 1} + \sum_{k=1}^{i} \frac{f_{k,t} \cdot k}{\sum_{j=1}^{\infty} f_{j,t} \cdot j} \cdot \frac{1 - p}{\lambda + 1} \cdot \frac{2 \cdot k \cdot (i - k + 1)}{\left(\sum_{j=1}^{\infty} f_{j,t} \cdot j\right)^2 - \sum_{j=1}^{\infty} f_{j,t} \cdot j},$$

with the convention that $p_{0,t} = \mathbb{P}(T_1) = \frac{\lambda}{\lambda + 1}$.

Then, let $f_{i,t} \to f_i$ a.s. as $t \to \infty$. Since the RG model can be mapped to the Polya process with parameter $\gamma = 1$ by Lemma 1, the limit $\sum_{j=1}^{\infty} f_j \cdot j$ exists and is equal the average bin size, which we will denote by $\overline{C}$. Thus, the aforementioned assumptions also hold for the RG model. Using this and defining $c = \frac{p_{i-1} - p_i}{f_i}$, we find

$$c \cdot f_i = p_{i-1} - p_i,$$

$$= \frac{f_{i-1} \cdot (i-1)}{\overline{C}} \cdot \frac{p}{\lambda+1} + \sum_{k=1}^{i-1} \frac{f_k \cdot k}{\overline{C}} \cdot \frac{1-p}{\lambda+1} \cdot \frac{2 \cdot k \cdot (i-k)}{\overline{C} \cdot (\overline{C}-1)},$$

$$- \left(\frac{f_i \cdot i}{\overline{C}} \cdot \frac{p}{\lambda+1} + \sum_{k=1}^{i} \frac{f_k \cdot k}{\overline{C}} \cdot \frac{1-p}{\lambda+1} \cdot \frac{2 \cdot k \cdot (i-k+1)}{\overline{C} \cdot (\overline{C}-1)} \right),$$

$$= \frac{p}{\lambda+1} \cdot \frac{f_{i-1} \cdot (i-1) - f_i \cdot i}{\overline{C}} + \frac{1-p}{\lambda+1} \cdot$$

$$\left(\sum_{k=1}^{i-1} \frac{f_k \cdot k}{\overline{C}} \cdot \frac{2 \cdot k \cdot (i-k)}{\overline{C} \cdot (\overline{C}-1)} - \sum_{k=1}^{i} \frac{f_k \cdot k}{\overline{C}} \cdot \frac{2 \cdot k \cdot (i-k+1)}{\overline{C} \cdot (\overline{C}-1)} \right),$$

$$= \frac{p}{\lambda+1} \cdot \frac{f_{i-1} \cdot (i-1) - f_i \cdot i}{\overline{C}} - \frac{1-p}{\lambda+1} \cdot \left(\frac{f_i \cdot i}{\overline{C}} \cdot \frac{2 \cdot i}{\overline{C} \cdot (\overline{C}-1)} + \sum_{k=1}^{i-1} \frac{f_k \cdot k}{\overline{C}} \cdot \frac{2 \cdot k}{\overline{C} \cdot (\overline{C}-1)} \right),$$

$$\leq \frac{p}{\lambda+1} \cdot \frac{f_{i-1} \cdot (i-1) - f_i \cdot i}{\overline{C}} - \frac{1-p}{\lambda+1} \cdot \frac{f_i \cdot i}{\overline{C}} \cdot \frac{2 \cdot i}{\overline{C} \cdot (\overline{C}-1)},$$

$$= \frac{p \cdot f_{i-1} \cdot (i-1) + \left[\left(\frac{2 \cdot i}{\overline{C} \cdot (\overline{C}-1)} - 1 \right) \cdot p - \frac{2 \cdot i}{\overline{C} \cdot (\overline{C}-1)} \right] \cdot f_i \cdot i}{(\lambda+1) \cdot \overline{C}}.$$

And therefore, for $i \geq 2$ it holds that

$$f_i \leq \frac{p \cdot (i-1)}{(\lambda+1) \cdot c \cdot \overline{C} - \left[\left(\frac{2 \cdot i}{\overline{C} \cdot (\overline{C}-1)} - 1 \right) \cdot p - \frac{2 \cdot i}{\overline{C} \cdot (\overline{C}-1)} \right] \cdot i} \cdot f_{i-1}.$$

Using this expression and defining $f_i \propto g(i)$ as $f_i = c(1 + o(1))g(i)$, we find that

$$f_i \leq f_1 \cdot \prod_{j=2}^{i} \frac{p \cdot (j-1)}{(\lambda+1) \cdot c \cdot \overline{C} - \left[\left(\frac{2 \cdot j}{\overline{C} \cdot (\overline{C}-1)} - 1 \right) \cdot p - \frac{2 \cdot j}{\overline{C} \cdot (\overline{C}-1)} \right] \cdot i},$$

$$\propto \prod_{j=2}^{i} \frac{p \cdot (j-1)}{\lambda+1+p \cdot j} = \prod_{j=2}^{i} \frac{j-1}{j + \frac{\lambda+1}{p}} \propto \frac{\Gamma(i)}{\Gamma\left(i+1+\frac{\lambda+1}{p}\right)} \propto i^{-\left(1+\frac{\lambda+1}{p}\right)}. \quad (5)$$

which indicates power-law behaviour.

Validation of Results. To validate these results, we ran multiple simulations using our model and plotted the probability density function (pdf) for each of these runs. We compare these simulations to the Yule distribution, with parameters α and $x_{\min}$. Since we are analysing the distribution of component sizes, it follows that $x_{\min} = 1$. Then, from Eq. 5, we find that $\alpha = \frac{\lambda+1}{p} + 1$. Let $\Gamma(\cdot)$ denote the Gamma function, by [7], the pdf of this distribution is as follows,

$$f(x) = \left(\frac{\lambda+1}{p} \right) \frac{\Gamma\left(\frac{\lambda+1}{p} + 1\right)}{\Gamma(1)} \frac{\Gamma(x)}{\Gamma\left(x + \frac{\lambda+1}{p} + 1\right)}. \quad (6)$$

In Fig. 2 we depict the results for several values of p of the simulations with $t = 100,000$, $\lambda = \frac{1}{3}$ and $q = 0.9$ as values for the other parameters of the RG model. Also depicted in Fig. 2 as black squares are the values of the pdf of the Yule distribution, shown in Eq. 6.

In Fig. 2 we see that for every run, there is one really large component. In [24], we named these components the Largest Connected Component (LCC) and we mention the fraction of nodes in the LCC in the legend of Fig. 2. Note that all the values for the other component sizes are slightly below the Yule distribution. This fact supports our claim that the component size distribution shows power-law behaviour. These values are slightly below the Yule distribution, since Eq. 5 is an upper bound for f_i.

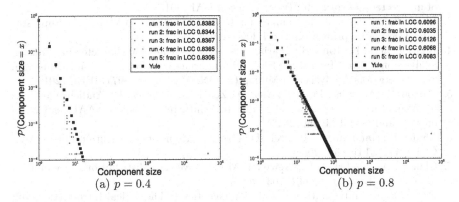

(a) $p = 0.4$ (b) $p = 0.8$

Fig. 2. Plots of the pdf of the component size distribution. For these simulations we used $t = 100,000$, $\lambda = \frac{1}{3}$ and $q = 0.9$.

5 Conclusion and Discussion

In this paper, in which we have extended our previous work on the RG model, we derived the limiting behaviour of the component sizes. Through a mapping of the RG model to the Polya process, we found that the distribution of component sizes shows power-law behaviour. Note that Corrolary 3 is identical to Theorem 4 when we fill in $p = 1$. Thus, interestingly enough, the possibility of merging components does not seem to affect this limiting behaviour greatly. The validation in this paper is based on simulated results, thus the model has currently not been tested to *Twitter* datasets.

Moreover, the model used in this paper can also easily be extended to a less general setting. For instance, the superstar parameter q is assumed to be equal for every message tree. This can be easily extended to an individual superstar parameter per message tree q_i. This addition does not change the result of the analysis shown in this paper and therefore is not included here.

Another aspect that could be taken into account in future work, is the weight of an edge. Given that there are multiple retweets between u and v, this can be taken into account by adding a weight to every edge. A last extension that could prove to be interesting, is to use time-varying parameters.

We plan to explore these aspects in our future research.

References

1. Altshuler, Y., Pan, W., Pentland, A.S.: Trends prediction using social diffusion models. In: Yang, S.J., Greenberg, A.M., Endsley, M. (eds.) SBP 2012. LNCS, vol. 7227, pp. 97–104. Springer, Heidelberg (2012)
2. Bauckhage, C., Kersting, K., Hadiji, F.: Parameterizing the distance distribution of undirected networks. In: Proceedings of UAI (2015)
3. Bhamidi, S., Steele, J.M., Zaman, T.: Twitter Event Networks and the Superstar Model. arXiv preprint arXiv:1211.3090 (2012)
4. Bhattacharya, D., Ram, S.: Sharing news articles using 140 characters: a diffusion analysis on twitter. In: 2012 IEEE/ACM International Conference on Advances in Social Networks Analysis and Mining (ASONAM), pp. 966–971. IEEE (2012)
5. Carton, S., Adar, E., Park, S., Mei, Q., Zeffer, N., Resnick, P.: Audience analysis for competing memes in social media. In: Ninth International AAAI Conference on Web and Social Media (2015)
6. Chung, F., Handjani, S., Jungreis, D.: Generalizations of polya's urn problem. Ann. Comb. **7**(2), 141–153 (2003)
7. Clauset, A., Shalizi, C.R., Newman, M.E.: Power-law distributions in empirical data. SIAM Rev. **51**(4), 661–703 (2009)
8. Ewens, W.J.: Mathematical Population Genetics 1: Theoretical Introduction, vol. 27. Springer Science & Business Media, New York (2012)
9. Ferrara, E., JafariAsbagh, M., Varol, O., Qazvinian, V., Menczer, F., Flammini, A.: Clustering memes in social media. In: 2013 IEEE/ACM International Conference on Advances in Social Networks Analysis and Mining (ASONAM), pp. 548–555. IEEE (2013)
10. Friggeri, A., Adamic, L., Eckles, D., Cheng, J.: Rumor cascades (2014). http://www.aaai.org/ocs/index.php/ICWSM/ICWSM14/paper/view/8122
11. Gleeson, J.P., Cellai, D., Onnela, J.P., Porter, M.A., Reed-Tsochas, F.: A simple generative model of collective online behavior. Proc. Natl. Acad. Sci. **111**(29), 10411–10415 (2014)
12. Guille, A., Hacid, H., Favre, C., Zighed, D.A.: Information diffusion in online social networks: a survey. ACM SIGMOD Rec. **42**(2), 17–28 (2013)
13. Hoang, T.A., Lim, E.P.: Virality and susceptibility in information diffusions. In: ICWSM (2012)
14. Iwata, T., Shah, A., Ghahramani, Z.: Discovering latent influence in online social activities via shared cascade poisson processes. In: Proceedings of the 19th ACM SIGKDD International Conference on Knowledge Discovery and Data Mining, KDD 2013, pp. 266–274. ACM, New York (2013). http://doi.acm.org/10.1145/2487575.2487624
15. Kupavskii, A., Ostroumova, L., Umnov, A., Usachev, S., Serdyukov, P., Gusev, G., Kustarev, A.: Prediction of retweet cascade size over time. In: Proceedings of the 21st ACM International Conference on Information and Knowledge Management, pp. 2335–2338. ACM (2012)

16. Lehmann, J., Gonçalves, B., Ramasco, J.J., Cattuto, C.: Dynamical classes of collective attention in Twitter. In: Proceedings of the 21st International Conference on World Wide Web, pp. 251–260. ACM (2012)

17. Lerman, K., Ghosh, R.: Information Contagion: An Empirical Study of the Spread of News on Digg and Twitter Social Networks (2010)

18. Pemantle, R., et al.: A survey of random processes with reinforcement. Probab. Surv. **4**, 1–79 (2007)

19. Rattanaritnont, G., Toyoda, M., Kitsuregawa, M.: A study on relationships between information cascades and popular topics in twitter. DEIM Forum **7**(5), 1–6 (2012). http://db-event.jpn.org/deim2012/proceedings/final-pdf/c7-5.pdf

20. Redner, S.: How popular is your paper? an empirical study of the citation distribution. Eur. Phys. J. B Condens. Matter Complex Syst. **4**(2), 131–134 (1998). http://dx.doi.org/10.1007/s100510050359

21. Romero, D.M., Meeder, B., Kleinberg, J.: Differences in the mechanics of information diffusion across topics: idioms, political hashtags, and complex contagion on Twitter. In: Proceedings of the 20th International Conference on World Wide Web, pp. 695–704. ACM (2011)

22. Sadikov, E., Martinez, M.M.M.: Information propagation on Twitter. CS322 Project Report (2009)

23. Simon, H.A.: On a class of skew distribution functions. Biometrika **42**, 425–440 (1955)

24. ten Thij, M., Ouboter, T., Worm, D., Litvak, N., van den Berg, H., Bhulai, S.: Modelling of trends in twitter using retweet graph dynamics. In: Bonato, A., Graham, F.C., Prałat, P. (eds.) WAW 2014. LNCS, vol. 8882, pp. 132–147. Springer, Heidelberg (2014)

25. Watts, D.J.: A simple model of global cascades on random networks. Proc. Natl. Acad. Sci. **99**(9), 5766–5771 (2002)

26. Wu, S., Raschid, L.: Prediction in a microblog hybrid network using bonacich potential. In: Proceedings of the 7th ACM International Conference on Web Search and Data Mining, WSDM 2014, pp. 383–392. ACM, New York (2014). http://doi.acm.org/10.1145/2556195.2556247

27. Yule, G.U.: A mathematical theory of evolution, based on the conclusions of Dr. J.C. Willis, F.R.S. Philos. Trans. R. Soc. Lond. Ser. B Containing Pap. Biol. Character **213**, 21–87 (1925)

28. Zaman, T.R., Herbrich, R., Stern, D.: Predicting information spreading in twitter. In: Social Science and the Wisdom of Crowds Workshop, vol. 55, pp. 1–4. Citeseer (2010). http://research.microsoft.com/pubs/141866/NIPS10_Twitter_final.pdf

29. Zubiaga, A., Spina, D., Fresno, V., Martínez, R.: Classifying trending topics: a typology of conversation triggers on Twitter. In: Proceedings of the 20th ACM International Conference on Information and Knowledge Management, pp. 2461–2464. ACM (2011)

Exploiting Content Quality and Question Difficulty in CQA Reputation Systems

Adrian Huna, Ivan Srba[✉], and Maria Bielikova

Faculty of Informatics and Information Technologies, Slovak University
of Technology in Bratislava, Ilkovicova 2, 842 16 Bratislava, Slovakia
{xhunaa,ivan.srba,maria.bielikova}@stuba.sk

Abstract. Community Question Answering (CQA) systems (e.g. Stack-Overflow) have gained popularity in the last years. With the increasing community size and amount of user generated content, a task of expert identification arose. To tackle this problem, various reputation mechanisms exist, however, they estimate user reputation especially according to overall user activity, while the quality of contributions is considered only secondary. As the result, reputation usually does not reflect the real value of users' contributions and, moreover, some users (so called reputation collectors) purposefully abuse reputation systems to achieve a high reputation score. We propose a novel reputation mechanism that focuses primarily on the quality and difficulty of users' contributions. Calculated reputation was compared with four baseline methods including the reputation schema employed in Stack Exchange platform. The experimental results showed a higher precision achieved by our approach, and confirmed an important role of contribution quality and difficulty in estimation of user reputation.

Keywords: Community Question Answering · User reputation · Expertise estimation

1 Introduction

The Internet is an enormous source of information which helps lots of people every day. Despite the amount of information available, there are still situations in which it is difficult to find specific information, or to answer a question that is too complex to be understood by a search engine. These types of situations led to creation of online communities whose members are focused on helping each other in a specific area. In the past years, especially many Community Question Answering (CQA) systems have appeared and gained popularity among users. They are essentially based on social interactions through asking and answering questions. In addition, all members of CQA communities can vote on the provided answers with the aim to select the most useful one among them. Moreover, the asker can pick any answer and mark it as the best answer, what also serves as an expression of its quality. All questions and answers are publicly available, and thus CQA systems serve as valuable centers of community knowledge. In general,

© Springer International Publishing Switzerland 2016
A. Wierzbicki et al. (Eds.): NetSci-X 2016, LNCS 9564, pp. 68–81, 2016.
DOI: 10.1007/978-3-319-28361-6_6

we can distinguish two types of CQA systems: universal systems consisting of categories from physics, to love or psychology (e.g. Yahoo! Answers); and specialized systems, which focus only on a specific area (e.g. StackOverflow that concerns with programming).

Users in CQA systems exhibit different kinds of behavior and thus create various internal structures of their communities. A traditional problem in systems that employ user generated knowledge is how to simply distinguish authoritative and expert users, who have a great impact on the evolution of the community, from newcomers or less experienced users. Most CQA systems include some kind of method to calculate user reputation as a way to rank users. Identification of high-reputation users is important in order to extend their rights in managing the community, to mentor them for better engagement with the site, or to route hard questions. In addition, visualization of reputation in the user interface allows users to easily recognize users' overall expertise.

These reputation mechanisms, however, often employ very simple principles based primarily on the amount of user activity in the system (regardless the real quality and difficulty of carried out contributions), what leads to an inaccurate reflection of user expertise and their overall value for the community. Moreover, these reputation mechanisms can be very easily abused by so called reputation collectors. There are many sources of data in CQA systems that can be analyzed in order to calculate users' reputation more accurately. It is possible to observe users' behavior in terms of asking and answering questions, look at feedback provided by a community, or study a social graph between askers and answerers. We suppose, that especially by utilization of the community-perceived quality and estimated difficulty of users' contributions, we will be able to measure user reputation more precisely than reputation schemas currently employed in the CQA systems or than methods proposed in the previous works.

2 Related Work

In the current CQA literature, problem of expert identification is commonly based on estimation of various user-related measures, such as:

1. user topical expertise (also termed as a user knowledge profile [4]),
2. user authority, and
3. user reputation.

These measures and their denominations are often used interchangeably and thus the differences between them are commonly neglected. In this paper, we distinguish between these terms as follows:

1. *Differences in Meaning:* In general, the common characteristic of all three measures is that they are indicators of user expertise and capture an amount of user knowledge and his/her potential to provide high-quality answers. User reputation as well as user authority refers to a *global* value of the user to the community that depends on quality of his/her contributions and activity in

the system. In other words, the more expert answers a user can provide, and the more frequently he/she participates in the question answering process, the more authority and reputation he/she should have. On the other side, user topical expertise relates to a *particular topic* (i.e. a user assigned tag/category or an automatically extracted topic).

2. *Differences in Representation:* Both user authority and user reputation are usually represented by a *single value* that provides simple comprehensive information about the user and thus it can be easily displayed in the user interface or utilized to rank users. On the other side, user topical expertise is rather a *more complex variable* that naturally depends on particular topics. It can be used in situations when identification of experts on a certain topic is important, for example in recommendation of recently posted questions to potential answerers (so called question routing).

3. *Differences in Calculation:* We can broadly divide the existing methods to expert identification into graph-based and feature-based approaches. The graph-based approaches work with a social graph underlying users' interactions in CQA systems (mainly between askers and answerers). Various graph-based algorithms (e.g. algorithms developed to rank websites, such as PageRank and HITS) are then applied on these graphs in order to identify authoritative and expert users in the community. The second group of feature-based approaches is based on historical question-answering records about users as well as about content created by them. Consequently, various mostly numerical methods are employed to derive user expertise.

User authority methods belong to graph-based approaches as they are based on *link analyses*. On the contrary, user reputation methods can be characterized as feature-based approaches – reputation can be calculated either by *reputations schemas* (rule-based mechanisms commonly employed in the existing CQA systems) or *numerically derived* from users' question answering history. Finally, user topical expertise methods can employ either graph-based or feature-based approaches, however, with data limited only to particular topics.

2.1 Reputation Schemas in the Existing CQA Systems

In spite of the large body of research publications on CQA systems, just few of them tackle explicitly with their reputation schemas. The most popular CQA systems utilize user reputation as a part of their gamification systems in order to provide users with motivation to actively participate on question answering.

Users in CQA system Yahoo! Answers are divided into 8 categories based on their reputation score. Each level has limitations in a number of questions and answers a user can contribute each day. Users gain and lose reputation based on their actions in the system. The reputation schema of CQA systems in Stack Exchange platform also work on point based reputation rules[1]. The actions and corresponding reputation changes are displayed in Table 1.

---

[1] http://stackoverflow.com/help/whats-reputation.

Table 1. Reputation rules in Stack Exchange platform

Action	Reputation change
Answer is voted up	+10
Question is voted up	+5
Answer is accepted	+15 (+2 to acceptor)
Question is voted down	−2
Answer is voted down	−2 (−1 to voter)
Experienced Stack Exchange user	onetime +100
Accepted answer to bounty	+bounty
Offer bounty on question	−bounty

Analyses of Stack Exchange reputation schema and its influence on user behavior has been performed by Bosu et al. [1] and Movshovitz-Attias et al. [6]. Bosu et al. [1] focused on exploring the ways how users earn reputation in Stack-Overflow community. They provide an analysis of variations in community's activity between different topics as well as throughout different days during a week and hours during a day. The results of this analysis consist of recommendations how users in StackOverflow can build reputation quickly and efficiently, such as by answering questions related to tags with lower expertise density, answering questions promptly or being active during off peak hours. Differently, Movshovitz-Attias et al. [6] analyzed behavior of users with both high and low reputation. The results showed that high reputation users provide the majority of all answers. On the other hand, the majority of all questions is asked by low reputation users, nevertheless high reputation users ask in average more questions as low reputation ones. Authors also demonstrated the application of their results in a prediction whether a user will become an influential long-term contributor by consideration of contributions in the first months of his/her activity in the system.

Paul et al. [7] studied reputation and its influence on user behavior in CQA system Quora. Quora does not employ any kind of public reputation schema or a visual representation of user reputation, however, there is available another implicit measure of reputation by means of number of user's followers. The lack of reputation system is also compensated by users' individual feeling of satisfaction as well as competency.

Reputation schemas employed in the existing popular CQA systems are based on simple rules in order to be transparent for a community. In addition, system administrators can simply influence the community behavior by gamification in order to promote insufficient actions in the system (e.g. by giving them more reputation points).

2.2 Measuring User Authority and Reputation

Besides rule-based reputation schemas applied in the existing popular CQA systems, it is possible to find several more or less simple measures of user expertise in the research papers concerned with CQA systems. In the following review, we focus primarily on methods aimed to estimate user authority and user reputation as their common goal is to calculate the global value of users while they differ only in the employed calculation approach.

An early attempt in expert identification in CQA systems was made by Jurczyk et al. [3] who compared performance of two graph-based approaches on different types of graphs and with data from different categories in Yahoo! Answers, particularly HITS algorithm and a simple degree measure (a difference between a number of ingoing and outgoing connections in the question answering graph). The results revealed that HITS algorithm achieved substantially unbalanced performance, it worked well in some categories, while in others its performance was quite week.

Zhang et al. [11] studied users' expertise in a system called Java Forum. Authors proposed the graph-based algorithm named ExpertiseRank, which is inspired by PageRank. However, the biggest influence for further research in this area comes from their proposal of a new feature-based reputation measure called Z-score. It is based only on a number of answers and questions a user contributed:

$$Z_{score} = \frac{a - q}{\sqrt{a + q}} \tag{1}$$

where a represents a number of posted answers and q is a number of asked questions. The authors also provided a comparison between graph-based and feature-based approaches, in which a simple Z-score metric performs better than other graph-based methods.

Liu et al. [5] proposed another graph-based approach that utilizes pairwise competition, i.e. the relationship between the best answerer and other answerers supposing that the best answerer has a higher expertise as other answerers. In comparison with the previous graph-based approaches, algorithms for ranking players (e.g. TrueSkill) were employed. The effectiveness of these ranking methods was compared with traditional graph-based algorithms (PageRank and HITS) and also with simple feature-based approaches (number of answers, number of best answers, best answer ratio and smoothed best answer ratio). The results showed that the proposed competition-based approach achieved very similar performance as much simpler feature-based metric best answer ratio.

2.3   Influence of Activity on User Expertise Estimation

Yang et al. [10] pointed out a problem that is present in standard expert identification methods. These methods very often misclassify very active users (denoted by authors as sparrows) for experts (denoted as owls). While sparrows generate most of the content, owls provide valuable answers to questions that are perceived as important by the community. The existing expert identification methods, however, targeted mainly sparrows as they focused mainly on the amount of users' activity in the system rather than on quality of their contributions. As the result, methods for topical expertise, authority as well as reputation estimation suffer with a serious issue - the calculated estimation of user expertise does not usually reflect real users' knowledge level.

The similar problem is present also in reputation schemas employed in the existing CQA systems. The negative consequences of these reputation schemas, which also favor user activity, lie in reputation abuse. As we showed in our previous case study [9] aimed to analyze user behavior in StackOverflow, we can observe increasing population of reputation collectors and other kinds of undesired types of users. Reputation collectors intentionally abuse the reputation system in order to collect reputation by answering as many questions as possible (commonly regardless their insufficient knowledge on the particular question topic).

To address these drawbacks, it is necessary to propose novel methods that balance the influence of user activity and quality of contributions. At first, Yang et al. [10] focused on the quality of users' contributions for topical expertise estimation. Authors proposed a metric called Mean Expertise Contribution which takes question debatableness and answer utility into calculation in order to distinguish sparrows and owls more precisely.

Instead of contribution quality, question difficulty was taken into consideration by Hanrahan et al. [2] in order to identify expert users more precisely. Authors decided to use duration between the time when the question was asked and the time when an answer was marked as the best answer as the measure for question difficulty. Authors, however, did not propose any method for reputation estimation, only observed correlation between question difficulty and user expertise represented by StackOverflow reputation and Z-score.

The conclusions from the analyzed state-of-the-art approaches to user expertise estimation provide directions for a proposal of our method. At first, feature-based approaches not only perform better than graph-based ones but also are computationally more efficient. Secondly, in feature-based approaches, it is essential to distinguish between user activity and quality of contributions. In spite of that, the most of existing approaches give a priority on the amount of user activity. An exception is the method by Yang et al. [10] that addressed this issue in estimation of *user topical expertise*. On the other side, we are not aware of any similar solution proposed for user reputation estimation.

3 Calculating User Reputation with Content Quality and Difficulty

Our main goal is to model users' reputation with accentuation on the quality of users' contributions, not their activity as it is done in the reputation schemas employed in the popular CQA systems and in the existing feature-based methods, in order to estimate user reputation with better success rate.

In our approach, reputation of a user consists of reputation gained for:

1. providing answers on questions asked by the rest of the community, as well as for
2. asking new questions.

It is in the contrast to methods for user topical expertise estimation (e.g. [10]) that usually consider only providing answers. The reason is that answering a question can be perceived as an expression of expertise on question topics, while asking a question, on the other side, can be perceived as a lack of expertise. However, in estimation of user reputation, asking popular questions as well as providing good answers is important.

A user gains greater reputation for asking difficult and useful questions and for providing useful answers on other difficult questions. The gained reputation for such actions is added to previously earned reputation. Final reputation R of a user u can thus be expressed as a sum of reputations gained for asking questions R_q, summed up with a sum of reputations gained for answering questions R_a. Formula (2) represents the formal expression of the final reputation:

$$R(u) = \sum R_q(q) + \sum R_a(a, q) \tag{2}$$

We also propose an alternative formula in order to completely suppress an influence of an amount of users' activity:

$$R(u) = \frac{\sum R_q(q) + \sum R_a(a, q)}{|q| + |a|} \tag{3}$$

where $|q|$ is the number of questions a user asked and $|a|$ is the number of answers he/she provided.

3.1   Reputation for Asking Questions

Inspired by the work [2], we propose to calculate reputation for asking questions based on question difficulty D_q in a combination with question utility QU. We suppose that the longer it takes for the first answer to be added (time to answer a question q - $TTA(q)$), the more difficult the question is. In order to take into account differences between various topics in CQA systems, we normalize this time by maximum time to add the first answer for questions assigned to the same topic t ($TTA_{max}(t)$). If a question belongs to more topics, we calculate D_q for each topic, and then average the results. We decided to use a logarithm of TTA values in order to solve a long tail distribution of the values. The binary logarithm is used because it performed better than the natural and the common (decadic) logarithm. Question difficulty D_q for a question q is computed as:

$$D_q(q) = \frac{\log_2(TTA(q))}{\log_2(TTA_{max}(t))} \tag{4}$$

The second factor for calculating reputation for asking questions is question utility QU. Our formula for question utility is an adaptation of an idea in the work [10]. We calculate question utility as *Score* (number of positive votes minus number of negative votes) normalized by a maximum value of scores - *MaxScore*(t) on questions in the same topic t to reflect differences in popularity between topics in CQA systems. If a question belongs to more than one topic, we calculate QU for every topic, and then we average the results. In addition similarly as for question difficulty, a logarithm of scores is used because we can observe a long tail distribution also for questions' scores.

$$QU(q) = \frac{\log_2 (Score(q))}{\log_2 (MaxScore(t))} \tag{5}$$

In the calculation, we had to solve several specific situations. At first, if a question receives negative score, question utility will be negative too. To calculate negative utility more accurately, we use absolute value of minimum question score for a topic t in the place of $MaxScore(t)$. Secondly, if a score of a question is zero and $MaxScore(t)$ is zero as well, QU will be equal one. Finally, we adapted the logarithm calculation in order to be able to handle negative values and zero. The logarithm of negative values is calculated as $-\log_2(-x)$ and the logarithm of zero is zero.

The final form of formula for reputation obtained for asking questions consists of sum of question difficulty and question utility. Formula (6) displays the final relationship for calculating reputation R_q for asking a question q:

$$R_q(q) = D_q(q) + QU(q). \tag{6}$$

3.2 Reputation for Answering Questions

The second part of our reputation system, which is responsible for calculating reputation for answering questions, utilizes question difficulty (4) as described in the previous section, and combines it with answer utility which adapts an idea from the work [10]. Answer utility $AU(a, q)$ for an answer a in a question q is calculated as:

$$AU(a, q) = \frac{\log_2 (Score(a))}{\log_2 (MaxAnswerScore(q))} \tag{7}$$

where $Score(a)$ is a score of an answer a, and $MaxAnswerScore(q)$ represents a maximum score from all answers provided for a question q. If an answer receives a negative score, answer utility will be negative too, as the same approach as for question utility is used. If $Score$ and $MaxAnswerScore$ are both equal zero, and the answer is labelled as *the best* then answer utility is equal one, otherwise zero. The best answer status, however, has no effect on answer utility for answers with nonzero score. The reason for using logarithm of answers' scores is the same as for logarithm of questions' scores with the same rules for negative values.

As well as in (6), we use the sum of question difficulty and answer utility for calculating reputation gained for answering a question:

$$R_a(a, q) = D_q(q) + AU(a). \tag{8}$$

4   Evaluation

4.1   Experiment Setup

In order to evaluate the proposed reputation system, we conducted an offline experiment in which we used two datasets from CQA systems Programmers[2] (collected in September 2014) and Sharepoint[3] (collected in August 2015), which are parts of Stack Exchange network. The data are publicly available to download on archive.org[4].

We are not aware of any gold standard available for the Stack Exchange datasets that could be used to evaluate the calculated users' reputations against. At first, there is not such a thing as an absolute value representing real user reputation since all existing scoring metrics are calculated according to a certain heuristic method that itself can be considered as an approach to estimate user reputation. In addition, datasets do not contain a global list of all users in the community sorted relatively according to their reputation either. Utilization of human judgements is not applicable here because it is not possible to manually evaluate so many users and all their previous activities in the system [11].

As the result of missing gold standard, many alternative approaches have been already employed in the previous works. The most objective way to evaluate the performance of user reputation estimation without manual data labelling, which is not applicable on large datasets, is a utilization of partial rankings of users. More specifically, it is possible to compare two sorted lists of users for each question separately. The first list is sorted according to calculated reputation, while the second one is sorted according to the score of answers as accumulated in the CQA system (if two answers have the same score, we consider the newer as better one assuming that the previous one did not answer the question sufficiently). This gives us the ability to evaluate how many users are in their correct position as well as examine the difference in rankings between these two lists.

As a baseline for comparison, we chose four feature-based approaches:

1. Firstly, we have reconstructed the original user reputation based on Stack Exchange reputation rules.
2. As the second method for comparison, we chose Best Answer Ratio (BAR) for each user, which performed as the best in the previous works.
3. As the third method, we chose Z-score, as proposed by Zhang et al. [11].
4. Finally, we employed a number of previously posted answers, which reflects only user activity and totally ignores quality of provided contributions.

As our method works with question difficulty, which is based on time to answer a question, we can take into consideration only those questions that have at least one answer. Moreover, we evaluated the performance of all methods for only those questions which have at least two answerers with calculated reputation, so we could perform a comparison between the lists of users (users with

---

[2] http://programmers.stackexchange.com/.

[3] http://sharepoint.stackexchange.com/.

[4] https://archive.org/details/stackexchange.

unknown reputation were left out from the comparison). For these reasons, we report our results on about 20 000 questions even though there are 33 052 questions in the Programmers dataset, and on about 11 000 questions from total number of 47 136 questions in the Sharepoint dataset respectively.

The evaluation was performed employing an experimental infrastructure, a part of CQA system Askalot [8] which is being developed at Faculty of Informatics and Information Technologies at Slovak University of Technology in Bratislava. The infrastructure enables us to reconstruct events as they happened in time, thus allows us to perform the chronological evaluation process.

4.2   Evaluation Metrics

Standard information retrieval metrics are applied in order to compare the performance of our method and baselines:

- Precision at N (P@N): The proportion of top N users who are ranked at the correct position.

$$P@N = \frac{r}{N} \tag{9}$$

  where r is the number of users in the correct position.
- Mean Reciprocal Rank (MRR): The reciprocal rank is the inverse of position (according to the ground truth) for the user with highest reputation (evaluated by the proposed method). The mean reciprocal rank is the average of reciprocal ranks for all questions evaluated:

$$MRR = \frac{1}{|Q|} \sum_{i=1}^{|Q|} \frac{1}{rank_i} \tag{10}$$

  where $|Q|$ is the number of questions, and $rank_i$ is the position of the user.
- Normalized Discounted Cumulative Gain (nDCG): A method which uses graded relevance as a measure of usefulness. Positions of users in the beginning of the list are more important than positions in the end of the list. The formula stands as follows:

$$nDCG = \frac{DCG_p}{IDCG_p} \tag{11}$$

where DCG_p is Discounted Cumulative Gain, and $IDCG_p$ is the ideal possible DCG - it is DCG of the ground truth, while DCG_p is Discounted Cumulative Gain of users sorted according a method being evaluated. We use alternative formulation of DCG:

$$DCG_p = \sum_{i=1}^{p} \frac{2^{rel_i} - 1}{\log_2 (i + 1)} \tag{12}$$

where p is a rank position evaluated, rel_i is relevance of a user at a position i.

4.3   Evaluation Results

In order to evaluate how individual components of the proposed method for reputation calculation contribute to user reputation, we evaluated its performance in two steps. Firstly, we worked only with reputation gained for answering questions (labeled as *Answers only*). Secondly, we employed also reputation for asking questions (i.e. the full variant of the proposed method). We also examined two configurations of our method in order to completely eliminate activity factor (Formula (3) labeled as *average*), and Formula (2) labeled as *sum* in the results.

Table 2 reports the results of our experiments on the Programmers dataset and Table 3 on the Sharepoint dataset, respectively. We present performance of Precision@1 (P@1), Precision@2 (P@2), Mean Reciprocal Rank (MRR) and Normalized Discounted Cumulative Gain (nDCG). The last column displays the number of questions which were evaluated.

Table 2. Comparison of the performance of the methods on the Programmers dataset

	P@1 (%)	P@2 (%)	MRR (%)	nDCG (%)	Questions
Full variant *(sum)*	40.093	38.074	65.538	83.162	20552
Full variant *(average)*	**43.971**	**41.154**	**66.278**	84.511	20552
Answers only *(sum)*	40.179	38.267	63.632	83.233	20324
Answers only *(average)*	43.623	40.926	66.182	**84.521**	20324
Stack Exchange Reputation	**42.080**	39.279	**64.850**	**83.888**	20558
Best Answer Ratio	41.881	**40.078**	64.585	83.728	20324
Z-score	38.388	37.022	62.322	82.534	20558
Number of answers	38.570	37.308	62.481	82.647	20324

Table 3. Comparison of the performance of the methods on the Sharepoint dataset

	P@1 (%)	P@2 (%)	MRR (%)	nDCG (%)	Questions
Full variant *(sum)*	36.005	37.324	65.554	85.429	11451
Full variant *(average)*	**50.004**	**49.563**	**73.145**	**88.671**	11451
Answers only *(sum)*	35.754	37.017	65.450	85.410	11042
Answers only *(average)*	45.634	45.707	70.753	87.692	11042
Stack Exchange Reputation	34.895	36.397	64.904	85.168	11483
Best Answer Ratio	**40.481**	**41.441**	**67.870**	**86.425**	11042
Z-score	35.313	36.693	65.177	85.309	11483
Number of answers	35.020	36.424	65.016	85.235	11042

The results show that our method outperformed all baseline methods. The interesting observation is that the variant which completely eliminates user activity performed as the best. This result confirms the significant influence of the quality of user contributions. It is especially true for the Sharepoint dataset, for which the methods that emphasize user activity perform clearly worse than the ones that suppress it (i.e. best answer ratio and our method in average variant).

In addition, we observe differences also between the full and partial (i.e. answers only) variant of our method. The full variant reflects user reputation better because it captures reputation gained from answering as well as asking questions. While on the Programmers dataset the differences are not so obvious, the full variant outperforms the answers only variant by almost 4.5 % (for P@1 metric) in the Sharepoint dataset.

Since Stack Exchange reputation outperformed best answer ratio on the Programmers dataset, we were interested in the distribution of calculated reputation among the community. We provide a comparison between the best variant of our method (i.e. the full variant that calculates reputation for answering as well for asking questions, and eliminates an influence of amount of users' activity) and Stack Exchange reputation rules. In order to eliminate a long tail problem with reputation distribution in Programmers CQA system, we decided to group reputation by range of two (0–1, 2–3, etc.) and cut the high end of reputation.

The charts in Figs. 1 and 2, which contain histograms of reputation distributions calculated by our method and Stack Exchange reputation system respectively, clearly show that we were able to distinguish between the expertise of users better. Reputation calculated by our method follows Gaussian distribution what is expected, since we can naturally presume the majority of users to have average skills and knowledge. Another advantage of our approach is that we are able to better identify users with negative reputation.

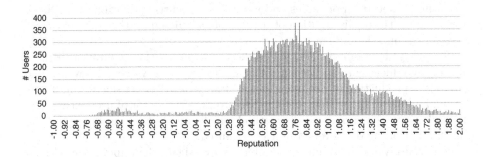

Fig. 1. Distribution of reputation calculated by our method

Overall computational complexity of our method is the same or similar as for the previous reputation metrics or reputation schemas. However, as our method normalizes values of users contributions, it does not provide so good transparency for the end users as simple rule-based reputation schemas (e.g. they cannot easily verify why and how much of their reputation changed because they do not have simple access to all information required to make the calculation). Finding an optimal balance between precision and transparency of methods for user reputation calculation provides an interesting direction for further research.

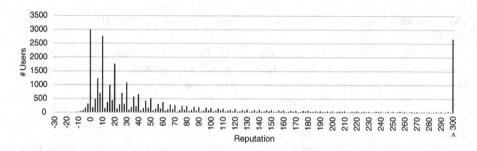

Fig. 2. Distribution of reputation calculated by Stack Exchange reputation system

5 Conclusions

In this paper, we introduced a method for estimating user reputation in CQA systems. Our main goal was to strengthen the importance of quality of user's contributions when calculating reputation. It is done by employing question difficulty and utility of questions and answers. The performance of our method was compared with other feature-based approaches on two datasets gathered from CQA systems provided by Stack Exchange platform. Our method outperformed all baselines, and thus we can confirm our assumption that consideration of content quality and difficulty plays an important role in estimation of user reputation. Moreover, we evaluated the distribution of calculated reputation among the community. We found out that reputation calculated by our method follows a continuous spectrum of values and a naturally occurring distribution, what is in contrast with the distribution of reputation calculated by the standard Stack Exchange reputation schema.

Encouraged by our results, we applied our method for reputation estimation in the educational and organizational CQA system Askalot [8], where it is running in production environment since May 2015. After consideration of educational nature of the system and the need to preserve factor of user activity, we decided to use the variant of our method which utilizes the sum of reputations for all questions and answers a user contributed.

For future work, it would be possible to investigate the importance of question difficulty and question/answer utility on the performance of our method. We can do this by assigning weight parameters to each component and observe differences in the performance when adjusting these values. Another possibility to improve our method lies in using clustering algorithms to find topics in CQA systems and do not rely on tags a user provided. We could also utilize an advanced method for content quality evaluation instead of the votes from the community. The problem of missing reputation gained for questions with no answers (due to unavailable estimation of question difficulty) could be solved by using average values of time to solve in the question's topic.

Acknowledgment. This work was partially supported by grants. No. VG 1/0646/15, VG 1/0774/16 and KEGA 009STU-4/2014 and it is the partial result of collaboration within the SCOPES JRP/IP, No. 160480/2015.

References

1. Bosu, A., Corley, C.S., Heaton, D., Chatterji, D., Carver, J.C., Kraft, N.A.: Building reputation in stackoverflow: an empirical investigation. In: Proceedings of the 10th Working Conference on Mining Software Repositories, MSR 2013, pp. 89–92. IEEE Press, Piscataway (2013)
2. Hanrahan, B.V., Convertino, G., Nelson, L.: Modeling problem difficulty and expertise in stackoverflow. In: Proceedings of the ACM 2012 Conference on Computer Supported Cooperative Work Companion, CSCW 2012, pp. 91–94. ACM, New York (2012)
3. Jurczyk, P., Agichtein, E.: Discovering authorities in question answer communities by using link analysis. In: Proceedings of the Sixteenth ACM Conference on Information and Knowledge Management, CIKM 2007, pp. 919–922. ACM, New York (2007)
4. Liu, D.R., Chen, Y.H., Kao, W.C., Wang, H.W.: Integrating expert profile, reputation and link analysis for expert finding in question-answering websites. Inf. Process. Manage. **49**(1), 312–329 (2013)
5. Liu, J., Song, Y.I., Lin, C.Y.: Competition-based user expertise score estimation. In: Proceedings of the 34th International ACM SIGIR Conference on Research and Development in Information Retrieval, SIGIR 2011, pp. 425–434. ACM, New York (2011)
6. Movshovitz-Attias, D., Movshovitz-Attias, Y., Steenkiste, P., Faloutsos, C.: Analysis of the reputation system and user contributions on a question answering website: stackoverflow. In: Proceedings of the 2013 IEEE/ACM International Conference on Advances in Social Networks Analysis and Mining, ASONAM 2013, pp. 886–893. ACM, New York (2013)
7. Paul, S.A., Hong, L., Chi, E.H.: Who is authoritative? understanding reputation mechanisms in quora. CoRR abs/1204.3724 (2012)
8. Srba, I., Bielikova, M.: Askalot: community question answering as a means for knowledge sharing in an educational organization. In: Proceedings of the 18th ACM Conference Companion on Computer Supported Cooperative Work, CSCW 2015, pp. 179–182. ACM, New York (2015)
9. Srba, I., Bielikova, M.: Why stack overflow fails? preservation of sustainability in community question answering. IEEE Softw. (2015, accepted)
10. Yang, J., Tao, K., Bozzon, A., Houben, G.-J.: Sparrows and owls: characterisation of expert behaviour in stackoverflow. In: Dimitrova, V., Kuflik, T., Chin, D., Ricci, F., Dolog, P., Houben, G.-J. (eds.) UMAP 2014. LNCS, vol. 8538, pp. 266–277. Springer, Heidelberg (2014)
11. Zhang, J., Ackerman, M.S., Adamic, L.: Expertise networks in online communities: structure and algorithms. In: Proceedings of the 16th International Conference on World Wide Web, WWW 2007, pp. 221–230. ACM, New York (2007)

Analysis of Co-authorship Ego Networks

Valerio Arnaboldi[1]([✉]), Robin I.M. Dunbar[2,3], Andrea Passarella[1],
and Marco Conti[1]

[1] IIT-CNR, Via Moruzzi 1, 56124 Pisa, Italy
{valerio.arnaboldi,andrea.passarella,marco.conti}@iit.cnr.it
[2] Department of Experimental Psychology, University of Oxford,
South Parks Road, Oxford OX1 3UD, UK
robin.dunbar@psy.ox.ac.uk
[3] Department of Information and Computer Science, Aalto University School
of Science, Konemiehentie 2, 02150 Espoo, Finland

Abstract. The availability of co-authorship data from large-scale electronic databases is paving the way for new analyses on human collaboration networks. The complex network of co-authorships can identify specific features that characterise the behaviour of researchers, and impact on their production and performance. In this paper, we analyse a large sample of data regarding scientific publications from Google Scholar. The aim of our analysis is to study a fundamental aspect of co-authorship networks, i.e. the structure of authors' ego networks. Specifically, we highlight the existence of a hierarchical organisation of these networks in a series of concentric circles, quite similar to that found in general human social networks. In addition, we highlight some properties of the correlation between the ego network structure and the authors scientific productivity, measured in terms of h-index.

Keywords: Collaboration networks · Ego networks · Optimal team size · Scientific productivity · H-index

1 Introduction

Co-authorship networks represent the patterns of human collaborations in the production of scientific knowledge. The analysis of these networks is gaining momentum, due to the increasing availability of co-authorship data from electronic databases like Google Scholar, Scopus or Microsoft Academic Search, and to the gradual shift in science from an individual based model (i.e. where individuals have the main role in the production of knowledge) to a teamwork model [18].

In this paper, we study the structural properties of a large number of co-authorship *ego networks* extracted from Google Scholar. In this context, the ego network of a given author is the network formed by linking that author

This work was partially funded by the EC under the H2020-INFRAIA SoBigData (654024) project.

© Springer International Publishing Switzerland 2016
A. Wierzbicki et al. (Eds.): NetSci-X 2016, LNCS 9564, pp. 82–96, 2016.
DOI: 10.1007/978-3-319-28361-6_7

with all its co-authors, and weighing each link with a measure of strength of their collaboration. The main goal of this work is understanding whether similar structures found in general human ego networks are also present in co-authorship ego networks. The main intuition is that the structure of human ego networks is determined by cognitive and time constraints that limit the number and intensity of social relationships each person can maintain. Scientific collaboration can be seen as one specific type of human social relationship, which is in principle also affected by cognitive and time constraints. Therefore, we ask ourselves if those constraints result in similar structures also in the co-authorship networks.

The structure of ego networks is a well-investigated topic in the area of social networking. The effect of cognitive and time constraints leads, in human social networks, to the formation of a typical hierarchical structure around each ego. According to this structure, *alters* (i.e. people with whom the individual or ego is connected) are arranged into inclusive groups. The size of these groups averages 1.5, 5, 15, 50, 150 respectively, with a scaling ratio of ~3 [6,19]. In this hierarchy, Dunbar's Number (150) represents the average limit on the total number of social contacts that humans can actively maintain in their networks [5]. The structural pattern found in ego networks is consistent among different social environments, including online social networks (OSNs) such as Facebook and Twitter [6], and other types of social organisation, such as the land armies of many countries [19]. This indicates a natural hierarchical grouping of everyday social structures, optimising the cognitive processing of within-group interactions [19].

Although the properties of ego networks have been largely studied in the literature, there are still no conclusive results about the relation between the hierarchy found in ego networks and the collaboration strategies in organisations and team work in general. To the best of our knowledge, there are no studies that characterise the hierarchical structure of ego networks in collaboration environments and that analyse the relation between this structure and scientific productivity. In addition, most of the experiments on collaboration networks are related to small-sized samples, often in controlled and limited environments.

In this paper, we aim to bridge this gap by analysing the structural properties of a large number (313,207) of co-authorship ego networks extracted from Google Scholar. We find that a hierarchical structure similar to that found in other types of human social ego networks is also present in co-authorship ego networks, suggesting that human cognitive and time constraints may play a significant role in shaping collaborations. In addition, we start to characterise the impact of these structures on scientific productivity. We study the correlation between the structural properties of the authors' ego network and their h-index. In particular, we find a significant correlation between the ego network size and the h-index, and we briefly discuss the main reasons that could explain this property.

2   Related Work

One of the most significant contributions to the analysis of co-authorship networks is the work on large-scale collaboration databases by Mark E.J. Newman (see for example [12,13]). Newman applied standard social network analysis tools to complete co-authorship graphs (not limited to ego networks), and his results are the first indication that co-authorship networks have high clustering coefficient and small average distance between pairs of nodes, thus being "small-world" networks. In addition, he found that statistics of individual authors can vary significantly in different fields.

Katz and Hicks [10] found that the number of co-authors has a positive impact on the number of citations of papers. Moreover, collaborations with foreign institutions bring to the highest impact. In a similar study, Guimerà and colleagues found that team "diversity" is one of the key aspects of success [8].

Abbasi and colleagues [1] analysed data related to five American Universities, by acquiring information regarding scientific publications from Google Scholar, ACM portal, and DBLP. They built complete co-authorship networks and calculated standard centrality measures (e.g. node degree, closeness, betweenness) for each node (author). They found that centrality measures have a high correlation with productivity (g-index). Moreover, authors embedded in clusterised parts of the network have lower performances than other authors.

Abbasi et al. also analysed ~8,000 co-authorship ego networks from the Scopus database [2]. The results show that several ego network measures (e.g. density, Burt's constraint, ego-betweenness, effective size) correlate with author performances (g-index). This is in accordance with the results of the analysis by Ortega [14] on a large dataset collected from Microsoft Academic Search (MSA) with ~32,000 authors, which also highlights differences in the properties of co-authorship ego networks in different research fields. These results also confirm similar findings on smaller co-authorship datasets [11].

Compared to these studies, our work is focused on the detailed analysis of the structural properties of ego networks, and their impact on scientific productivity.

3   Co-authorship Data

3.1   Data Statistics

We analysed 313,207 author profiles accessed from Google Scholar in November 2013. For each author, we have information about the categories (research areas) manually indicated in their personal profiles as one or more freely assigned labels (for a total of 188,657 categories), and all the publications indexed by Scholar (for a total of 19,420,220 publications, of which 378,305 are patents). In addition, we have all the statistics calculated by Scholar, e.g. the total number of citations for each author and the h-index. We accessed the authors' profiles starting from a single category ("computer science"). Then, we accessed all the categories found in the visited profiles, iterating the procedure until no new categories were found. The distribution of the category size, depicted in Fig. 1a, clearly shows a power-law shape. The largest category, "machine learning", has been indicated by 8,122 authors. The distribution of the number of citations of the authors and that of their h-index are depicted in Fig. 1b and d respectively, while the distribution of the number of citations of the papers in our sample is

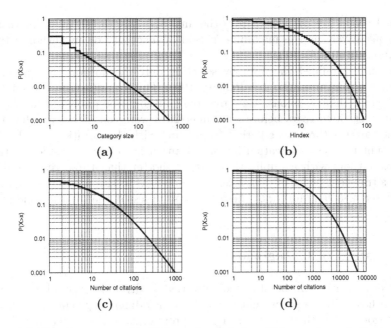

Fig. 1. CCDFs of category size (1a), author h-index (1b), number of citations per paper (1c), and number of citations per author (1d)

depicted in Fig. 1c. The number of co-authors in the papers ranges between 1 and 150. The limit of 150 is imposed by Google Scholar. Papers with more than 150 co-authors are limited to 150. Nevertheless, the number of papers with 150 co-authors is only 6.5 % of the total number of papers.

3.2 Data Preprocessing

For the analysis presented in the rest of the paper, it is important to know the dates of the publications. Scholar derives them from the hosting web site of the paper or from the pdf file directly. For some papers, dates are wrongly read from fields related to author's personal information (e.g. the zip code of the author's affiliation). These cases, although rare, usually lead to inconsistent dates or a date far from the other publication dates of the author and are thus easy to be identified and corrected. We discarded dates in the future (i.e. after the date when the paper's data were accessed) and dates too far from the rest of the publication dates of the author. Specifically, for each author, we ordered its publication dates in a descending order and we calculated the difference between subsequent dates. We formed groups by putting together all dates such that the distance between two consecutive dates is lower than 20 years, and we consider as relevant publications of an author only those belonging to its largest group. Therefore, the first date (in temporal order) of this group is taken as the first publication date of the author. Publications with dates that are outside the obtained group are discarded from the analysis. The threshold of 20 years is chosen intuitively as the maximum period of inactivity of an author between two subsequent publications.

We further refined the data by selecting only the authors who published their first paper after the 1st January 1900. This ensures that the analysed data are more homogeneous. Moreover, only authors who published for the first time at least three years before November 2013 were considered for the analysis, since after a three year period (coinciding with the duration of a Ph.D in most countries) the publication history of an author can be considered stable, whereas authors with a publication history shorter than three years could be still in a transient phase of their scientific career. After this preprocessing phase, we selected 285, 577 authors. These authors represent the final sample of our analysis.

4   Clusters of Categories

To better analyse co-authorship ego networks, we divided authors into separate research fields. To do so, we clustered them into different groups according to the categories that they declared in their profiles. Note that in Google Scholar categories are simple free-text strings that users associate to their profile. Therefore, it is not possible to simply group users by the same category. Instead, we applied a clustering algorithm on the bipartite graph G representing the relations between authors and categories. More formally, we defined $G = (A, C, E)$ as a bipartite graph where A is the set of authors, C is the set of categories, and E is the set of edges connecting elements of A to elements in C. An edge between an author $a \in A$ and category $c \in C$ exists if a has declared c in her profile. We applied a community detection algorithm (a greedy algorithm based on network modularity for bipartite graphs [4]) on G to group together similar categories. We obtained a set of 6, 779 clusters of categories. Table 1 reports the properties of the first six clusters ordered by total number of authors (i.e. the sum of the number of authors of all the categories in the cluster). In the table, the main category of each cluster (i.e. the one with the highest number of authors) is placed along with the first six sub-categories (ordered by number of authors), the total number of authors in the cluster, and the number of sub-categories.

The results reported in the table confirm that the clustering algorithm is effectively able to group together categories belonging to the same research field. Another important feature of the clustering algorithm is that it is able to correctly place duplicates of the same category in the same cluster (e.g. categories with small differences in the naming such as *Consumer Behavior* and *Consumer Behaviour*). This is possible since most of the authors indicating one of the two names in their profiles also indicate other categories that are in common with the other label, and this permits to identify a strong overlap between the two.

In some cases, clusters group together topics that would seem to be not that overlapping. This is the case for example of "economics" and "entrepreneurship", that are grouped in a neuroscience/psychology cluster. This is likely an effect

Table 1. Properties of the first six clusters of categories found in Google Scholar ordered by number of authors.

Main category	First 6 sub-categories (by size)	no. of authors	no. of sub-categories
Machine learning	Artificial intelligence, computer vision, data mining, image processing, robotics, software engineering	81, 409	23, 615
Physics	Nanotechnology, optimization, biochemistry, biophysics, chemistry, materials science	80, 491	27, 666
Neuroscience	Economics, psychology, education, innovation, cognitive neuroscience, enterpreneurship	59, 609	24, 219
Bioinformatics	Computational biology, genomics, molecular biology, evolution, genetics, conservation biology	59, 428	19, 802
Ecology	Climate change, remote sensing, gis, gis&t, hydrology, geology	47, 519	21, 965
Molecular biology	Microbiology, medicine, hiv aids, biotechnology, immunology, epidemiology	20, 431	19, 738

of strong inter-disciplinary relationships among those topics. In other cases, the main category seems, at a first glance, not the best description of an area. This is the case, for example, for the "machine learning" cluster, that also contains "computer science". This is perhaps not so counterintuitive, as computer science is a very broad field and computer scientists may prefer to indicate more specific categories in their profile rather than a generic one.

We give here a more detailed description of the dataset leveraging the clusters that we obtained. In particular, we look at the relation between the h-index of the authors in the different clusters and the properties derived form their profile (i.e. the average number of co-authors per paper and their index of multidisciplinarity – defined in the following). To be able to perform a detailed analysis of the different clusters, we only considered the first six clusters in terms of size (number of authors) and we omitted the remaining clusters.

4.1   H-Index vs. Average Number of Co-authors per Paper

Figure 2a depicts the average number of co-authors per paper (considering all the authors) as a function of their h-index. The average number of co-authors per paper is distributed around 5 (the horizontal line in Fig. 2a), with higher variability for low values of h-index. Nevertheless, there are some authors with a very high average number of co-authors per paper with high h-index (up to 120). This could be due to the presence of authors working in fields where publications with many co-authors are common. When dividing the authors into the different clusters (Fig. 2b), it is clear that for some clusters (e.g. neuroscience) this effect disappears.

This first result tells us that although scientists may have a large number of collaborations, they tend to work in groups of 6 members (5 plus the ego). This is particularly true for authors with very high performance (i.e. with h-index > 120). Notably, the result is consistent for all the clusters. This is in accordance with the results in the organisational literature, which identify 6 as the best team size for productivity [9]. Nevertheless, having an optimal team size is clearly not enough to perform well in scientific publications, as demonstrated by the large number of authors working on average with other 5 co-authors, but having a low value of h-index.

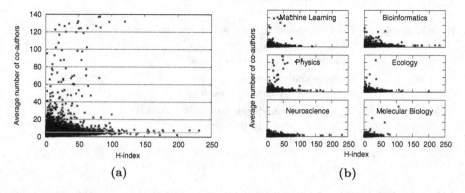

Fig. 2. H-index as a function of the average number of co-authors for all the authors (2a) and the first six clusters (2b).

4.2   H-index and Mono- or Multi-disciplinarity

We calculated a measure of multi-disciplinarity for each author as the similarity between the categories that each author declared in her Google Scholar profile. Specifically, we defined $O(C_i, C_j)$, the overlap coefficient between category C_i and category C_j as follows.

$$O(C_i, C_j) = \frac{|C_i \cap C_j|}{min(|C_i|, |C_j|)}. \tag{1}$$

Then, we averaged the overlap for all the possible pairwise combinations of categories in each profile to obtain a measure of multidisciplinarity m_a, for each author a, defined as follows.

$$m_a = \frac{\sum_{\{C_i, C_j\} \in [S_a]^2} O(C_i, C_j)}{|[S_a]^2|}, \tag{2}$$

where S_a is the set of categories of author a, and $[S_a]^2$ is the set of 2-subsets of S_a. Authors with high values of m work in categories tightly connected to each other that share a high percentage of authors. This indicates research fields very close to each other or different terms used to describe the same field. On the other hand, a low value of m indicates that the author works in research fields that are far from each other, with a very low number of authors working in both fields. The authors in categories with very low values of similarity are often the few people working at the same time in those fields, thus representing bridges between them.

Figure 3a depicts the h-index of the authors as a function of the average similarity of their categories. Figure 3b depicts the same scatterplot but considering the first six clusters of categories separately. The figures show a more random pattern for low values of h-index than for high values. Interestingly, in the latter case, two strategies seem to prevail, and authors tend to: (i) be completely focused on one subject or (ii) spread the effort on subjects that are completely separate from each other. Other mid-way strategies are not adopted by the most successful authors, and are only used by authors with lower h-index. This is visible also when the analysis is applied to the different clusters, with compatible patterns across the different fields. Of course, this aspect needs to be further investigated in the future to draw definitive conclusions.

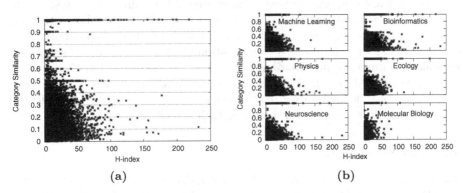

(a)   (b)

Fig. 3. H-index as a function of the average category similarity for all the authors (3a) and the first six clusters (3b).

5   The Structure of Co-authorship Ego Networks

5.1   Definitions

In a co-authorship ego network, an author is the *ego*, and the people with whom she co-authored at least a paper are her *alters*. Note that we use the most simple definition of ego network, without considering mutual connections between alters. To extract the set of alters from the metadata of the articles in Scholar, we looked at the co-authors in the papers of each author and we performed a lexicographic match of their names. Thus, for a given author, we cannot discriminate possible different co-authors with the same name, that are considered as one co-author only. However, intuitively the probability of this case should be very low. In different articles, the same authors may appear with slightly different names or abbreviations. To find these differences, we matched the names using either the first name and the surname or the first letter of the first name and the surname, case insensitive. Then, we defined the strength of a collaboration relationship between an ego i and one of her alters j, $ts_{i,j}$, as follows.

$$ts_{i,j} = \frac{1}{d_{i,j}} \sum_{p \in \{P(i) \cap P(j)\}} \frac{1}{k(p) - 1}, \tag{3}$$

where $d_{i,j}$ is the duration of the relationship between i and j, measured as the time span (in years, between the first article that the ego and her alter published together and the last article published by the ego), $P(i)$ is the set of papers where i appears as a co-author, and $k(p)$ is the number of co-authors of paper p. Intuitively, this measure of tie strength is a frequency of co-authorship, measured as the number of joint publications, where each publication is "weighted" by the number of co-authors to estimate the level of collaboration between the ego and a specific alter in that collaboration. Being a frequency, the total number of (weighted) publications is divided by the number of years during which the ego and the alter are supposed to have collaborated. This definition of tie strength embodies the fact that a small number of co-authors generally implies a stronger collaboration between these than the case of high number of co-authors. We considered only the relationships with duration greater than six months to avoid possible bias due to approximation on too short relationships. Finally, for each author, we define the ego network size as the number of its co-authors. Note that, because we have defined a tie strength on each link, ego networks are *weighted* networks, which is the basis for analysing their structure.

5.2   Ego Network Size

The average ego network size is 104.01. Remarkably, this value is not too far from Dunbar's Number, and compatible with other sizes found in offline [19] and online environments [6,7]. The probability density function of the ego network size, depicted in Fig. 4a, indicates that, although there are many large ego networks (note that we have limited the x axis, and the maximum size is 12,070) the highest density is around 5. Moreover, the density function resembles in its shape the function of the active network size found in social networks [3]. Figure 4b depicts the density function of the ego network size for the first six largest clusters of categories. The size varies sensibly among the clusters, with "machine learning" and "neuroscience" showing a more picked density than "bioinformatics" and "physics", in which the size is more uniformly distributed. This difference is probably due to the fact that in machine learning and neuroscience publications are typically done by a small group of authors, while in fields such as physics and bioinformatics, where sometimes large experiments involving a high number of people are needed, publications with many co-authors are more common.

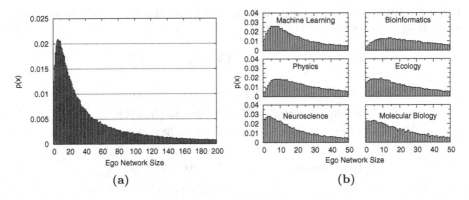

Fig. 4. Density of ego network size for all the authors (4a) and the first six clusters (4b).

5.3 Average Tie Strength vs. Ego Network Size

The average tie strength of ego networks is negatively correlated with ego network size ($r = -0.23$ considering all the authors, $r = -0.60$ when the variables are log-transformed). This is visible also when the clusters are analysed separately ($r = -0.20$ and $r = -0.60$ for machine learning without and with log-transformation respectively, $r = -0.24$ and $r = -0.62$ for physics, $r = -0.23$ and $r = -0.59$ for neuroscience, $r = -0.26$ and $r = -0.59$ for bioinformatics, $r = -0.22$ and $r = -0.53$ for ecology, and $r = -0.25$ and $r = -0.6$ for molecular biology). Interestingly, correlation values are quite homogeneous across research fields. This suggests that this property may depend on some general mechanism underpinning collaboration, rather than on the specific ways of collaborations in different fields, which may vary from topic to topic (see Fig. 4(b)). Indeed, this result is in accordance with the general findings on social ego networks and in organisational studies, that show that the constraints on our social behaviour limit the number of alters that we can maintain at a certain level of intimacy, and people with larger ego networks must inevitably have, on average, relationships with lower levels of intensity [15].

Taken together, these results (distribution of ego network size, and correlation between ego network size and tie strength) provide a first indication that cognitive mechanisms similar to those governing typical social relationships may also determine the development of scientific collaborations. In particular, the negative correlation between tie strength and ego network size is a classical "capacity shrinkage" effect: as the total amount of cognitive resources we can allocate to scientific collaboration is limited, the more intense collaboration are for an author, the lower is the number of active collaboration they can sustain.

5.4 Ego Network Circles

Remember from Sect. 1 that one of the fingerprints of the general structure of ego networks is the presence of concentric layers, of a very well defined average size, containing alters with whom the ego maintains social relationships

Table 2. Properties of ego network circles found by applying k-means on the set of tie strengths of each ego with a fixed $k = 5$.

Cluster	C1	C2	C3	C4	C5
Size					
All authors	2.0	6.3	15.8	37.9	116.8
Machine learning	1.9	5.7	14.2	33.5	102.6
Physics	2.0	6.4	16.1	38.6	119.5
Neuroscience	1.8	5.5	13.3	31.1	100.1
Bioinformatics	2.2	7.5	19.6	49.2	150.9
Ecology	2.0	6.2	15.4	36.3	105.5
Molecular biology	2.1	6.2	15.0	34.3	97.0
Minimum tie strength					
All authors	0.77	0.40	0.20	0.09	0.02
Machine learning	0.88	0.46	0.24	0.10	0.03
Physics	0.83	0.43	0.22	0.10	0.02
Neuroscience	0.75	0.38	0.20	0.09	0.02
Bioinformatics	0.65	0.33	0.16	0.07	0.02
Ecology	0.67	0.34	0.18	0.08	0.02
Molecular biology	0.64	0.33	0.17	0.08	0.02

at a decreasing intensity. To further investigate possible similarities between generic ego networks in social environments and in scientific collaborations, we analysed whether such a structure can also be identified in co-authorship ego networks. Previous studies in other social environments (such as Online Social Networks) have shown that the typical number of layers is 5, with average sizes approximately equal to 1.5, 5, 15, 50, 150 [6]. Therefore, we applied two different clustering algorithms (k-means and DBSCAN) to the tie strengths of each ego network, with a number of cluster equal to 5, and analysed the sizes of the obtained layers. Note that, for each ego network, this means applying k-means and DBSCAN clustering on a mono-dimensional variable (the tie strength). For k-means, we used the `Ckmeans.1d.dp` algorithm [16], which ensures that the clustering procedure converges to a unique and optimal solution. For DBSCAN, we implemented an iterative procedure to find the value of ϵ that gives a number of cluster equal to the chosen k. In addition, we fixed $MinPts$ parameter to 2 to eliminate possible noisy points in the data. This is the same technique used, among others, in [6].

The sizes of the resulting layers found by k-means (nesting the subsequent groups of alters identified) are reported in Table 2. The last circle (C5) may sometimes appear larger than the average ego network size because ego networks with less than 5 different values of tie strength were not considered. The results in Table 2 indicate that co-authorship ego networks have a very similar pattern to social ego networks. Specifically, the sizes of the circles are similar to those found in generic social networks. Although in some cases (typically for C4 and C5) the sizes are below the reference values (50 and 150, respectively), it must be noted that the actual values of ego network circles in *specific* social environments have been found to vary quite significantly around those reference values. The scaling factors between consecutive layers are approximately close to 3 (namely, they average 2.8 for all the authors taken together, 2.7 for machine learning, 2.8 for physics, 2.8 for neuroscience, 2.9 for bioinformatics, 2.7 for ecology, and 2.6 for molecular biology). This is another reference fingerprint of ego network structures in many other social environments. The table also shows the minimum tie strength for an alter to be part of each circle (averaged across all egos). Remember that, based on our definition of tie strength (which is essentially an annual frequency of co-authorship, normalised by the number of co-authors in each publication), a value of 1 would mean that the ego and the alter publish together a joint paper with 2 authors only every year. Interestingly, the results show that the intensity of co-authorship for the inner-most layer are quite close to this value of frequency, indicating indeed a particularly strong intensity of collaboration inside C1.

The results found by DBSCAN, reported in Table 3, are similar to those obtained by k-means and are compatible with the pattern found in social networks [6]. However, DBSCAN tends to place more alters in the outermost circle (C5), where the density is much higher than in the other circles. As a consequence, C3 and C4 are smaller than C3 and C4 of k-means. This difference between the two clustering algorithms has been found also in Twitter and Facebook ego networks [6]. Note that the size of C1 is affected by the choice of having the parameter MinPts set to 2. This eliminates single element clusters, but allows us to detect noisy data. In addition, the somewhat larger values of C5 could be a by-product of our iterative procedure, which is in some (few) cases unable to produce the desired number of clusters, especially for very small networks. As these networks are not considered in the analysis, the values of C5 might be slightly biased towards larger ego networks. The scaling ratios obtained by DBSCAN clustering are also in this case close to 3 (3.4 for all the authors taken together, 3.3 for machine learning, 3.3 for physics, 3.3 for neuroscience, 3.4 for bioinformatics, 3.2 for ecology, and 2.9 for molecular biology). The values of the minimum tie strengths are slightly lower than those found by k-means, in particular for C1, which is again a side effect of the minimum cluster size we have imposed.

These results are another strong indication that the same cognitive and time constraints may regulate also scientific collaboration networks. If this results could be further generalised to other types of collaboration networks, this might be a first step towards a convergence between the results in social network analysis and in organisational research.

5.5 Author H-index and Ego Network Properties

Having characterised the structure of co-authorship ego networks, we now study whether there is any sensible correlation between the scientific productivity

Table 3. Properties of ego network circles found by applying DBSCAN on the set of tie strengths of each ego with a fixed $k = 5$.

Cluster	C1	C2	C3	C4	C5
Size					
All authors	2.8	6.4	11.2	19.3	152.8
Machine learning	2.7	6.2	10.8	18.4	138.3
Physics	2.9	6.5	11.5	19.8	146.7
Neuroscience	2.8	6.3	11.1	19.2	139.8
Bioinformatics	3.0	7.0	12.5	22.1	172.5
Ecology	2.8	6.4	11.4	19.8	135.3
Molecular biology	2.9	6.7	11.7	20.2	121.4
Minimum tie strength					
All authors	0.46	0.29	0.20	0.14	0.02
Machine learning	0.49	0.31	0.22	0.14	0.02
Physics	0.44	0.28	0.20	0.13	0.02
Neuroscience	0.43	0.27	0.19	0.12	0.01
Bioinformatics	0.36	0.24	0.17	0.11	0.01
Ecology	0.41	0.26	0.18	0.12	0.01
Molecular biology	0.36	0.23	0.16	0.11	0.01

of authors, measured through the h-index, and structural elements of the co-authorship network. Specifically, we analyse the correlation between the h-index and the ego network size.

H-index and ego network size are highly correlated ($r = 0.56$ without transformations and $r = 0.79$ when both variables are log-transformed). The correlation values for the different clusters are $r = 0.47$ without transformations and $r = 0.79$ with logarithmic transformation for machine learning, $r = 0.56$ and $r = 0.80$ for physics, $r = 0.57$ and $r = 0.77$ for neuroscience, $r = 0.64$ and $r = 0.82$ for bioinformatics, $r = 0.58$ and $r = 0.80$ for ecology, and $r = 0.68$ and $r = 0.77$ for molecular biology. These results tell us that the larger the ego network of an author, the higher her h-index, with an exponential function controlling the relation between the two variables (because of the higher correlation of log-transformed variables). This could indicate that a high number of collaborations brings more information sources, thus increasing innovativeness and creativity of the ego. In the management literature, this is typically seen as one factor determining a successful career [17]. Another possible explanation of this correlation is that having more opportunities of collaborating facilitates more extensive productivity, and a higher impact on the respective scientific communities. Or, that authors with high h-index attract more and more collaborators, thus increasing their network size. Discriminating between these possible factors would require longitudinal studies on the evolution of the ego network and h-index over time, which is part of future work. Finally, also in this case, note that the correlation values are quite consistent across the different disciplines. Again, this suggests that the reason behind this property may be a general human behaviour underpinning scientific collaboration and productivity, rather than a feature of specific disciplines.

6 Conclusion

We analysed a large set of co-authorship ego networks from Google Scholar. These networks show a hierarchical structure based on the intensity of collaboration with the ego. This structure is similar to those found in other social environments, and known to be the result of the cognitive and time constraints in humans. The size and the scaling ratio between the sizes of the identified layers are quite similar to those found in other social networks, both offline and online. Moreover, the size of the ego network is negatively correlated with the average intensity of collaboration of the ego. This property is another fingerprint of ego networks in general social networks. In addition, we found a direct relation between these structural properties and the performance of each author. In particular, the size of an author's ego network is positively correlated with her h-index. This property does not depend on the specific research field where authors are active, suggesting that this might be a general feature of human scientific collaboration. We think that the results presented in this paper contribute to bridge the gap between organisational studies of team work and social network analysis, giving interesting and new insights into the nature of collaboration networks and social (ego) networks in general.

References

1. Abbasi, A., Altmann, J., Hossain, L.: Identifying the effects of co-authorship networks on the performance of scholars: a correlation and regression analysis of performance measures and social network analysis measures. J. Inf. 5(4), 594–607 (2011). http://dx.doi.org/10.1016/j.joi.2011.05.007
2. Abbasi, A., Chung, K.S.K., Hossain, L.: Egocentric analysis of co-authorship network structure, position and performance. Inf. Process. Manag. 48(4), 671–679 (2012). http://dx.doi.org/10.1016/j.ipm.2011.09.001
3. Arnaboldi, V., Guazzini, A., Passarella, A.: Egocentric online social networks: analysis of key features and prediction of tie strength in Facebook. Comput. Commun. 36(10–11), 1130–1144 (2013)
4. Doormann, C.F., Strauss, R.: A method for detecting modules in quantitative bipartite networks. Methods Ecol. Evol. 5(1), 90–98 (2013)
5. Dunbar, R.I.M.: Neocortex size and group size in primates: a test of the hypothesis. J. Hum. Evol. 28(3), 287–296 (1995). http://www.sciencedirect.com/science/article/pii/S0047248485710214
6. Dunbar, R.I.M., Arnaboldi, V., Conti, M., Passarella, A.: The structure of online social networks mirrors those in the offline world. Soc. Netw. 43, 39–47 (2015)
7. Gonçalves, B., Perra, N., Vespignani, A.: Modeling users' activity on Twitter networks: validation of Dunbar's Number. PloS One 6(8), e22656 (2011)

8. Guimerà, R., Uzzi, B., Spiro, J., Amaral, L.A.N.: Team assembly mechanisms determine collaboration network structure and team performance. Science **308**(5722), 697–702 (2005)
9. Guzzo, R.A., Shea, G.P.: Group performance and and intergroup relations in organizations. In: Dunnette, M.D., Hough, L.M. (eds.) Handbook of Industrial and Organizational Psychology, 2nd edn. Consulting Psychologists Press, Palo Alto (1992)
10. Katz, J.S., Hicks, D.: How much is a collaboration worth? A calibrated bibliometric model. Scientometrics **40**(3), 541–554 (1997)
11. Li, E.Y., Liao, C.H., Yen, H.R.: Co-authorship networks and research impact: a social capital perspective. Res. Policy **42**(9), 1515–1530 (2013). http://dx.doi.org/10.1016/j.respol.2013.06.012
12. Newman, M.E.J.: The structure of scientific collaboration networks. Proc. Nat. Acad. Sci. USA **98**(2), 404–409 (2001). http://www.ncbi.nlm.nih.gov/pubmed/11149952
13. Newman, M.E.: Coauthorship networks and patterns of scientific collaboration. PNAS **101**(Suppl), 5200–5205 (2004)
14. Ortega, J.L.: Influence of co-authorship networks in the research impact: ego network analyses from Microsoft academic search. J. Inf. **8**(3), 728–737 (2014). http://dx.doi.org/10.1016/j.joi.2014.07.001
15. Sutcliffe, A., Dunbar, R.I.M., Binder, J., Arrow, H.: Relationships and the social brain: integrating psychological and evolutionary perspectives. Br. J. Psychol. **103**(2), 149–68 (2012)
16. Wang, H., Song, M.: Clustering in one dimension by dynamic programming. R J. **3**(2), 29–33 (2011)
17. Wiersema, M.F., Bantel, K.A.: Top management team demography and corporate strategic change. Acad. Manag. **35**(1), 91–121 (2010)
18. Wuchty, S., Jones, B.F., Uzzi, B.: The increasing dominance of teams in production of knowledge. Science **316**(5827), 1036–1039 (2007)
19. Zhou, W.X., Sornette, D., Hill, R.A., Dunbar, R.I.M.: Discrete hierarchical organization of social group sizes. Biol. Sci. **272**(1561), 439–444 (2005)

Studying the Role of Diversity in Open Collaboration Network: Experiments on Wikipedia

Katarzyna Baraniak[1]([✉]), Marcin Sydow[1,4], Jacek Szejda[2],
and Dominika Czerniawska[3]

[1] Polish-Japanese Academy of Information Technology, Warsaw, Poland
katarzyna.baraniak1@pjwstk.edu.pl, msyd@poljap.edu.pl
[2] Educational Research Institute, Warsaw, Poland
jacek.szejda@gmail.com
[3] Interdisciplinary Centre for Mathematical and Computational Modelling,
University of Warsaw, Warsaw, Poland
d.czerniawska@icm.edu.pl
[4] Institute of Computer Science, Polish Academy of Sciences, Warsaw, Poland

Abstract. This paper presents some empirical study towards understanding the role of diversity of individual authors and whole teams of authors on the quality of the articles they co-edit in open collaboration environments like Wikipedia. We introduce a concept of *diversity of interests* or *versatility* of a Wikipedia editor and Wikipedia teams and examine how it is correlated with the quality of their production. Our experiments indicate that editor's and team's diversity seems to have bigger impact on quality of their work than other properties.

Keywords: Diversity of interest · Team diversity · Wikipedia · Article quality · Open collaboration

1 Introduction

Open-collaboration environments like Wikipedia produce outcome of varying quality. It is important to study what properties of community members and their teams increase chances for high-quality results of their work. Such studies can help in future in developing tools that improve and support open-collaboration team-building process. For example, it is interesting to study whether editors that have *diverse* interests tend to create better Wikipedia articles. Diversity has proved to play important role in multiple fields of applications: text summarisation, web search [2], databases [12], recommender systems and semantic entity summarisation [10]. Recently, the concept of diversity has attracted interest also in the domain of open collaboration research [1].

In this paper we introduce a quantitative measure of *diversity of interests* of a member of an open-collaboration environment such as Wikipedia and aim to study how versatility influences the work quality. The measure is based on the

© Springer International Publishing Switzerland 2016
A. Wierzbicki et al. (Eds.): NetSci-X 2016, LNCS 9564, pp. 97–110, 2016.
DOI: 10.1007/978-3-319-28361-6_8

information-theoretic concept of entropy. We demonstrate on Wikipedia data that versatility of editor seems to be correlated with the quality of articles they co-edit. We also extend the notion of interest diversity on whole teams of authors and study how it impacts the work quality compared to their productivity and experience. In case of teams the reported experimental findings are similar: team's diversity is correlated with quality.

The original contributions of this paper include:

- the concept of team versatility and other measures of team diversity
- experiments on two dumps of Wikipedia. The results confirm the previous preliminary findings from a short paper [11] including new experiment with multinomial model and experiments with logistic regression model based on various predictors, that confirm versatility of teams is correlated with quality and presents relationships of quality with other variables.

2   Sociological Background

Team diversity is one of the fundamental issues in social and organisational studies that has been broadly researched on. It has been broadly theorised and tested on virtual communities. One of the most burning questions concerns team coherence vs efficiency. There are two competing theories describing efficient team organisation: modularity and integrity. The first was introduced by David Parnas who suggested that co-dependence between components (in our context, a module corresponds to an article on Wikipedia) should be eliminated by limiting the communication [8]. In this approach participation in a module does not require knowledge about the whole system or other modules, e.g. Wikipedia users can co-author articles about social science without knowing anything about life sciences or mathematics. It leads to higher specialization and less diversity in individual performance. Modular approach enables more flexibility and decentralized management [9].

The integral approach to organizations is characterized by smoother adaptation to new environments and to new cooperation rules as well as it gives better results when it comes to fine-tuning of the system [6]. In the integral mode the team members have diverse knowledge and skills. We aim to study whether modular/specialized or integral collaboration pattern is more successful in creating high-quality Wikipedia articles.

2.1   Related Work

Important role of diversity was noticed early not only in complex systems but also in other fields like Operation Research or Information Retrieval [5]. One of the earliest successful applications of diversity-aware approach was reported in [3] in the context of text summarisation. Recently, diversity-awareness has gained increasing interest in other information-related areas where the actual user's information need is unknown and/or the user query is ambiguous. Examples range from databases [12] to Web search [2] or very recently to the quite novel problem of graphical entity summarisation in semantic knowledge graphs [10].

From the open collaboration point of view, diversity can be considered from many perspectives, for example as a team diversity vs homogeneity or a single editor's diversity of interest (Integrity) vs specialisation (Modularity). For example, the positive role of team diversity was studied in [4], but the used definitions of diversity and its measures (e.g. Blau index) are different than in our paper, where it is based on the concept of *entropy*. Most importantly, in contrast to our work, the mentioned work studies the influence of diversity on amount of accomplished work and withdrawal behaviour rather than the work quality that is considered here. In contrast to our work most of previous works focus on diversity of editor teams in terms of categories such as culture, ethnicity, age, etc. [7] studies how the content diversity influences online public spaces in the context of local communities. A recent example, with a special emphasis on ad-hoc "swift" teams where the members have very little previous interactions with each other is [1].

3   Editor's Topical Versatility

In this section we explain the model of editor's interest diversity that we apply in our approach. We use Wikipedia terminology, to illustrate the concepts, however our model can be adapted to other, similar open-collaboration environments.

Let X denote a group of Wikipedia editors. Editors participate in editing Wikipedia articles. Each article can be mapped to one or more categories from a pre-defined *set of categories* $C = \{c_1, \ldots, c_k\}$ that represent topics.

Each editor $x \in X$ in our model is characterised by their editing activity i.e. all editing actions done by x. We assume that the interests of an editor x can be represented by the amount of work that x committed to articles in particular categories.

Let $t(x)$ denote the total amount of textual content (in bytes) that x contributed to all articles editor co-edited and let $t_i(x)$ denote the total amount of textual content that editor x contributed to the articles belonging to a specific category c_i.[1]

Now, lets introduce the following denotation: $p_i(x) = t_i(x)/t(x)$ and interpret it as representing x's *interest in category* c_i. Henceforth, we will use a shorter denotation p_i for $p_i(x)$ whenever x is understood from the context.

3.1   Editor's Interest Profile

Finally, we define the *interest profile* of the editor x, denoted as $ip(x)$, as the *interest distribution vector* over the set of all categories:

$$ip(x) = (p_1(x), \ldots, p_k(x)) \tag{1}$$

---

[1] Since a single article can be assigned to multiple categories, we split the contribution equally for all the categories of the article.

Notice that according to the definition the interest profile represents a valid distribution vector i.e. its coordinates sum up to 1.

3.2 Example

Assume that the set of categories C consists of 8 categories: $\{c_i\}_{1 \leq i \leq 8}$ and that editor x has contributed $t(x) = 10\,kB$ of text in total, out of which $t_2(x) = 8\,kB$ of text has been contributed to articles in category c_2, $t_5(x) = 2\,kB$ in category c_5 and nothing to articles that were not assigned to c_2 nor c_5. Thus the $x's$ interest in c_2 is $p_2(x) = t_2(x)/t(x) = \frac{4}{5}$, in c_5 is $p_5(x) = t_5(x)/t(x) = \frac{1}{5}$ and is equal to 0 for all other categories. The interest profile of this user is:

$$ip(x) = (0, \frac{4}{5}, 0, 0, \frac{1}{5}, 0, 0, 0).$$

3.3 Editor's Versatility Measure

There are many possible ways of measuring diversity. Since the interest profile $ip(x)$ is modelled as a distribution vector over categories, we define *diversity of interests* (or equivalently *versatility*) of x, $V(x)$, as the *entropy of interest profile* of x:

$$V(x) = H((p_1, p_2, \ldots, p_k)) = \sum_{1 \leq i \leq k} -p_k \lg(p_k) \tag{2}$$

Where lg denotes binary logarithm. The value of entropy ranges from 0 (extreme specialisation, i.e. total devotion to a single category) to $lg(k)$ (extreme diversity, i.e. equal interest in all categories).

3.4 Example

The versatility of user x from Sect. 3.2 has the following value:

$$V(x) = -p_2 lg(p_2) - p_5 lg(p_5) = 0.8 \times 0.32 + 0.2 \times 2.32 = 0.256 + 0.464 = 0.72$$

Now assume that another user x' has contributed equally to the four first categories, i.e. user's interest profile is: $ip(x') = (\frac{1}{4}, \frac{1}{4}, \frac{1}{4}, \frac{1}{4}, 0, 0, 0, 0)$. The versatility value for this editor has the following value:

$$H(ip(x')) = -4 \times 0.25 \times (log_2(0.25)) = 2$$

Notice that the versatility measure of x' is higher than that of x and that this is according to the intuition since x' has similar interest in four different categories and x only in two (mostly in one). In other words, x' is more versatile while x is more specialised. Maximum versatility for eight categories would have value of 3, for an editor that is equally interested in all categories.

4   Data

Wikipedia shares latest dumps on https://dumps.wikimedia.org/. The hypothesis on impact of editors' versatility on the quality of their work was tested using a dataset built from the Polish Wikipedia from March 2015.[2] Data size for Polish Wikipedia is presented in Table 1. For greater reliability of the results, similar experiments were also executed on another dataset extracted from German Wikipedia. For each contributor we counted the number of pages he edited, the number of edits they made, the number of characters by which they modified Wikipedia articles (regardless of whether modifications were additions or deletions), the number of both "good" and "featured" articles he edited.

Table 1. Data size for Polish Wikipedia

Measure	Size
The number of authors	126,406
The number of all articles	947,080
The number of regular articles	944,585
The number of good articles	1,889
The number of featured articles	606
The number of editions	16,084,290

German dataset contained a random-uniform sample of 10,000 registered contributors. Sampling frame was restricted to contributors who made at least one edition during the Wikipedia project lifetime. Input of editors was distributed among twelve main content categories for Polish Wikipedia and eight for German Wikipedia accessible from the front page. We show them in Table 2.

Table 2. Wikipedia main content categories

Dataset	Main content categories
Polish Wikipedia	Humanities and social sciences, Natural and physical sciences, Art & Culture, Philosophy, Geography, History, Economy, Biographies, Religion, Society, Technology, Poland
German Wikipedia	Art & Culture, Geography, History, Knowledge, Religion, Society, Sport, Technology

Wikipedia articles are usually not directly tagged with any of these high-level categories. Only the most specific categories are assigned to articles by Wikipedia community. Those are subcategories of more general categories, creating tree-like

---

[2] Dataset used for analysis in this paper is available on e-mail request.

structure. We employed a method that sought main content categories iteratively among parents of categories directly describing any given page. If the article was mapped to more than one category, contribution size was split equally among them. Articles that couldn't be classified were excluded from the dataset, as well as users whose production consisted of such articles exclusively. Also, only editions of the pages in the primary namespace were taken into account (that is, articles *per se* and not –for example – discussion pages), because only these pages are evaluated with regard to their quality.

In the reported experiments the quality of articles is modelled based on the information given by Wikipedia community, who evaluate articles as *good* and *featured* based on the following criteria: well-written, comprehensive, well-researched, neutral, stable, illustrated, and additionally for featured article: length and style guidelines including a lead, appropriate structure and consistent citation. More precisely, we utilise two kinds of information regarding the articles' quality: some articles are marked by Wikipedia editors as *featured* and, independently, some as *good*.

In experiments concerning teams, we used Polish Wikipedia dumps. We define team as a group of authors who made any change in one article. We precomputed three components of the data shown in Table 3, and integrated into one dataset.

Table 3. Datasets

Components of the dataset	Description
Single edition	article id, the size of single edition in bytes made by one author and the total size of edition made by this author to all articles, quality of article
Tenure of contributions	contributor id, article id, the number of days spent on article and the number of days on Wikipedia, the quality of article
Diversity of interest	mean contribution of team members to twelve categories presented in part about individual editors and its entropy, article id, the quality of article

5 Experiments Concerning Editors

In this section we report experiments conducted on data extracted from Wikipedia that reflect recorded activity of its editors. In this part of experiments, entropy of editor's partial contributions to each category was calculated as a measure of their **versatility,** or thematic breadth of their contributions as explained in Sect. 3. The number of bytes by which they modified Wikipedia content was used to measure their **productivity.** The goal is to experimentally study the dependence between editors' versatility and the quality of articles they co-edit.

Table 4. Analysed groups of editors

Editor group	Co-edited
N	(regular) neither good nor featured article
G	(good) at least one good article
F	(featured) at least one featured article
GF	(good and featured) at least one good and one featured article

5.1   Analysis of Editor's Productivity and Versatility

We analysed four groups of editors and denoted them as presented in Table 4.
Notice that the four groups represent a graded "hierarchy" of high-quality editors, with the *GF* representing the highest-quality editors in some way. For
each of the four groups we computed some statistics concerning versatility measure $V()$ (Eq. 2), including mean, median and quartiles. The results for Polish
Wikipedia are presented on Figs. 1 and 2, where one can observe a noticeable
regularity that indicates clear positive connection between editors versatility and

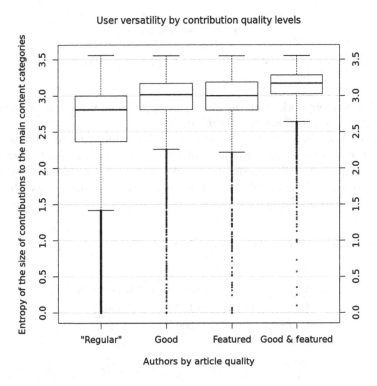

Fig. 1. Versatility vs quality for Polish Wikipedia

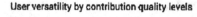

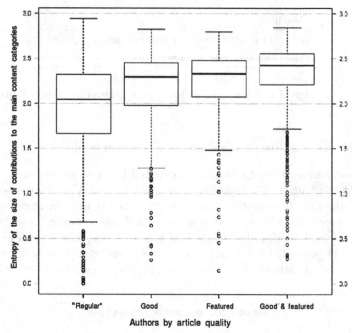

Fig. 2. Versatility vs quality for German Wikipedia (denotations as on Fig. 1)

the quality of their work. More precisely, the aggregated versatility statistics for the groups N, G, F, GF are strictly increasing.

Table 5 shows how median versatility and productivity of editors differs between the four categories of quality of articles. For better quality articles we can observe slightly higher median versatility. Productivity column shows more significant results. Better quality of articles has positive relationship with editors of higher median productivity.

Table 5. Median of versatility and productivity of editors vs. quality for Polish Wikipedia

Quality	Versatility	Productivity
Good and featured	3.1720	159300
Featured	3.000	2322
Good	3.016	3347
Regular	2.807	237

5.2   Explaining Quality with Multinominal Model

The simple statistics presented in Table 5 might indicate that productivity is not less important factor than diversity in the context of article quality. To futher examine this signal, we decided to compare the influence of interest versatility and productivity on quality in a more quantitative way. We did this experiments on Polish Wikipedia. Editors were again classified into 4 groups as presented in Table 4. We built multinomial model with versatility, productivity and their interaction as explanatory variables. Model was applied to 4 categories according to the number of edited pages: edited up to 5 pages, edited 5 to 10 pages, edited 10 to 20 pages, edited more than 20 pages. The group N (regular editors) is used as a referential group in all models.

The results are presented in Table 6. In each model versatility has significant correlation with quality. There is positive relationship between versatility of

Table 6. The multinomial model for 4 categories Polish Wikipedia

Model 1: Up to 5 edited pages				Model 2: 6 to 10 edited pages			
Estimate	Sd. Err	P-val	Odds	Estimate	Sd. Err	P-val	Odds
"(Intercept)"				"(Intercept)"			
G -5.221	0	0***	0.005	G -3.343	0	0***	0.035
F -5.465	0	0***	0.004	F -4.170	0	0***	0.050
GF -10.157	0	0***	0	GF -6.231	0	0***	0.001
Versatility				Versatility			
G **0.312**	0	0***	1.367	G **0.146**	0	0***	1.156
F **0.185**	0	0***	1.204	F **0.229**	0	0***	1.256
GF **0.728**	0	0***	2.071	GF **0.279**	0	0***	1.322
Productivity				Productivity			
G 0	0	0.889	1	Good art. 0	0	0.069	1
F 0	0	0.125	1	F 0	0	0.535	1
GF 0	0	0***	1	GF 0	0	0.230	1
Interaction: vers.*prod.				Interaction: vers.*prod.			
G 0	0	0.932	1	G 0	0	0.251	1
F 0	0	0.188	1	F 0	0	0.634	1
GF 0	0	0.005*	1	GF 0	0	0.202	1
Model 3: 10 to 20 edited pages				Model 4: More than 20 edited pages			
Estimate	Sd. Err	P-val	Odds	Estimate	Sd. Err	P-val	Odds
"(Intercept)"				"(Intercept)"			
G -2.737	0	0***	0.064	G -2.170	0	0***	0.114
F -3.479	0	0***	0.030	F -3.252	0	0***	0.038
GF -6.219	0	0***	0.002	GF -4.331	0	0***	0.013
Versatility				Versatility			
G **0.189**	0	0***	1.208	G **0.357**	0	0***	1.429
F **0.205**	0	0***	1.227	F **0.471**	0	0***	1.602
GF **0.695**	0	0***	2.005	GF **1.033**	0	0***	2.810
Productivity				Productivity			
G 0	0	0.997	1	G 0	0	0.138	1
F 0	0	0.857	1	F 0	0	0***	1
GF 0	0	0.002*	1	GF 0	0	0***	1
Interaction: vers.*prod.				Interaction: vers.*prod.			
G 0	0	0.719	1	G 0	0	0***	1
F 0	0	0.821	1	F 0	0	0***	1
GF 0	0	0.007*	1	GF 0	0	0***	1

Signif. codes: $p<0$ '***', $p<0.001$ '**', $p<0.01$ '*', $p<0.05$ '.', $p<0.1$ ' '
all values are approximated to 3 decimal places

editor and the better quality of article. In each group, the results indicate that the more versatile editors are, the better quality articles they produce.

Productivity in this models has no significant influence, except the most productive group. Even in this group the observed relationship between quality and productivity is weak. Also we can't observe positive relationship of productivity and its interaction with versatility on quality. We can observe that productivity for F and GF quality groups has statistical significance in relation with quality but still there is no positive correlation.

Also for interaction of versatility and productivity we can't observe positive correlation with quality for G, F and GF categories of quality. To sum up, the results indicate that only versatility in this model is an important factor explaining higher quality of articles.

6   Experimental Results for Teams

The experimental results presented in Sect. 5 indicate that productivity of authors seems to have weak relationship with the article quality, but their diversity of interest seems to have more impact on it. Encouraged by these observations, in the remaining part of this work, we make a step further and extend the study on whole *teams* of authors. More precisely, we analyse how productivity and diversity of teams impact the quality of articles they create. Also, as literature [4] suggests, productivity and diversity of teams may be defined more widely and other variables may have influence on the quality of article, we introduce another term - tenure of authors on Wikipedia in the article measured as a number of days spent on editing Wikipedia articles. In this part we divided teams into three categories depending on article quality they contributed to: featured (F), good (G) and normal (N) (similarly as for single editors).

6.1   Brief Data Analysis

At the beginning of experiments we did a brief analysis of some team properties and their relationship with quality and found some of them interesting (Table 7). One can see that higher team size seems to have positive relation with work quality. Median edition size is slightly decreasing for better quality articles. The next column concerns how experience of contribution measured as total time spent on Wikipedia and on individual articles is related with quality. It can be observed that teams of better quality articles have longer tenure of editors than regular quality teams. Next, we apply standard deviation of tenure as a measure of its diversity. One can observe, that better quality articles have more diverse teams in aspect of tenure. These results seem to show that 'new' and 'old' editors through exchanging their experience create articles of better quality.

6.2   Explaining Quality with Logistic Regression Model for Teams

Experiments from previous section show some interesting results about factors correlated with the quality of articles. We used aggregated data from previous

Table 7. Median of team features vs. quality articles

Quality	Team size	Edition size	Mean tenure in article	Std. dev. tenure in article	Std. dev. tenure in Wikipedia
Featured	33	37	79.69	234.82	921.1369
Good	17	39	77.52	225.58	906.6
Regular	4	45	5.00	33.94	804.8

Table 8. Features of logistic regression model for teams on Polish Wikipedia

Name	Description
Versatility	for every article we count the mean amount of contribution in bytes of all team members (using data about editors interests distribution) to 12 main categories for Polish Wikipedia (Table 2). Then we count versatility as entropy of distribution vector over these categories
Mean productivity in article	mean amount of editors' contribution in bytes to individual article. Counted as sum of all bytes contributor change in one article
Mean total productivity	mean amount of editors' contribution in bytes to all articles on the Wikipedia. Counted as sum of all bytes contributor change in all articles in Wikipedia
The size of team	the number of editors who contributes in one article
Mean tenure in article	mean number of days spent on individual article, counted as the amount of days between first and the last contribution of editor to a given article
Mean tenure in Wikipedia	mean number of days spent on the Wikipedia, counted as the amount of days between the first and the last contribution of editor contribution to all articles on the whole Wikipedia
Std. dev. productivity in art	standard deviation of the number of editors' contribution bytes to individual article
Std. dev total productivity	standard deviation of editors' contribution bytes to all articles on the Wikipedia
Std. dev tenure in article	standard deviation of number of days between the first and the last editors contribution to individual article
Std. dev tenure in wikipedia	standard deviation of number of days between the first and the last editors contribution to all articles on the Wikipedia

Table 9. Logistic regression model for teams on Polish Wikipedia

	Estimate	Std. Error	z value	Pr($> \|z\|$)	
(Intercept)	−7.753e+00	5.333e−01	−14.539	<2e−16	***
Versatility	**7.984e−01**	1.668e−01	4.787	1.69e−06	***
Mean productivity in article	−2.502e−04	1.685e−05	−14.851	<2e−16	***
Mean total productivity	2.832e−08	9.191e−09	3.081	0.00206	**
Size of team	**1.179e−02**	5.052e−04	23.336	<2e−16	***
Mean tenure in article	**−1.242e−02**	5.198e−04	−23.896	<2e−16	***
Mean tenure in wikipedia	−3.169e−04	5.974e−05	−5.304	1.13e−07	***
Sd productivity in art	1.638e−04	6.122e−06	26.754	<2e−16	***
Sd total productivity	−9.191e−08	9.522e−09	−9.652	<2e−16	***
Sd tenure in article	7.450e−03	2.239e−04	33.272	<2e−16	***
Sd tenure in wikipedia	−6.709e−04	8.746e−05	−7.672	1.70e−14	***

Signif. codes: p<0 '***', p<0.001 '**', p<0.01 '*', p<0.05 '.', p<0.1 ' '

section and built an additional logistic regression model based on analysed data. Detailed description of 10 explanatory variables is presented in Table 8. Table 9 shows coefficient estimates for this model. A response variable is the quality of article which can take two values 0, which represents regular quality or 1, for both good and featured quality. In other words we want to predict the probability of being a good/featured article produced by a team over the regular quality article.

Table 9 shows that all variables are statistically significant. It indicates that each of these variable is associated with the probability of better quality article. An estimated coefficient of versatility shows that it has positive impact on quality. The more diverse interests of team members are, the better articles they produce. If team members contribute in articles of different categories, the probability of better quality of their work results is higher than if they were highly specialised. This confirms our thesis that diversity of team has positive relationship with the better quality of articles.

Second interesting result is that the size of a team is positively correlated with better quality. It may indicate that better quality articles become more popular for editors or topics of better articles are better known so more authors can join to edit them.

The least relevant variable in our experiment is the mean team tenure in an article. It has negative relationship with quality. It indicates that teams of editors who edit articles for the longer period of time produce worse quality articles. This is quite surprising and is somehow opposite to the effect that we observe in the previous section in Table 7. Mean tenure in article seems to be correlated with other predictors. The teams that edit articles for a longer period of time seem to increase their quality in general.

Mean productivity in an article and mean total productivity does not have big impact on quality. Their p-value indicates statistical significance but the coefficients are close to 0. This means that better articles and regular articles are created by authors of the same productiveness. Also mean tenure in Wikipedia shows that the amount of time spent on editing articles on the whole Wikipedia has very weak relationship with quality. Logistic regression model shows that any of standard deviation of productivity and any standard deviation of tenure are strongly correlated with quality. Although all of them have small p-values, their coefficients indicates that there is no strong dependence. This means that the diversity of productivity and editors' experience does not influence the quality. Table 9 shows that practically only three of the analysed variables are correlated with the quality. The most important fact is that we can observe strong relationship between versatility and quality. This further confirms our hypothesis that the diversity of interests has positive impact on the quality of articles.

7   Conclusions and Future Work

We proposed a model of user interests and entropy-based measure of interest diversity of a single Wikipedia editor and extend our experiments for teams introducing other predictors into our model. Literature review suggests that the diversity of interests might have positive impact on the quality of performance. To verify this hypothesis we fit the multinomial model for Wikipedia editors with 3- categorical independent variable modelling the quality of the produced articles and two explanatory variables: versatility of interests and productivity. The results indicate significant, positive dependence between versatility and quality and no strong relation between productivity and quality. The model was applied to 4 productivity categories to verify the consistency of the observations among editors with different levels of engagement. Next, we extended our study on whole teams of editors and introduced new explanatory variables to indicate if there are any other features related to article quality. Our experiments show that the interest diversity of teams has positive influence on their work quality.

This result might be interpreted so that in some organizational contexts the integral approach emerges spontaneously and might serve as a more efficient organisational mode. We can speculate that users with a broader expertise play a different role in the community. They act as ties between community subgroups, which is a crucial factor for maintaining a group coherence. The integral approach to organization also helps to adapt to new environments and to change the cooperation rules.

In future work it would be interesting to study other features and deeper investigate the problem. It would be also interesting in future to develop an intelligent decision-support tool for suggesting how to build a successful editor team in order to produce high-quality articles. We believe that our work would serve as one of the steps towards achieving such a goal in future.

Acknowledgements. The work is partially supported by the Polish National Science Centre grant 2012/05/B/ST6/03364.

References

1. Aggarwal, A.: Decision making in diverse swift teams: an exploratory study. In: Proceedings of the 2014 47th Hawaii International Conference on System Sciences, HICSS 2014, pp. 278–288. IEEE Computer Society, Washington, DC (2014)
2. Agrawal, R., Gollapudi, S., Halverson, A., Ieong, S.: Diversifying search results. In: Proceedings of the Second ACM International Conference on Web Search and Data Mining, WSDM 2009, pp. 5–14. ACM, New York (2009)
3. Carbonell, J., Goldstein, J.: The use of mmr, diversity-based reranking for reordering documents and producing summaries. In: Proceedings of the 21st Annual International ACM SIGIR Conference on Research and Development in Information Retrieval, SIGIR 1998, pp. 335–336. ACM, New York (1998)
4. Chen, J., Ren, Y., Riedl, J.: The effects of diversity on group productivity and member withdrawal in online volunteer groups. In: Proceedings of the SIGCHI Conference on Human Factors in Computing Systems, CHI 2010, pp. 821–830. ACM, New York (2010)
5. Goffman, W.: A searching procedure for information retrieval. Inf. Storage Retrieval $2(2)$, 73–78 (1964)
6. Langlois, R.N., Garzarelli, G.: Of Hackers and Hairdressers: Modularity and the Organizational Economics of Open-source Collaboration. Working papers 2008–53, University of Connecticut, Department of Economics (2008)
7. López, C.A., Butler, B.S.: Consequences of content diversity for online public spaces for local communities. In: Proceedings of the 2013 Conference on Computer Supported Cooperative Work, CSCW 2013, pp. 673–682. ACM, New York (2013)
8. Parnas, D.L.: On the criteria to be used in decomposing systems into modules. Commun. ACM $15(12)$, 1053–1058 (1972)
9. Sanchez, R., Mahoney, J.T.: Modularity, flexibility, and knowledge management in product and organization design. Strateg. Manag. J. 17, 63–76 (1996)
10. Sydow, M., Pikula, M., Schenkel, R.: The notion of diversity in graphical entity summarisation on semantic knowledge graphs. J. Intell. Inf. Syst. 41, 109–149 (2013)
11. Szejda, J., Czerniawska, D., Sydow, M.: Does a "Renaissance Man" create good wikipedia articles? In: Proceedings of the International Conference on Knowledge Discovery and Information Retrieval, (KDIR-2014), pp. 425–430. SCITEPRESS (2014)
12. Vee, E., Srivastava, U., Shanmugasundaram, J., Bhat, P., Yahia, S.A.: Efficient computation of diverse query results. In: Proceedings of the 2008 IEEE 24th International Conference on Data Engineering, ICDE 2008, pp. 228–236. IEEE Computer Society, Washington, DC (2008)

On the Evaluation Potential of Quality Functions in Community Detection for Different Contexts

Jean Creusefond[1]([✉]), Thomas Largillier[1], and Sylvain Peyronnet[2]

[1] Normandy University, Caen, France
jean.creusefond@unicaen.fr
[2] Qwant and ix-labs, Rouen, France

Abstract. Due to nowadays networks' sizes, the evaluation of a community detection algorithm can only be done using quality functions. These functions measure different networks/graphs structural properties, each of them corresponding to a different definition of a community. Since there exists many definitions for a community, choosing a quality function may be a difficult task, even if the networks' statistics/origins can give some clues about which one to choose.

In this paper, we apply a general methodology to identify different **contexts**, *i.e.* groups of graphs where the quality functions behave similarly. In these **contexts** we identify the best quality functions, *i.e.* quality functions whose results are consistent with expectations from real life applications.

Keywords: Quality functions · Social networks · Community detection

1 Introduction

Every community detection algorithm is justified by the search for particular substructures, *i.e.* communities, defined by a particular purpose in a particular network. This combination of structured data and purpose makes the field complex and fuzzy, but drives research to unravel the different meanings that the word "community" bears.

As a result, a large number of desirable properties of communities have been discovered. To measure them, many works aimed at designing functions quantifying these properties in order to evaluate the goodness of a community. Called quality functions, these mathematical tools are not only useful for evaluation purposes but can also be used in greedy algorithms as community detection methods directly.

However, evaluating an algorithm may be difficult because it implies choosing between quality functions that often output contradictory results. The structural properties of the network and of the communities being looked for may strongly differ from one case to the other. It is then of the utmost importance to identify the right quality function for each graph. In order to do that we define the notion of **context** which is a group of graphs where quality functions behave similarly.

© Springer International Publishing Switzerland 2016
A. Wierzbicki et al. (Eds.): NetSci-X 2016, LNCS 9564, pp. 111–125, 2016.
DOI: 10.1007/978-3-319-28361-6_9

One then only needs to identify the right quality function for a `context` and the means to identify which `context` a graph is part of.

In this paper we identify some `contexts` for community detection, and select quality functions that feature behavior that is coherent with real-world data. To achieve this goal, we compare 10 functions from relatively recent literature, using 10 datasets featuring ground-truth, 7 community detection algorithms and 2 extrinsic evaluation functions. We look at the correlation between quality functions and real-world data: do they rank higher clusterings that are close to the ground-truth, and conversely? We then identify `contexts` when quality functions rank different graphs in the same way.

2   Related Work

The rise of community detection as a research field has inevitably given birth to a variety of works on meta analysis. They feature a wide range of methods, but all of them are aimed to identify quality functions with desirable properties.

Van Laarhoven and Marchiori [28] designed six axioms that qualify intuitive good behavior of quality functions. They show that modularity does not satisfy two of them, partly because of the resolution limit [14].

Yang and Leskovec [30] studied 12 quality functions that could be applied at cluster level. They classified them into four groups depending on how they were correlated when applied to real-world graphs, and these groups corresponded to the measured structural property. They designed "goodness metrics" that measure only one property of a cluster and compared how the quality functions fared in order to identify what property were measured by which function.

Almeida *et al.* [2] compared the result of 5 quality functions when applied to 5 real-world graphs. They applied 4 parameterized algorithms on these networks and changed the parameters to get different number of communities. They observed that some metrics have the tendency to favor bigger clusters while others favor the opposite.

Our approach differs from previous works by the scale and purpose of our work: to the best of our knowledge, we are the first to focus on the identification of `contexts` for quality functions. Chakraborty *et al.* [9] have already applied part of this methodology in the context of community detection in order to experimentally demonstrate the efficiency of the quality function they proposed.

3   Quality Functions

Throughout the rest of this paper we use the following notations.

A quality function is an application $f(G, C) \rightarrow \mathbb{R}$, whose purpose is to quantify the quality of a clustering on a graph. For brevity, we omit the graph input. Note that quality functions are different from comparison methods, the latter comparing two clusterings.

In order to ease comparisons, we normalize some quality functions. We categorize the functions depending on the locality of information they use. We

General	
$G = (V, E)$	Undirected graph (set of vertices, edges)
n, m	# of vertices (= nodes) and edges
$N_{v \in V}$	Set of neighbors of a node v
$k_{v \in V}$	# of neighbors (degree) of a node v
k_m	Median degree
Set-specific	
$m(S \subseteq V)$	# of internal edges of S
$m(S \subseteq V, S' \subseteq V)$	# of edges with one end in S and another in S'
$N_{v \in V, S \subseteq V}$	Internal neighborhood of v in S
$k_{S \subseteq V}$	Size of a cluster S
$Vol(S \subseteq V)$	Volume of a cluster S (sum of the degrees of the vertices)
$diam(S \subseteq V)$	Internal diameter of a cluster S
Clusterings	
$\mathcal{C}, \mathcal{L}$	Clustering, set of sets of nodes whose union is V
$C(v \in V), L(v \in V)$	Set of clusters in which a node v belongs to in $\mathcal{C}/\mathcal{L}$

identify three classes of locality: vertex-level, community-level and graph-level. The formula for each quality function can be found in Table 1.

Vertex-Level Quality Functions. Compute a quality for every node in the graph and output the average as the total quality of the clustering on the graph. Let $v \in V$ be the considered node, and $C \in \mathcal{C}$ be the community of v.

The **Local internal clustering coefficient** [29] (called clustering coefficient from now on) of a node is the probability that two of his neighbors that are in the same community are also neighbors. The clustering property of communities is actually one of the most well-known in the field, and is explained by the construction of social networks by homophily.

This property is included in **Permanence** [9], where it is combined with a notion of equilibrium for the nodes concerning their membership to their community. A node has a lower Permanence if there is another community than its own that highly attracts it, *i. e.* to which it is very connected compared to its connection to its community.

The **Flake-ODF** [13] compares internal to external degree. It is similar to the **Fraction Over Median Degree** [30] (FOMD), that compares internal degree and the median degree in the whole graph.

Community-Level Quality Functions. Compute a score for each cluster and output the sum as the quality of the clustering.

The **Conductance** [17] and the **Cut-ratio** are concerned with the external connectivity of the community. The Cut-ratio normalizes it with the number of potential edges between the individuals of the community and the remainder of the network. On the other hand, the Conductance is normalized by the same potential number of edges but takes into account the degrees in the community (few edges may reach a community of consisting of a few nodes with small degree). We weight these local measures with the size of the community so that each vertex in the networks has the same level of participation in the measure.

The **Compactness** [11] measures the potential speed of a diffusion process in a community. Starting from the most eccentric node, the function captures the number of edges reached per time step by a perfect transmission of information. The underlying model defines community as a group of people within which communication quickly reaches everyone.

Modularity [21] is the difference between the number of internal edges of the community versus the expected number of edges. This expectancy is expressed using the configuration model, a graph model guaranteeing the same degree distribution as the original one but with randomized edges. Assuming that this model ignores community structure, a high difference between expectancy and reality would indicate an abnormal density, *ergo* community structure.

Graph-Level Quality Functions. Output the score of the whole graph. **Surprise** [1] (in its asymptotical approximation [26]) and **Significance** [27] are based on the computation of an asymmetric difference, the Kullback-Leibler divergence, between two-points probability distributions (only one event and its complement). Considering x/y indifferently as one of the two probabilities featured in the reference/non-reference distribution, the divergence is: $D(x\|y) = x\log(x/y) + (1-x)\log((1-x)/(1-y))$.

The reference distribution of Surprise models the probability that an edge is internal to a community, and the non-reference is the event that a couple of nodes are inside the same community. Significance features one reference distribution per community that corresponds to the event that a random couple of nodes inside the same community are linked by an edge. The non-reference distribution is the same value for the whole graph.

4   Networks with Ground-Truth

To identify `contexts` for community detection, we need some real-life information on what a community actually is. We therefore pulled 10 networks with known community structure from literature. To compare them with the algorithms that classify all nodes, vertices with no ground-truth communities are removed and only the largest connected component is considered. We note $\rightarrow$ for directed networks and $\textcircled{D}$ for overlapping communities.

Collaboration Networks (cf Table 2). The networks represent people working together in certain organizations. They have a strong underlying bipartite structure.

The Computer Science (CS) network comes from the same source as the DBLP network, but it features only computer scientists and a different kind of

Table 1. Quality functions

Name	Function
Local clustering coefficient	$f_{clus}(v, C) = \dfrac{2 * |\{u \in N_{v,C}, w \in N_{v,C} \setminus \{u\}, (u,w) \in E\}|}{|N_{v,C}|(|N_{v,C}| - 1)}$
Permanence	$f_{perm}(v, C) = \dfrac{m(v, C)}{max_{C' \in \mathcal{C} \setminus \{C\}}(m(v, C')) \times k_v} + f_{clus}(v, C) - 1$
1-Flake-ODF	$f_{flak}(v, C) = \begin{cases} 1 & \text{when } m(v, C) > m(v, V \setminus C) \\ 0 & \text{otherwise} \end{cases}$
FOMD	$f_{FOMD}(v, C) = \begin{cases} 1 & \text{when } m(v, C) > d_m \\ 0 & \text{otherwise} \end{cases}$
1-Cut ratio	$f_{cut}(C) = \left(1 - \dfrac{m(c, V \setminus C)}{k_C(n - k_C)}\right) \times \dfrac{k_C}{n}$
1-Conductance	$f_{cond}(C) = \left(1 - \dfrac{m(v, V \setminus C)}{Vol(C)}\right) \times \dfrac{k_C}{n}$
Compactness	$f_{comp}(C) = \dfrac{m(C)}{diam(C)}$
Modularity	$f_{mod}(C) = \dfrac{m(C)}{m} - \left(\dfrac{Vol(C)}{2m}\right)^2$
Surprise	$f_{surp}(C) = D\left(\dfrac{\sum_{C \in \mathcal{C}} m(C)}{m} \middle\| \dfrac{\sum_{C \in \mathcal{C}} \binom{k_C}{2}}{\binom{n}{2}}\right)$
Significance	$f_{sign}(C) = \sum_{C \in \mathcal{C}} \binom{k_C}{2} D\left(\dfrac{m(C)}{\binom{k_C}{2}} \middle\| \dfrac{m}{\binom{n}{2}}\right)$

Table 2. Collaboration networks

Name	n	m	Nodes	Edges	Communities
DBLP[a] [30]	129981	332595	authors	co-authorships	publication venues Ⓞ
CS [7,8]	400657	1428030	authors	co-authorships	publication domains Ⓞ
Actors (imdb)[b] [5]	124414	20489642	actors	co-appearances	movies Ⓞ
Github[b,c]	39845	22277795	developers	co-contributions	projects Ⓞ

[a]http://snap.stanford.edu/data/
[b]http://konect.uni-koblenz.de
[c]https://github.com/blog/466-the-2009-github-contest

ground-truth. Furthermore, the actors and github networks are constructed from bipartite graphs, and therefore form cliques inside of the communities.

Online Social Networks (OSNs) (cf Table 3). Most of these networks are originally directed but due to the high reciprocity the original authors considered safe to set all links as undirected.

Table 3. Online social networks

Name	n	m	Nodes	Edges	Communities
LiveJournal[a] [30]	1143395	16880773	bloggers	following $\rightarrow$	explicit groups Ⓓ
Youtube[a] [30]	51204	317393	youtubers	following $\rightarrow$	explicit groups Ⓓ
Flickr [20]	368285	11915549	users	following $\rightarrow$	explicit groups Ⓓ

[a]http://snap.stanford.edu/data/

Table 4. Social-related networks

Name	n	m	Nodes	Edges	Communities
Amazon[a] [30]	147510	267135	products	frequent co-purchases	categories
Football [15]	115	613	football teams	> 1 one disputed match	divisions
Cora[b] [25]	23165	89.156	scientific papers	citations $\rightarrow$	categories

[a]http://snap.stanford.edu/data/
[b]http://konect.uni-koblenz.de

Social-Related Networks (cf Table 4). Nodes in these networks do not represent people, but their connections are created by social interaction.

Artificial Benchmarks. We use the Lancichinetti-Fortunato-Radicchi (LFR) [19] benchmark as a validation method for our methodology.

On this benchmark, we may chose the number of nodes, the average degree ($\hat{k}$), the maximum degree (k_{max}), the mixing parameter (μ), the coefficients of the power laws of degree and community size distributions (respectively t_1 and t_2), the average clustering coefficient ($\hat{cc}$), the number of nodes belonging to multiple communities (on) and the number of communities they belong to (om).

Table 5. The parameters of the five classes of synthetic LFR networks

Name	n	$\hat{k}$	k_{max}	μ	t_1	t_2	$\hat{cc}$	on	om
LFRa	10 000	50	1 000	0.1	2.5	2.5	0.2	8 000	4
LFRb	100 000	50	2 500	0.1	2.5	2.5	0.2	8 000	4
LFRc	10 000	100	500	0.4	2.1	2.0	0.1	8 000	5
LFRd	10 000	50	1 000	0.1	2.5	2.5	0.2	0	0
LFRe	10 000	100	500	0.4	2.1	2.0	0.1	0	0

As presented in Table 5, we have 5 classes of networks. The a class represents a standard social network, with common values for each parameter. We note that the mixing parameter is quite low (the communities should be well-cut) and the communities are overlapping. The b class is the same as the a class but with ten times more nodes. The c class is however completely different, with all its parameters changed except size (but it is still overlapping). The $d(e)$ class is the same as the $a(c)$ class but without any overlapping community.

5   Comparison Methods

A comparison method (or extrinsic clustering evaluation metric [3]) is an application $f(\mathcal{C}, \mathcal{L}) \rightarrow [-1; 1]$, whose purpose is to evaluate the closeness of two clusterings.

The **Normalized Mutual Information (NMI)** measures the quantity of information gained by the knowledge of one clustering compared to the other. The version that we use was introduced by Lancichinetti *et al.* [18].

The **F-BCubed (fb3)** [4] precision measures for each element e the proportion of its associates (*e.g.* individuals that are in the same cluster) in $\mathcal{C}$ that are still its associates in $\mathcal{L}$, and takes the average among all e. Amigó *et al.* [3] extended this metric for overlapping clustering, taking into account the number of clusters in common that e and its associates have. They define BCubed overlapping precision and recall as follows:

$$prec(C, L) = Avg_e \left[Avg_{\substack{e' \\ C(e) \cap C(e') \neq \emptyset}} \left(\frac{min(|C(e) \cap C(e')|, |L(e) \cap L(e')|)}{|C(e) \cap C(e')|} \right) \right] \quad (1)$$

$$recall(C, L) = prec(L, C) \quad (2)$$

$$F\text{-}BCubed(C, L) = \frac{1}{\dfrac{1}{2 * prec(C, L)} + \dfrac{1}{2 * recall(C, L)}} \quad (3)$$

Amigó *et al.* [3] also gave an extensive comparison of evaluation metrics by designing intuitive properties of goodness. Their conclusion was that the F-BCubed measure satisfied all of them, while the other common metrics fail at least on of these axioms.

6   Experimental Setup

In this section, we describe our experiments. We first cover the methodology, then present the community detection algorithms used to generate clusterings and finally tools we used to keep tractable the number of operations.

6.1   Methodology

The methodology has two goals: to identify `contexts` in which quality functions behave in the same way, and to identify the best quality functions for each `context`. For each graph with ground-truth communities (cf Sect. 4), we execute the following steps:

1. Apply various community detections methods on the base graph (cf Sect. 6.2).
2. Compute quality functions over the resulting clusterings (cf Sect. 3).
3. Compare the communities found to the ground-truth, creating a gold standard value for each clustering (cf Sect. 5).

4. Compare for each graph the ranking of the clusterings given by the gold standard value to the ranking of clusterings measured by quality functions with Spearman's coefficient. For each graph, each quality now have a score.
5. For each couple of graphs, compute the correlation of the previous scores using Spearman's coefficient.

The rationale behind step 4 is that a quality function fits a ground-truth if the clusterings that are the closest to the ground-truth are highly ranked with the quality, and conversely. Therefore, at this step we can conclude which quality function is the best for each graph. We also need to go through step 5 in order to identify contexts: the graphs are compared on their ranking from the quality functions, and contexts may be identified as sets of graphs that are highly correlated.

6.2 Community Detection Algorithms

Since we consider large graphs, we decided to use community detection algorithms that have sub quadratic time and space complexity. We chose several methods, based on their availability, efficiency, originality and/or spread.

We classify the algorithms we use in three groups:

- Modularity optimization: Louvain [6], Clauset [10].
- Random walks: MCL [12], Infomap [23].
- Heuristics: LexDFS [11], 3-core [24], label propagation [22].

6.3 Computation Time Management

Three kinds of measures are computation-heavy in our experimental setup: triangle computation, diameter and fb3. Fb3 needs $O(|C|^2)$ operations to compute the values for the community C. f_{clus} and f_{perm} need the computation of all internal triangles, which is very demanding for highly clustered graphs.

We therefore sample our dataset and average these two values over the sample. We use the Hoeffeding bound [16] (our samples are $i.i.d$ and in the $[0, 1]$ interval) to get the number of samples t needed ensure that there is a small probability p that the error resulting in our sampling is not bounded by ϵ.

$$P(|\overline{X} - E[X]| < \epsilon) = p \geq 2e^{-2n\epsilon^2} \Leftrightarrow n \geq \frac{ln(p/2)}{-2\epsilon^2} \qquad (4)$$

We use 5000 samples, meaning that $p \leq 5\%$ and $\epsilon \leq 0.02$. Of course, the bound is a worst-case: in practice, we observe errors of about 10^{-4}, which is too small to disturb the rankings.

The diameter computation, needed by f_{comp}, is in $O(|C|^2)$. We use the standard approximate algorithm based on two BFSs to compute it in near-linear time. The first BFS starts at a random point of the community, and the last node visited by this BFS is used as the origin of another BFS. This heuristic searches for an eccentric point which is likely to feature at the end of a maximum-distance path.

Due to the process of ranking quality functions and comparison methods, even bounded errors may have unbounded impact on the results if the approximated values are too close to each other. On top of that, some of the community detection algorithms make nondeterministic choices, which implies an incontrollable potential difference in results. To gain confidence that the randomness of the processes involved does not influence the results too much, we ran the whole process multiple times. We obtained very close results in every run.

7   Experimental Results

7.1   Correlations in LFR

We first study the results of the methodology when applied to LFR graphs. In order to assess its stability, we create three benchmark graphs from different random seeds for each class of LFR graphs described in Sect. 4. In order to judge behavioral similarity of quality functions between graphs, we compute Spearman's coefficient of each couple of graphs (as presented in Sect. 6.1, step 5) and report the results in Table 6 (resp. Table 7) for NMI (resp. for fb3).

In Table 6, we see that quality functions of the same class behave in the same way when compared to NMI. However, this positive view is tarnished by some exceptions: c1 seems to relate more to graphs of the a class than from its own class, and the same can be said from e3. We assume that these exceptions are due to the random nature of the generative model, which might produce networks that have some structural properties that vary significantly enough to disturb comparison with NMI.

Table 6. The correlation between the ranking of quality functions (with NMI ranking) for synthetic graphs (A colored version is available on the authors' webpage).

file\file	a1	a2	a3	b1	b2	b3	c1	c2	c3	d1	d2	d3	e1	e2	e3
a1	-	1.00	1.00	0.98	0.99	0.45	0.40	-0.23	-0.09	0.53	0.53	0.53	0.69	0.31	0.95
a2	-	-	1.00	0.98	0.99	0.45	0.40	-0.23	-0.09	0.53	0.53	0.53	0.69	0.31	0.95
a3	-	-	-	0.98	0.99	0.45	0.43	-0.22	-0.07	0.53	0.53	0.53	0.69	0.31	0.94
b1	-	-	-	-	0.99	0.48	0.35	-0.15	0.01	0.53	0.53	0.53	0.69	0.31	0.92
b2	-	-	-	-	-	0.46	0.34	-0.21	-0.07	0.53	0.53	0.53	0.69	0.31	0.94
b3	-	-	-	-	-	-	0.29	0.03	0.21	0.15	0.15	0.15	0.67	0.56	0.42
c1	-	-	-	-	-	-	-	0.07	0.15	0.27	0.27	0.27	0.30	0.25	0.41
c2	-	-	-	-	-	-	-	-	0.90	0.34	0.34	0.34	-0.12	0.05	-0.32
c3	-	-	-	-	-	-	-	-	-	0.22	0.22	0.22	-0.03	0.20	-0.16
d1	-	-	-	-	-	-	-	-	-	-	1.00	1.00	0.47	0.12	0.47
d2	-	-	-	-	-	-	-	-	-	-	-	1.00	0.47	0.12	0.47
d3	-	-	-	-	-	-	-	-	-	-	-	-	0.47	0.12	0.47
e1	-	-	-	-	-	-	-	-	-	-	-	-	-	0.76	0.70
e2	-	-	-	-	-	-	-	-	-	-	-	-	-	-	0.35
e3	-	-	-	-	-	-	-	-	-	-	-	-	-	-	-

Table 7. The correlation between the ranking of quality functions (with FB3 ranking) for synthetic graphs

file\file	a1	a2	a3	b1	b2	b3	c1	c2	c3	d1	d2	d3	e1	e2	e3
a1	-	0.99	1.00	0.95	0.94	0.96	-0.23	-0.50	-0.44	0.72	0.72	0.72	0.89	0.89	0.88
a2	-	-	0.99	0.94	0.93	0.94	-0.26	-0.48	-0.42	0.70	0.70	0.70	0.89	0.87	0.88
a3	-	-	-	0.95	0.94	0.96	-0.23	-0.50	-0.44	0.72	0.72	0.72	0.89	0.89	0.88
b1	-	-	-	-	1.00	1.00	-0.26	-0.49	-0.44	0.80	0.80	0.80	0.90	0.92	0.93
b2	-	-	-	-	-	1.00	-0.27	-0.48	-0.43	0.80	0.80	0.80	0.90	0.92	0.93
b3	-	-	-	-	-	-	-0.25	-0.49	-0.43	0.80	0.80	0.80	0.90	0.91	0.92
c1	-	-	-	-	-	-	-	0.62	0.76	-0.27	-0.27	-0.27	-0.42	-0.38	-0.37
c2	-	-	-	-	-	-	-	-	0.90	-0.26	-0.26	-0.26	-0.49	-0.51	-0.37
c3	-	-	-	-	-	-	-	-	-	-0.31	-0.31	-0.31	-0.47	-0.47	-0.39
d1	-	-	-	-	-	-	-	-	-	-	1.00	1.00	0.75	0.78	0.79
d2	-	-	-	-	-	-	-	-	-	-	-	1.00	0.75	0.78	0.79
d3	-	-	-	-	-	-	-	-	-	-	-	-	0.75	0.78	0.79
e1	-	-	-	-	-	-	-	-	-	-	-	-	-	0.983	0.963
e2	-	-	-	-	-	-	-	-	-	-	-	-	-	-	0.96
e3	-	-	-	-	-	-	-	-	-	-	-	-	-	-	-

It was expected that the *a* class would be rated in the same way as the *b* and *d* class, and would be different from the other two. If the correct similarities are observed, surprisingly, the *e* class seems to behave similarly to the *a* class, and this is even clearer with the fb3 measure (cf Table 7). This is probably because the distribution difference and the mixing parameter have less influence in the structural properties of the network than the overlapping nature. We conclude that the comparison with NMI is globally efficient, but it is very sensitive to noise and overlapping difference.

In Table 7, we see that the comparison with fb3 is much more clear-cut than the one with NMI: there is no value between −0.2 and 0.6, which would indicate medium to weak correlations. It is also very clear that the *c* class is considered as differently ranked for fb3 than the other ones. As stated above, the fb3 measure does not identify the model difference in the generation of the *e* class.

We note that the c1 and the e3 networks that did not behave like the others when compared with NMI measure behave in the same way when looking at the fb3 measure. We conclude that comparing networks through the measure is less sensitive than NMI to random variations due to network generation processes, the downside being that it may show resemblance between two networks that are actually very different.

7.2   Correlations in Real World Data

Just as with the LFR benchmark, we start by identifying groups of networks where quality functions behave approximately in the same way. Unlike LFR, the only classification available for these networks is their representation of reality, and not the underlying model.

Table 8. Spearman's coefficient of the rows of Table 10 (NMI, Real-world)

file\file	CS	actors	amazon	cora	dblp	flickr	football	github	lj	youtube
CS	-	0.923	0.281	0.972	0.302	0.103	0.245	0.014	0.253	-0.187
actors	-	-	0.264	0.899	0.276	0.168	0.318	0.105	0.262	-0.077
amazon	-	-	-	0.280	0.965	-0.231	0.523	-0.033	-0.269	-0.336
cora	-	-	-	-	0.327	0.115	0.213	0.052	0.334	-0.191
dblp	-	-	-	-	-	-0.238	0.453	0.031	-0.241	-0.357
flickr	-	-	-	-	-	-	0.180	0.367	0.808	0.759
football	-	-	-	-	-	-	-	0.350	-0.191	0.117
github	-	-	-	-	-	-	-	-	0.329	0.549
lj	-	-	-	-	-	-	-	-	-	0.587
youtube	-	-	-	-	-	-	-	-	-	-

Real-life data are less clear-cut than controlled benchmark networks. However, we see in Tables 8 and 9 that the connections (cora, CS) and (lj, youtube, flickr) appear with both comparison methods as high, which means that these networks are consistently close with the ranking of their ground-truth. This observation is consistent with our knowledge of these networks. Cora and CS both correspond to scientific publication and their ground-truthes both correspond to publication domains. Interestingly, neither the overlapping nature of CS nor the size difference seem to affect this outcome, which comforts us in the robustness of the method. Youtube, flickr and lj have similar connection (someone follows someone) and ground-truth (explicit membership) mechanics. The other correlation relationships differ given the considered comparison method.

NMI: We notice first that the tuple (cora, CS) is extended to **(cora, CS, actors)**, which brings another collaboration network close to the first two. We note, however, that the github network is not correlated with them. We notice that the structural difference with github, where an individual belongs to more

Table 9. Spearman's coefficient of the rows of Table 11 (FB3, Real-world)

file\file	CS	actors	amazon	cora	dblp	flickr	football	github	lj	youtube
CS	-	-0.070	0.920	0.970	0.502	0.224	-0.434	-0.344	-0.351	-0.035
actors	-	-	-0.052	-0.157	0.472	-0.091	0.776	0.774	0.434	0.227
amazon	-	-	-	0.935	0.411	0.189	-0.455	-0.378	-0.316	-0.105
cora	-	-	-	-	0.409	0.358	-0.456	-0.381	-0.266	0.040
dblp	-	-	-	-	-	0.250	0.163	0.187	0.143	0.456
flickr	-	-	-	-	-	-	0.154	0.156	0.533	0.790
football	-	-	-	-	-	-	-	0.911	0.719	0.497
github	-	-	-	-	-	-	-	-	0.654	0.414
lj	-	-	-	-	-	-	-	-	-	0.760
youtube	-	-	-	-	-	-	-	-	-	-

Table 10. Spearman's coefficient of the NMI (ground truth, algorithms) compared to the results of quality functions. Real-world dataset

file\quality	cc	fb3	mod	nmi	perm	sign	cond	FOMD	comp	cut_ratio	f-odf	sur
CS	0.00	0.82	-0.25	1.00	0.00	-0.14	0.14	0.61	-0.04	0.32	0.00	-0.46
actors	-0.54	0.46	-0.89	1.00	-0.21	-0.50	-0.21	-0.21	-0.39	-0.21	-0.32	-0.57
amazon	-0.30	0.03	-0.57	1.00	-0.57	-0.12	-0.57	-0.57	0.03	-0.96	-0.57	-0.44
cora	0.06	0.69	-0.06	1.00	0.06	-0.06	0.19	0.69	0.06	0.44	0.19	-0.06
dblp	-0.43	0.89	-0.96	1.00	-0.96	-0.32	-0.89	-0.57	0.18	-0.88	-0.86	-0.46
flickr	0.00	-0.71	0.75	1.00	0.61	0.07	0.61	0.07	0.14	-0.01	0.61	-0.79
football	0.38	0.38	0.10	1.00	0.88	0.38	-0.37	0.56	0.38	-0.87	-0.33	0.38
github	-0.29	-0.36	-0.11	1.00	-0.07	0.11	-0.11	-0.04	-0.43	-0.14	0.07	-0.04
lj	-0.21	-0.86	0.43	1.00	0.21	-0.18	0.50	0.25	0.32	0.35	0.50	-0.32
youtube	0.36	-0.89	0.96	1.00	0.79	0.39	0.68	0.07	0.11	0.31	0.68	0.61

Table 11. Spearman's coefficient of the fb3 (ground truth, algorithms) compared to the results of quality functions. Real-world dataset

file\quality	cc	fb3	mod	nmi	perm	sign	cond	FOMD	comp	cut_ratio	f-odf	sur
CS	-0.50	1.00	-0.14	0.82	0.14	-0.57	0.39	0.75	-0.61	0.59	0.18	-0.57
actors	0.29	1.00	-0.07	0.46	-0.89	0.43	-0.64	-0.64	0.18	-0.64	-0.64	0.36
amazon	-0.86	1.00	-0.04	0.03	-0.04	-0.89	0.00	0.25	-0.93	-0.01	0.00	-0.46
cora	-0.64	1.00	0.04	0.69	0.29	-0.71	0.50	0.89	-0.75	0.79	0.50	-0.71
dblp	0.64	1.00	-0.71	0.89	-0.86	-0.57	-0.64	-0.32	-0.07	-0.57	-0.61	-0.46
flickr	0.18	1.00	-0.21	-0.71	0.07	0.04	0.07	0.46	0.39	0.60	0.07	0.29
football	1.00	1.00	0.68	0.38	0.25	1.00	-0.96	-0.05	1.00	-0.21	-0.95	1.00
github	-0.29	1.00	0.39	-0.36	-0.57	0.71	-0.61	-0.79	0.71	-0.57	-0.93	0.71
lj	0.29	1.00	-0.54	-0.86	-0.14	0.39	-0.46	-0.36	-0.11	-0.38	-0.46	0.32
youtube	0.04	1.00	-0.86	-0.87	-0.61	-0.07	-0.54	0.04	0.14	-0.19	-0.54	-0.32

groups than actors (7.8 compared to 3.8), resembles the difference between LFR a and c class, which was demoted by NMI.

An unexpected correlation is **(dblp, amazon)**: quality functions behave in similar ways in a co-purchase network and in a co-authorship network. As observed in Sect. 7.3, this result is due to the erratic behavior of the correlation between qualities with very low correlation values.

FB3: We notice a surprising correlation of the co-purchase network with scientific networks **(amazon, cora, CS)**.

The networks that are strongly defined by the underlying bipartite network, **(football, actor, github)**, are correlated with fb3. They have a similar structure, with a particularly high clustering coefficient inside of the communities.

We observe that the **(lj, football, github)** tuple appears as close to each other. It could be explained by the underlying bipartite model of lj (and the other two OSNs) that creates a weak correlation with the other networks that are structurally more defined by it.

7.3 Quality Functions in Contexts

We analyze the correlations between the quality functions and the comparison methods. Our aim is to find quality functions that give a consistent ranking that is highly correlated with the ground truth.

In the context of OSNs (flickr, youtube, lj), we see in Table 11 that the fb3 does not give us an answer on the best quality function to use since no satisfying correlation is observed. However, we see in Table 10 that NMI tells us that Modularity gives a consistently correlated score, while Permanence also behaves well while being more inconsistent (notably with lj).

Concerning scientific collaboration networks (cora, CS), the average FOMD consistently shows a strong correlation with the ground-truth, close to the Cut-ratio. This tendency is coherent with both comparison methods.

The networks with strong bipartite underlying structure (football, github, actor) do not show any particular outlier when compared with NMI with very weak correlations. However, fb3 outlines the performance of Signature and Surprise.

The last two networks, amazon and dblp, do not show any satisfying correlation with the selected quality functions. We suspect the quality functions that we use are not adapted to the contexts of these graphs.

8 Conclusion

In this paper, we introduced fb3 as a clustering comparison method for community detection algorithms. We gave evidence that quality functions are context-dependant. The application of a quality function comparison methodology resulted in the identification of three contexts and of the relevant quality functions. We also provided evidence that the methodology clearly differentiate contexts.

The methodology that has been presented here may very well be applied to overlapping/weighted quality functions that would measure the efficiency of overlapping/weighted community detection algorithms.

We are currently in the process of integrating all the functionalities presented in this paper in a tool that will be made available shortly to the public.

References

1. Aldecoa, R., Marín, I.: Surprise maximization reveals the community structure of complex networks. Scientific reports 3, January 2013
2. Almeida, H., Guedes, D., Meira Jr., W., Zaki, M.J.: Is there a best quality metric for graph clusters? In: Gunopulos, D., Hofmann, T., Malerba, D., Vazirgiannis, M. (eds.) ECML PKDD 2011, Part I. LNCS, vol. 6911, pp. 44–59. Springer, Heidelberg (2011)
3. Amigó, E., Gonzalo, J., Artiles, J., Verdejo, F.: A comparison of extrinsic clustering evaluation metrics based on formal constraints. Inf. Retrieval 12(4), 461–486 (2009)

4. Bagga, A., Baldwin, B.: Entity-based cross-document coreferencing using the vector space model. In: Proceedings of the 36th Annual Meeting of the Association for Computational Linguistics and 17th International Conference on Computational Linguistics, pp. 79–85. Association for Computational Linguistics (1998)
5. Barabási, A.L., Albert, R.: Emergence of scaling in random networks. Science **286**(5439), 509–512 (1999)
6. Blondel, V.D., Guillaume, J.L., Lambiotte, R., Lefebvre, E.: Fast unfolding of communities in large networks. J. Stat. Mech. Theor. Exp. **2008**(10), P10008 (2008)
7. Chakraborty, T., Sikdar, S., Tammana, V., Ganguly, N., Mukherjee, A.: Computer science fields as ground-truth communities: their impact, rise and fall. In: 2013 IEEE/ACM International Conference on Advances in Social Networks Analysis and Mining (ASONAM), pp. 426–433. IEEE (2013)
8. Chakraborty, T., Sikdar, S., Ganguly, N., Mukherjee, A.: Citation interactions among computer science fields: a quantitative route to the rise and fall of scientific research. Soc. Netw. Anal. Mining **4**(1), 1–18 (2014)
9. Chakraborty, T., Srinivasan, S., Ganguly, N., Mukherjee, A., Bhowmick, S.: On the permanence of vertices in network communities. In: Proceedings of the 20th ACM SIGKDD International Conference on Knowledge Discovery and Data Mining, KDD 2014, pp. 1396–1405. ACM, New York (2014). http://doi.acm.org/10.1145/2623330.2623707
10. Clauset, A., Newman, M., Moore, C.: Finding community structure in very large networks. Phys. Rev. E **70**(6), 066111 (2004)
11. Creusefond, J., Largillier, T., Peyronnet, S.: Finding compact communities in large graphs. In: 2015 Proceedings of SOMERIS, Workshop of Advances in Social Networks Analysis and Mining (ASONAM). IEEE (2015)
12. van Dongen, S.: Graph clustering by flow simulation. Ph.D. thesis (2000)
13. Flake, G.W., Lawrence, S., Giles, C.L.: Efficient identification of web communities, pp. 150–160. ACM Press (2000)
14. Fortunato, S., Barthelemy, M.: Resolution limit in community detection. Proc. Natl. Acad. Sci. **104**(1), 36–41 (2007)
15. Girvan, M., Newman, M.E.J.: Community structure in social and biological networks. PNAS **99**(12), 7821–7826 (2002)
16. Hoeffding, W.: Probability inequalities for sums of bounded random variables. J. Am. Stat. Assoc. **58**(301), 13–30 (1963)
17. Kannan, R., Vempala, S., Vetta, A.: On clusterings: good, bad and spectral. J. ACM (JACM) **51**(3), 497–515 (2004)
18. Lancichinetti, A., Fortunato, S., Kertsz, J.: Detecting the overlapping and hierarchical community structure in complex networks. New J. Phys. **11**(3), 033015 (2009)
19. Lancichinetti, A., Fortunato, S., Radicchi, F.: Benchmark graphs for testing community detection algorithms. Phys. Rev. E **78**(4), 046110 (2008)
20. Mislove, A., Marcon, M., Gummadi, K.P., Druschel, P., Bhattacharjee, B.: Measurement and analysis of online social networks. In: Proceedings of the 5th ACM/Usenix Internet Measurement Conference (IMC 2007), San Diego, CA (2007)
21. Newman, M.E., Girvan, M.: Finding and evaluating community structure in networks. Phys. Rev. E **69**(2), 026113 (2004)
22. Raghavan, U., Albert, R., Kumara, S.: Near linear time algorithm to detect community structures in large-scale networks. Phys. Rev. E **76**(3), 036106 (2007)
23. Rosvall, M., Bergstrom, C.T.: Maps of random walks on complex networks reveal community structure. Proc. Natl. Acad. Sci. **105**(4), 1118–1123 (2008)

24. Seidman, S.B.: Network structure and minimum degree. Soc. Netw. **5**(3), 269–287 (1983)
25. Šubelj, L., Bajec, M.: Model of complex networks based on citation dynamics. In: Proceedings of the 22nd International Conference on World Wide Web, pp. 527–530 (2013)
26. Traag, V.A., Aldecoa, R., Delvenne, J.C.: Detecting communities using asymptotical surprise. Phys. Rev. E **92**(2), 022816 (2015)
27. Traag, V.A., Krings, G., Van Dooren, P.: Significant Scales in Community Structure. Scientific reports 3, October 2013
28. Van Laarhoven, T., Marchiori, E.: Axioms for graph clustering quality functions. J. Mach. Learn. Res. **15**(1), 193–215 (2014)
29. Watts, D.J., Strogatz, S.H.: Collective dynamics of small-worldnetworks. Nature **393**(6684), 440–442 (1998)
30. Yang, J., Leskovec, J.: Defining and evaluating network communities based on ground-truth. Knowl. Inf. Syst. **42**(1), 181–213 (2012)

Predicting User Participation in Social Media

Fredrik Erlandsson[1]([⊠]), Anton Borg[1], Henric Johnson[1], and Piotr Bródka[2]

[1] Blekinge Institute of Technology, 37179 Karlskrona, Sweden
{fredrik.erlandsson,anton.borg,henric.johnson}@bth.se
[2] Wrocław University of Technology, 50-370 Wrocław, Poland
piotr.brodka@pwr.edu.pl

Abstract. Online social networking services like Facebook provides a popular way for users to participate in different communication groups and discuss relevant topics with each other. While users tend to have an impact on each other, it is important to better understand and analyze users behavior in specific online groups. For social networking sites it is of interest to know if a topic will be interesting for users or not. Therefore, this study examines the prediction of user participation in online social networks discussions, in which we argue that it is possible to predict user participation in a public group using common machine learning techniques. We are predicting user participation based on association rules built with respect to user activeness of current posts. In total, we have crawled and extracted 2,443 active users interacting on 610 posts with over 14,117 comments on Facebook. The results show that the proposed approach has a high level of accuracy and the systematic study clearly depicts the possibility to predict user participation in social networking sites.

1 Introduction

Online social networks are a large part of our society. Just Facebook alone attracts 1.3 billion users[1] with 640 million minutes spent each month. Facebook had a total revenue of \$12,466 M in 2014[1]. Consequently, discovering trending topics or influential users is of interest for many researchers, e.g. for marketing [6]. Several studies have tried to identify user influence, however most have used page rank [21] or centrality [5,17] based approaches to identify influential users.

In this article we argue that users, on Facebook groups, are following each other and that it is possible to detect influential users. E.g. if user A, B, C and D share common interests, the chance is that if A, B, and C already have commented on a topic, D also will comment on it. Therefore, this paper relates to how users perform actions (e.g. comments or likes) on posts in Facebook pages. In addition, we use association learning to discover relationships between variables, or in our case users, in the dataset [9]. Given a list of posts from a specific domain we extract users actions such as comments and likes.

---

[1] http://www.statisticbrain.com/facebook-statistics/.

© Springer International Publishing Switzerland 2016
A. Wierzbicki et al. (Eds.): NetSci-X 2016, LNCS 9564, pp. 126–135, 2016.
DOI: 10.1007/978-3-319-28361-6_10

Using association rule learning on the data, we argue that it is possible to predict if a particular user will or will not participate on a post discussion based on the other users activity.

For evaluation, a systematic study is conducted, which include building association rules that can be used to predict if a specific user will be active in a particular post. The prediction is done based on the activeness of users within current posts. Moreover, the scope of the paper is limited to user interactions on a subset of Facebook users on posts with a similar topic.

The paper is organized as follows: In Sect. 2 related work is discussed. Sections 3 and 5 presents the data and the methodology. Association rule learning and the evaluation metrics are discussed in Sect. 4. Finally, the results are presented in Sect. 6 and discussed in Sect. 7.

2   Related Work

Online social networks and social media analysis are one of the hottest areas of research in modern network science. Like in many different areas, scientists struggle to predict the future of online social network. The main focus in social network area is on link prediction [16] but different teams around the world work also on: (i) popularity prediction in social media based on comment mining [12], (ii) personality prediction for micro blog Users [29], (iii) churn prediction and its influence on the network [4,22], (iv) community evolution prediction [7,23], (v) using social media to predict real-world outcomes [3], (vi) predicting information cascade on social media [11], (vii) users features prediction using relational learning [14,15], (viii) predicting patterns of diffusion processes in social network [13], (ix) predicting friendship intensity [2,20], (x) affiliation recommendations [25,26], and many others.

Association rule mining has been previously used in social network and social media analysis. In [18], the authors explores the association rule between a course and gender in the Face book 100 university dataset. This was performed to discover the influence of gender in studying a specific course. [27] introduces the scheme for association rule mining of personal hobbies in social networks, while [24] tackle the problem of mining association rules in folksonomies and try to find out how association rule mining can be applied to analyze and structure folksonomies.

However, while online social network analysis is popular, there is according to our review a lack of research on using association rules for predicting user participation in online social media discussions.

3   Data Model

The data used in this study has been obtained from the crawler described by [8]. This crawler gathers complete posts from Facebook. In this context, the term complete stands for posts that contains all likes and comments. In addition, if a post is crawled, the dataset contains all likes, comments and interacting users up to the crawling time. Our current dataset, captured from public pages and groups on Facebook, consists of over 56 million posts, 560 million comments and 7.3 billion likes made by 820 million Facebook users. The crawled data is parsed and available from a SQL database, structured as described in [19], making all fields needed for our task available. In this study, we assume that the investigated posts will not get any new comments. We simplify the dynamics of social media by saying that the posts we are investigated are "dead" when the data was collected, in which the term of dead posts refers to posts that no longer attracts attention or new comments or likes.

We are limiting this study to only investigate a subset of groups available by the crawler. From these groups we exclude posts with less than 20 comments as these posts are considered to be of too low value and do not hold enough information.

3.1 Data Selection

To perform prediction of user interactions, we have selected the page OccypyTogether. This page was selected based on the following properties: it is active, it has a high number of users (~300 k), it has a reasonable high number of active users (~30,000 users with more than one comment) and it is political with a bias user group (most of the users are positive to the Occupy movement). From this page, only users that have made more than five comments are investigated. This ensures that the selected users are or have been fairly active in the community. The resulting dataset consists of 2,443 users interacting on 610 posts totaling in 14,117 comments.

4 Association Rules

As stated in Sect. 1, we are predicting user participation based on previous interactions with other users on common posts. We argue that if user A participates in all posts where B is participating, there is a high chance of A participating in a new post where B is already active. The method of matching items in different transactions is called association rule mining. We apply association rule mining to the domain of social media where we model the data as follows. Items correspond to users on Facebook and transactions correspond to posts. An user is considered to be active and part of the transaction, as an item, if the user comments on a post.

To build association rules from our dataset, we evaluated several implementations. [1] presented the Aprori algorithm, which was proven to be an efficient method for association rule learning. This algorithm is however proven to have efficiency issues in large datasets [10] and the identified implementation for Python is very slow (considering our dataset it was not possible to get a result within reasonable time). Hence, other algorithms were tested, and in particular the Eclat algorithm [28]. The Eclat algorithm quickly discards items with low frequency by considering a minimum of associations as input parameters.

From the selected dataset, described in Sect. 3.1, we firstly count the frequency of all posts where A and B are active respectively. Secondly, we count all posts where $A \cup B$, both participates. This gives us two measures, length (the number of participating users) and frequency (the sum of all posts where they are participating). These two steps can be summarized as, building frequent item-sets $(\mathcal{I})$. Finally, all possible rules from the computed $\mathcal{I}s$ are generated. In this step we also compute the evaluation metrics described below.

4.1 Evaluation Metrics

To understand the learned association rules, there exist a few metrics. First, we have *Support*, where we compute the frequency of a given item-set, $\mathcal{I}$, and divide it with the total number of transactions (posts) in $\mathcal{D}$. Or, the number occurrence of $\{A, B\}$ in our dataset, $\mathcal{D}$ divided by length of $\mathcal{D}$. As shown in (1).

$$support(\{A, B\}) = \frac{\{A, B\}}{|\mathcal{D}|} \tag{1}$$

Secondly, we have *Confidence*, which is an indicator saying that $\{A, B\} \Rightarrow C$ in the set of transactions in $\mathcal{D}$ is the proportions of transactions that contain $\{A, B\}$ also will contain C as illustrated in (2). Say that $\{A, B, C\}$ participates in 4 common posts and $\{A, B\}$ participates in 8 posts in total. This leads to $4/8 = 0.5$ i.e., the *confidence* that C will participate on a post where A and B already are active is 50%.

$$confidence(\{A, B\} \Rightarrow C) = \frac{support(\{A, B, C\})}{support(C)} \tag{2}$$

Thirdly, we have *lift*, a ratio of the interdependence of the observed values. As we see from (3), if lift is 1, it implies that the rule and the items are independent of each other. However, if the lift is > 1, the lift indicates the degree of dependency of our item-sets.

$$lift(\{A, B\} \Rightarrow C) = \frac{support(\{A, B, C\})}{support(\{A, B\}) \times support(\{C\})} \tag{3}$$

Finally, we have *conviction*, as the ratio of the expected *support* that $\{A, B\}$ occurs without C as shown in (4). Notable, *conviction* is infinite (due to division with zero) when the *confidence* is 1.

$$conviction(\{A, B\} \Rightarrow C) = \frac{1 - support(\{A, B\})}{1 - confidence(\{A, B\} \Rightarrow C)} \tag{4}$$

The described measures enable understanding of the learned rules in $\mathcal{D}$, where higher number of all four measures indicate that the learned rule has relevance for prediction.

5   Methodology

The final dataset used in the experiment consists of 2,443 users interacting on 610 posts and writing 14,117 comments. The selected users are or have been fairly active in the community, which reflect how we build the association rules.

The algorithm used for the association rule mining is the Eclat algorithm. The Eclat algorithm learns about all the frequent item-sets in our data. By using Eclat, it is possible to define a lower bound threshold and in our dataset a good trade-off between resolution and speed is 4, where lower frequency is ignored. The used implementation of Eclat is modified to sort the item-sets by participants so only $\{A, B, C\}$ is considered. Other combinations e.g., $\{B, C, A\}$ and $\{C, A, B\}$ are consolidated in the item-set $\{A, B, C\}$. Association rules supporting the hypothesis of user participation based on other users activities were computed from the calculated frequency item-sets. The results are measured using the evaluation metrics presented in Sect. 4.1.

6   Results

The resulting frequent item-sets are depicted in Fig. 1. This figure illustrates the length of elements (number of collaborating users) with respect to frequency (the number of occurrence for each item-set). The main scatter-plot illustrates how the *frequency* decreases when the number of users (*length*) increases, a natural feature of frequent item-sets.

Figure 1 also depicts the distribution as histograms. The top histogram shows the distribution of frequency and the histogram on the right hand side shows the distribution of the length of the learned item-sets. The top histogram illustrates a significant density of user collaboration to occur at low frequency, between 4–6. This is natural as the frequency of user participation decreases for most of the users. Noticeable on the length distribution is the fact that the density is higher for two and three participating users than for just one. This is because there exist more combinations of users than the number of single users.

Association rules supporting the hypothesis of user participation based on other users activities were computed from the calculated frequency item-sets. Resulting in 55,166 rules. Table 1 shows descriptive statistics for all the computed rules. It can be noted that although the confidence median and mean is low, the high level of lift indicates high dependency of the learned rules, i.e., the computed rules show that out hypothesis is valid and users tend to follow each other. As our dataset is big, with many users and many posts, the low support mean and median is expected. Moreover, it is noticeable that users are not active in all posts but more on a subset of them.

Figure 2 depicts the distribution, Confidence, Lift, Conviction and Frequency respectively in our learned model. The figures are illustrated as violin-plots which represents the kernel density (shown as height and depth) in addition to normal box-plots with outer quartiles as thin lines, the inner quartiles as bold lines and the mean as a white dot.

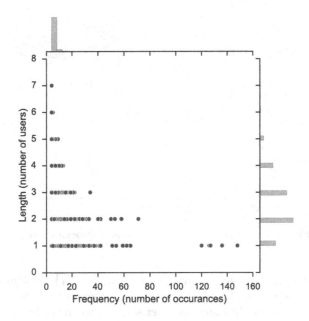

Fig. 1. Combined plot of number of users (Length) with respect to number of occurrence (Frequency). The upper and right axis illustrates histograms of the respective distributions

Table 1. Descriptive statistics of 55,166 computed rules.

	Mean	Median	Std
Support	0.05	0.02	0.07
Confidence	0.43	0.33	0.33
Lift	18.97	9.38	24.64
Conviction	1.83	1.32	1.18

Figure 2a shows a dense distribution of support at 0.025 and interestingly a higher density at 0.20. The confidence distribution is illustrated in Fig. 2b, interestingly there is a dense distribution around 1.0, i.e., there is a significant number of learned rules with high confidence that the rule is accurate. Figure 2c shows that the lift measure have a heavy tail distribution. Figure 2d illustrates a distribution of conviction to be concentrated between zero and five.

Table 2 presents learned rules in tree sections. Each section is sorted firstly by Confidence, Lift and Conviction respectively and secondly by the number of supporting users. The rule $\{u_{429}, u_{578}\} \Rightarrow \{u_{19}\}$ should be interpreted as user–429 together with user–578 influence participation of user–19. Notable, when sorting by confidence and lift, the conviction is infinite (this is due to the confidence of 1.0) as shown how conviction is calculated in (4). All of the rules in Table 2 have high confidence and show high dependency (via the lift metric), i.e., the top five rules sorted by either Confidence, Lift or Conviction are relevant for predicting user participation.

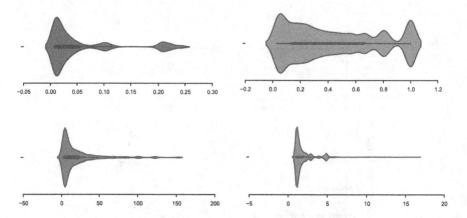

Fig. 2. Distribution of values in learned association rules.

The rule, $\{u_{580}, u_{861}, u_{1352}, u_{1466}\} \Rightarrow \{u_{896}, u_{1291}\}$ presented in Table 2 with confidence of 1.0 and lift of 152.5 strongly indicates that the left-hand-side user set influences the right-hand-side user set, i.e., when the left-hand-side user set is active on a post the right-hand-side user set also will be active. A confidence of 1.0 means that 100 % of the posts where the left-hand-side user set is active, the right user set also will be active. A lift value of 152.5, in this specific rule, shows that the right-hand-side user set is dependent on the left.

Considering rules where at least two separate users affect another user with a confidence of ≥ 95 %. We can reduce the 55,166 rules to 4,959 rules, which have a median lift of 4.80 and a median support of 21 %. In other words, we have close to 5,000 rules that strongly indicates that users are affected by each other when it comes to participating in online social networks. From learned rules, we can also identify influential users, i.e., the users that exists on the left side of multiple rules.

7   Conclusion and Discussion

Users within online social networks creates a large amount of generated data in form of interactions (comments and likes). Not enough attention has been put on the prediction of how users influence each other and how to predict the behavior of users within Facebook groups. Therefore, we have, in this paper, crawled a significant amount of user data and then by using machine learning, implemented and examined how users influence each other. Based on the results and analysis, we are able to determine that users influence other users to participate and interact in new groups.

From the group OccypyTogether, 2,443 active users have been extracted. They interact on 610 posts with a total of 14,117 comments. From this dataset, the association rules were computed. Resulting in almost 5,000 rules with high confidence of correctness, ≥ 95 %. These rules were proven to be dependent of the

Table 2. Top 5 rules sorted by different metrics

Rule	Confidence	Lift	Conviction
Confidence			
$\{u_{179}, u_{538}, u_{580}, u_{938}, u_{992}, u_{1090}\} \Rightarrow \{u_{11}\}$	1.00	10.17	inf
$\{u_{11}, u_{31}, u_{80}, u_{179}, u_{992}, u_{1093}\} \Rightarrow \{u_{580}\}$	1.00	4.80	inf
$\{u_{11}, u_{31}, u_{179}, u_{580}, u_{992}, u_{1093}\} \Rightarrow \{u_{80}\}$	1.00	9.53	inf
$\{u_{11}, u_{179}, u_{538}, u_{580}, u_{938}, u_{953}\} \Rightarrow \{u_{429}\}$	1.00	4.84	inf
$\{u_{179}, u_{1094}, u_{1096}, u_{1113}, u_{1171}, u_{1352}\} \Rightarrow \{u_{1378}\}$	1.00	101.67	inf
Lift			
$\{u_{580}, u_{861}, u_{1352}, u_{1466}\} \Rightarrow \{u_{896}, u_{1291}\}$	1.00	152.50	inf
$\{u_{580}, u_{861}, u_{1291}, u_{1352}\} \Rightarrow \{u_{896}, u_{1466}\}$	1.00	152.50	inf
$\{u_{31}, u_{80}, u_{179}, u_{580}\} \Rightarrow \{u_{11}, u_{992}, u_{1093}\}$	1.00	152.50	inf
$\{u_{19}, u_{64}, u_{673}, u_{685}\} \Rightarrow \{u_{54}, u_{581}\}$	1.00	152.50	inf
$\{u_{580}, u_{861}, u_{1291}, u_{1466}\} \Rightarrow \{u_{896}, u_{1352}\}$	1.00	152.50	inf
Conviction			
$\{u_{429}, u_{578}\} \Rightarrow \{u_{19}\}$	0.95	3.93	16.66
$\{u_{920}\} \Rightarrow \{u_{179}\}$	0.95	4.27	16.32
$\{u_{929}\} \Rightarrow \{u_{179}\}$	0.95	4.26	15.54
$\{u_{580}, u_{1093}\} \Rightarrow \{u_{179}\}$	0.94	4.22	13.21
$\{u_{580}, u_{938}\} \Rightarrow \{u_{179}\}$	0.94	4.22	13.21

active users, via the lift metric. Therefore, the hypothesis of user participation influences can be accepted. The results also proved that using association rule learning, influential users can be identified. Moreover, users on the left-hand-side, in a rule with high confidence and high lift, are influencing users on the right-hand-side to participate in the conversation.

At present, information on Facebook are filtered by a secret algorithm. This poses a potential validity threat to our results. Even external recommender systems might pose a threat as data might be bias since users can only see a subset of all posts.

For future work, it would be interesting to compare the results across different Facebook groups, e.g. politics-related Facebook group is different from news-related Facebook groups. Additionally, methods for association rule learning that supports number of occurrence and order of items in each transaction also needs to be investigated further. Finally, investigating the temporal aspects of users participation, e.g. whether users influence each other over time, or if a user participates throughout a discussion or only in the beginning, is something that needs to be considered and which could hopefully improve the prediction results.

Acknowledgement. This work was partially supported by the European Union's Seventh Framework Programme for research, technological development and demonstration under grant agreement no 316097 [ENGINE] and by The National Science Centre, the decision no. DEC-2013/09/B/ST6/02317.

References

1. Agrawal, R., Srikant, R.: Fast algorithms for mining association rules in large databases. In: Proceedings of the 20th International Conference on Very Large Data Bases, pp. 487–499. Morgan Kaufmann Publishers Inc., San Francisco (1994)
2. Ahmad, W., Riaz, A., Johnson, H., Lavesson, N.: Predicting friendship intensity in online social networks. In: Proceedings of the 21st Tyrrhenian Workshop on Digital Communications: Trustworthy Internet. Springer, September 2010
3. Asur, S., Huberman, B.A.: Predicting the future with social media. In: Proceedings of the 2010 IEEE/WIC/ACM International Conference on Web Intelligence and Intelligent Agent Technology, WI-IAT 2010, vol. 01, pp. 492–499. IEEE Computer Society, Washington, DC (2010)
4. Au, W.H., Chan, K.C., Yao, X.: A novel evolutionary data mining algorithm with applications to churn prediction. IEEE Trans. Evol. Comput. **7**(6), 532–545 (2003)
5. Bródka, P.: Key user extraction based on telecommunication data (aka. key users in social network. how to find them?) (2013). arXiv preprint arXiv:1302.1369
6. Cha, M., Haddadi, H., Benevenuto, F., Gummadi, P.K.: Measuring user influence in Twitter: the million follower fallacy. ICWSM **10**(10–17), 30 (2010)
7. De Meo, P., Ferrara, E., Rosaci, D., Sarne, G.M.L.: Trust and compactness in social network groups. IEEE Trans. Cybern. **45**(2), 205–216 (2015)
8. Erlandsson, F., Nia, R., Boldt, M., Johnson, H., Wu, S.F.: Crawling online social networks. In: 2015 European Network Intelligence Conference (ENIC), September 2015
9. Flach, P.: Machine Learning: The Art and Science of Algorithms that Make Sense of Data. Cambridge University Press, New York (2012)
10. Goethals, B.: Survey on frequent pattern mining. Technical report, University of Helsinki (2003)
11. Hakim, M., Khodra, M.: Predicting information cascade on Twitter using support vector regression. In: 2014 International Conference on Data and Software Engineering (ICODSE), pp. 1–6, November 2014
12. Jamali, S., Rangwala, H.: Digging digg: comment mining, popularity prediction, and social network analysis. In: International Conference on Web Information Systems and Mining, 2009, WISM 2009, pp. 32–38, November 2009
13. Jankowski, J., Michalski, R., Kazienko, P.: The multidimensional study of viral campaigns as branching processes. In: Aberer, K., Flache, A., Jager, W., Liu, L., Tang, J., Guéret, C. (eds.) SocInfo 2012. LNCS, vol. 7710, pp. 462–474. Springer, Heidelberg (2012)
14. Kajdanowicz, T., Kazienko, P., Indyk, W.: Parallel processing of large graphs. Future Gener. Comput. Syst. **32**, 324–337 (2014)
15. Kazienko, P., Kajdanowicz, T.: Label-dependent node classification in the network. Neurocomputing 75(1), 199–209 (2012), Brazilian Symposium on Neural Networks (SBRN 2010) International Conference on Hybrid Artificial Intelligence Systems (HAIS 2010)
16. Liben-Nowell, D., Kleinberg, J.: The link-prediction problem for social networks. J. Am. Soc. Inf. Sci. Technol. **58**(7), 1019–1031 (2007)
17. Musiał, K., Kazienko, P., Bródka, P.: User position measures in social networks. In: Proceedings of the 3rd Workshop on Social Network Mining and Analysis, SNA-KDD 2009, pp. 6:1–6:9. ACM, New York (2009)

18. Nancy, P., Geetha Ramani, R., Jacob, S.: Mining of association patterns in social network data through data mining techniques and methods. In: Meghanathan, N., Nagamalai, D., Chaki, N. (eds.) Advances in Computing and Information Technology. Advances in Intelligent Systems and Computing, vol. 178, pp. 107–117. Springer, Berlin, Heidelberg (2013)

19. Nia, R., Erlandsson, F., Bhattacharyya, P., Rahman, M.R., Johnson, H., Wu, S.F.: Sin: a platform to make interactions in social networks accessible. In: 2012 International Conference on Social Informatics (SocialInformatics), pp. 205–214. IEEE, December 2012

20. Nia, R., Erlandsson, F., Johnson, H., Wu, S.F.: Leveraging social interactions to suggest friends. In: 2013 IEEE 33rd International Conference on Distributed Computing Systems Workshops (ICDCSW), pp. 386–391. IEEE (2013)

21. Riquelme, F.: Measuring user influence on Twitter: a survey (2015). CoRR abs/1508.07951

22. Ruta, D., Kazienko, P., Bródka, P.: Network-aware customer value in telecommunication social networks. In: IC-AI, pp. 261–267 (2009)

23. Saganowski, S., Gliwa, B., Bródka, P., Zygmunt, A., Kazienko, P., Koźlak, J.: Predicting community evolution in social networks (2015). arXiv preprint arXiv:1505.01709

24. Schmitz, C., Hotho, A., Jäschke, R., Stumme, G.: Mining association rules in folksonomies. In: Batagelj, V., Bock, H.-H., Ferligoj, A. (eds.) Data Science and Classification, pp. 261–270. Springer, Heidelberg (2006)

25. Spertus, E., Sahami, M., Buyukkokten, O.: Evaluating similarity measures: a large-scale study in the orkut social network. ACM, New York, August 2005

26. Vasuki, V., Natarajan, N., Lu, Z., Savas, B., Dhillon, I.: Scalable affiliation recommendation using auxiliary networks. ACM Trans. Intell. Syst. Technol. (TIST) 3(1), 1157–1162 (2011). Article No. 3

27. Yu, X., Liu, H., Shi, J., Hwang, J.N., Wan, W., Lu, J.: Association rule mining of personal hobbies in social networks. In: 2014 IEEE International Congress on Big Data (BigData Congress), pp. 310–314, June 2014

28. Zaki, M.J.: Scalable algorithms for association mining. IEEE Trans. Knowl. Data Eng. 12(3), 372–390 (2000)

29. Seng, B.: ICT for sustainable development of the tourism industry in Cambodia. In: Zu, Q., Hu, B., Gu, N., Seng, S. (eds.) HCC 2014. LNCS, vol. 8944, pp. 1–14. Springer, Heidelberg (2015)

Computing Information Integration
in Brain Networks

Xerxes D. Arsiwalla[1(✉)] and Paul Verschure[1,2]

[1] Synthetic Perceptive Emotive and Cognitive Systems (SPECS) Lab,
Center of Autonomous Systems and Neurorobotics,
Universitat Pompeu Fabra, Barcelona, Spain
x.d.arsiwalla@gmail.com
[2] Institució Catalana de Recerca i Estudis Avançats (ICREA), Barcelona, Spain

Abstract. How much information do large brain networks integrate as
a whole over the sum of their parts? Can the complexity of such networks be quantified in an information-theoretic way and be meaningfully
coupled to brain function? Recently, measures of dynamical complexity
such as integrated information have been proposed. However, problems
related to the normalization and Bell number of partitions associated
to these measures make these approaches computationally infeasible for
large-scale brain networks. Our goal in this work is to address this problem. Our formulation of network integrated information is based on the
Kullback-Leibler divergence between the multivariate distribution on the
set of network states versus the corresponding factorized distribution over
its parts. We find that implementing the maximum information partition optimizes computations. These methods are well-suited for large
networks with linear stochastic dynamics. As an application to brain
networks, we compute the integrated information for the human brain's
connectomic data. Compared to a randomly re-wired network, we find
that the specific topology of the brain generates greater information complexity.

Keywords: Brain networks · Neural dynamics · Complexity measures

1 Introduction

From a computational neuroscience perspective, the brain is oftentimes
abstracted as a complex information processing network, that integrates sen-
sory inputs from multiple modalities in order to generate action and cognition.
In this paper, we ask a much simpler question: viewing the brain as a dynamical
network of neural masses, how can one compute the information integrated by
such networks in the course of dynamical transitions from one state to another? A
possible approach, among others, is to look at information-theoretic complexity
measures that seek to quantify information generated by all causal sub-processes
in such a network. One candidate measure exists and is called integrated information, usually denoted by Φ. It was first introduced in neuroscience as a complexity measure for neural networks, and by extension, as a possible correlate of

© Springer International Publishing Switzerland 2016
A. Wierzbicki et al. (Eds.): NetSci-X 2016, LNCS 9564, pp. 136–146, 2016.
DOI: 10.1007/978-3-319-28361-6_11

consciousness itself [19]. It is defined as the quantity of information generated by a network as a whole, due to its causal dynamical interactions, and one that is over and above the information generated independently by the disjoint sum of its parts. As a complexity measure, Φ seeks to operationalize the intuition that complexity arises from simultaneous integration and differentiation of the network's structural and dynamical properties. As such, the interplay of integration and differentiation in a network's dynamics is hypothesized to generate information that is highly diversified yet integrated, thereby creating patterns of high complexity. Our challenge in this paper, is to mathematically formalize this measure and apply it to compute integrated information for real connectivity data of the human brain.

We start by briefly reviewing the rich history of this field. The earliest proposals defining integrated information were made in the pioneering work of [17–19]. Since then, considerable progress has been made towards the development of a quantitative theory of integrated information in [4,6,8,15]. Similar information-based approaches have also been successfully applied to many-body problems in other domains, such as, for the problem of estimating microstates of statistical mechanical ensembles [2]. In fact, within integrated information theory itself, there are several candidate measures. For instance, the measure of [6] is only applicable to discrete-state, deterministic, Markovian systems with the maximum entropy distribution. On the other hand, the measure of [8] extends to include continuous-state, stochastic, non-Markovian systems and in principle, admits dynamics with any empirical distribution (although in practice, analytic results have only been shown for Gaussian distributions). However, the definition of [8] is based on mutual information rather than the Kullback-Leibler form of [6]. The Kullback-Leibler definition computes the information generated during state transitions and therefore has a more general interpretation of integrated information than the mutual information definition. In any case, both measures [6,8] make use of a normalization scheme in their formulations, which ultimately introduces ambiguities in computations of Φ itself. The normalization is used in determining the partition of the network that minimizes the integrated information, but a normalization dependent choice of partition ends up influencing the value and interpretation of Φ itself. An alternate measure based on the earth-mover distance was proposed in [15]. While this does away with the normalization, it lies outside the scope of standard information theory, in the sense that the proposed measure happens to be in units of bits^2, rather than bits. Currently, this version is still not applicable to continuous-state, stochastic non-Markovian systems. Moreover, all three of these definitions of Φ use what is called the minimum information partition or bi-partition (MIP/MIB), which also introduces a new problem: the combinatorics of all these algorithms explodes beyond networks of a handful of nodes. That makes the application of the above three measures computationally challenging for large-scale networks and that has thus far hindered applications to large biological or data networks. On the other hand, in earlier work [4], we have introduced a formulation of integrated information that overcomes both, the normalization and combinatorial problem by using a different partitioning of the network called the maximum information partition (MaxIP), thereby leading to the prospect of large-scale applications. However, the formulation in [4] was only applicable for uncorrelated node dynamics, which may not be realistic enough for many biological systems.

In this paper, we seek to go beyond [4], starting with an extension of the formalism to include node correlations. In order to do that, we solve the discrete-time Lyapunov equation, the solution of which, is then used to get an analytic expression for Φ with network correlations. We consider networks with linear stochastic dynamics, which generate multivariate time-series signals. Moreover, our networks are plastic, in the sense that connection weights are scalable using a global coupling parameter. We compute Φ as a function of this coupling. As proof of principle, we apply our formulation to the structural connectivity network of white matter fiber tracts in the human cerebral cortex, obtained from diffusion spectrum imaging [13,14]. This network has 998 nodes, representing neuronal populations. The edges are weighted fiber counts between populations. Implementing stochastic Gaussian dynamics on this network, we determine stationary solutions to the dynamical system from which we compute the information integrated in bits. To contrast with a null-model, we randomly re-wire the original network and repeat the computation. The original network scores higher on integrated information for all allowed couplings within the stationary limit.

2   Stochastic Integrated Information

2.1   Mathematical Formulation

We consider networks with linear stochastic dynamics. The state of each node is given by a random variable pertaining to a given probability distribution. These variables may either be discrete-valued or continuous. However, for many biological applications, Gaussian distributed, continuous-valued state variables are fairly reasonable abstractions (for example, aggregate neural population firing rate, EEG or fMRI signals). The state of the network $\mathbf{X_t}$ at time t is taken as a multivariate Gaussian variable with distribution $\mathbf{P_{X_t}}(\mathbf{x_t})$. $\mathbf{x_t}$ denotes an instantiation of $\mathbf{X_t}$ with components x_t^i (i going from 1 to n, n being the number of nodes). When the network makes a transition from an initial state $\mathbf{X_0}$ to a state $\mathbf{X_1}$ at time $t = 1$, observing the final state generates information about the system's initial state. The information generated equals the reduction in uncertainty regarding the initial state $\mathbf{X_0}$. This is given by the conditional entropy $\mathbf{H(X_0|X_1)}$. In order to extract that part of the information generated by the system as a whole, over and above that generated individually by its parts, one computes the relative conditional entropy given by the Kullback-Leibler divergence of the conditional distribution $\mathbf{P_{X_0|X_1=x'}}(\mathbf{x})$ of the system with respect to the joint conditional distributions $\prod_{k=1}^{r} \mathbf{P_{M_0^k|M_1^k=m'}}$ of its non-overlapping subsystems demarcated with respect to a partition $\mathcal{P}_r$ of the system into r distinct sub-systems. Denoting this as $\Phi_{\mathcal{P}_r}$, we have

$$\Phi_{\mathcal{P}_r}(\mathbf{X_0} \to \mathbf{X_1} = \mathbf{x'}) = D_{KL}\left(\mathbf{P_{X_0|X_1=x'}}\left\|\prod_{k=1}^{r} \mathbf{P_{M_0^k|M_1^k=m'}}\right.\right) \tag{1}$$

where for an r partitioned system, the state variable $\mathbf{X_0}$ can be decomposed as a direct sum of state variables of the sub-systems

$$\mathbf{X_0} = \mathbf{M_0^1} \oplus \mathbf{M_0^2} \oplus \cdots \oplus \mathbf{M_0^r} = \bigoplus_{k=1}^{r} \mathbf{M_0^k} \tag{2}$$

and similarly, $\mathbf{X_1}$ decomposes as

$$\mathbf{X_1} = \mathbf{M_1^1} \oplus \mathbf{M_1^2} \oplus \cdots \oplus \mathbf{M_1^r} = \bigoplus_{k=1}^{r} \mathbf{M_1^k} \tag{3}$$

For stochastic systems, it is useful to work with a measure that is independent of any specific instantiation of the final state $\mathbf{x'}$. So we average with respect to final states to obtain an expectation value from Eq. (1). After some algebra, we get

$$\langle\Phi\rangle_{\mathcal{P}_r}(\mathbf{X_0} \to \mathbf{X_1}) = -\mathbf{H}(\mathbf{X_0}|\mathbf{X_1}) + \sum_{k=1}^{r}\mathbf{H}(\mathbf{M_0^k}|\mathbf{M_1^k}) \tag{4}$$

This is our definition of integrated information, which we use in the rest of this paper. Note that the measure described in [6] is not applicable to networks with stochastic dynamics. They do use Eq. (1) as their definition but endow their nodes with only binary states. On the other hand, [8] uses a different definition of integrated information, where conditional entropies as in Eq. (4) are replaced by conditional mutual information. This definition only matches the definition of Eq. (1) in special cases but not in general for any distribution. From an information theory perspective, the Kullback-Leibler divergence offers a principled way of comparing probability distributions, hence we follow that approach in formulating our measure in Eq. (4).

The state variable at each time $t = 0$ and $t = 1$ follows a multivariate Gaussian distribution

$$\mathbf{X_0} \sim \mathcal{N}(\mathbf{\bar{x}_0}, \Sigma(\mathbf{X_0})) \qquad \mathbf{X_1} \sim \mathcal{N}(\mathbf{\bar{x}_1}, \Sigma(\mathbf{X_1})) \tag{5}$$

The generative model for this system is equivalent to a multi-variate auto-regressive process [7]

$$\mathbf{X_1} = \mathcal{A}\,\mathbf{X_0} + \mathbf{E_1} \tag{6}$$

where $\mathcal{A}$ is the weighted adjacency matrix of the network and E_1 is Gaussian noise. Next, taking the mean and covariance respectively on both sides of this equation, while holding the residual independent of the regression variables, yields

$$\mathbf{\bar{x}_1} = \mathcal{A}\,\mathbf{\bar{x}_0} \qquad \Sigma(\mathbf{X_1}) = \mathcal{A}\,\Sigma(\mathbf{X_0})\,\mathcal{A}^\mathbf{T} + \Sigma(\mathbf{E}) \tag{7}$$

In the absence of any external inputs, stationary solutions of a stochastic linear dynamical system as in Eq. (6) are fluctuations about the origin. Therefore, we can shift coordinates to set the means $\bar{\mathbf{x}}_0$ and consequently $\bar{\mathbf{x}}_1$ to the zero. The second equality in Eq. (7) is the discrete-time Lyapunov equation and its solution will give us the covariance matrix of the state variables.

The conditional entropy for a multivariate Gaussian variable was computed in [8]

$$\mathbf{H}(\mathbf{X}_0|\mathbf{X}_1) = \frac{1}{2}n\log(2\pi e) - \frac{1}{2}\log\left[\det \mathbf{\Sigma}(\mathbf{X}_0|\mathbf{X}_1)\right] \tag{8}$$

which is fully specified by the conditional covariance matrix. Inserting this in Eq. (4) yields

$$\langle \Phi \rangle_{\mathcal{P}_r}(\mathbf{X}_0 \to \mathbf{X}_1) = \frac{1}{2}\log\left[\frac{\prod_{k=1}^{r} \det \mathbf{\Sigma}(\mathbf{M}_0^k|\mathbf{M}_1^k)}{\det \mathbf{\Sigma}(\mathbf{X}_0|\mathbf{X}_1)}\right] \tag{9}$$

Now, in order to compute the conditional covariance matrix we make use of the identity (proof of this identity for the Gaussian case was demonstrated in [7])

$$\mathbf{\Sigma}(\mathbf{X}|\mathbf{Y}) = \mathbf{\Sigma}(\mathbf{X}) - \mathbf{\Sigma}(\mathbf{X},\mathbf{Y})\mathbf{\Sigma}(\mathbf{Y})^{-1}\mathbf{\Sigma}(\mathbf{X},\mathbf{Y})^{\mathbf{T}} \tag{10}$$

The appropriate covariance we will need to insert in this expression is

$$\mathbf{\Sigma}(\mathbf{X}_0,\mathbf{X}_1) \equiv \langle(\mathbf{X}_0 - \bar{\mathbf{x}}_0)(\mathbf{X}_1 - \bar{\mathbf{x}}_1)^{\mathbf{T}}\rangle = \mathbf{\Sigma}(\mathbf{X}_0)\mathcal{A}^{\mathbf{T}} \tag{11}$$

which gives for the conditional covariance

$$\mathbf{\Sigma}(\mathbf{X}_0|\mathbf{X}_1) = \mathbf{\Sigma}(\mathbf{X}_0) - \mathbf{\Sigma}(\mathbf{X}_0)\mathcal{A}^{\mathbf{T}}\,\mathbf{\Sigma}(\mathbf{X}_1)^{-1}\mathcal{A}\,\mathbf{\Sigma}(\mathbf{X}_0)^{\mathbf{T}} \tag{12}$$

And similarly for the sub-systems

$$\mathbf{\Sigma}(\mathbf{M}_0^k|\mathbf{M}_1^k) = \mathbf{\Sigma}(\mathbf{M}_0^k) - \mathbf{\Sigma}(\mathbf{M}_0^k)\mathcal{A}^{\mathbf{T}}\big|_k \mathbf{\Sigma}(\mathbf{M}_1^k)^{-1}\mathcal{A}\big|_k \mathbf{\Sigma}(\mathbf{M}_0^k)^{\mathbf{T}} \tag{13}$$

where k indexes the partition such that $\mathbf{M}_0^k$ denotes the kth sub-system at $t = 0$ and $\mathcal{A}\big|_k$ denotes the restriction of the adjacency matrix to the kth sub-network.

Further, for linear multi-variate systems, a unique fixed point always exists. We try to find stable stationary solutions of the dynamical system. In that regime, the multi-variate probability distribution of states approaches stationarity and the covariance matrix converges, such that

$$\mathbf{\Sigma}(\mathbf{X}_1) = \mathbf{\Sigma}(\mathbf{X}_0) \tag{14}$$

$t = 0$ and $t = 1$ refer to time-points taken after the system converges to the fixed point. Then the discrete-time Lyapunov equations can be solved iteratively for the stable covariance matrix $\mathbf{\Sigma}(\mathbf{X}_t)$. For networks with symmetric adjacency matrix and independent Gaussian noise, the solution takes a particularly simple form

$$\mathbf{\Sigma}(\mathbf{X}_t) = \left(1 - \mathcal{A}^2\right)^{-1}\mathbf{\Sigma}(\mathbf{E}) \tag{15}$$

and for the parts, we have

$$\Sigma(\mathbf{M_0^k}) = \Sigma(\mathbf{X_0})\big|_{\mathbf{k}} \tag{16}$$

given by the restriction of the full covariance matrix on the kth sub-network. Note that Eq. (16) is not the same as Eq. (15) on the restricted adjacency matrix as that would mean that the sub-network has been explicitly severed from the rest of the system. Indeed, Eq. (16) is precisely the covariance of the sub-network while it is still part of the network and $\langle \Phi \rangle$ yields the integrated and differentiated information of the whole network that is greater than the sum of these connected parts. Inserting Eqs. (12), (13), (15) and (16) into Eq. (9) yields $\langle \Phi \rangle$ as a function of network weights for symmetric and correlated networks[1].

2.2   The Maximum Information Partition

Following [4], the maximum information partition (MaxIP) is defined as the partition of the system into its irreducible parts. This is the finest partition and is unique as there is only one way to combinatorially reduce a system into all of its sub-units. Hence, this partition can directly be found by construction and therefore does not require any normalization scheme for sampling through the space of multi-partitions in order to search for the one that maximizes or minimizes the integrated information. Therefore, $\langle \Phi \rangle$ computed using the MaxIP, is independent of any normalization scheme. The reason it is called the maximum information partition is that it integrates the maximum information compared to any other bi-, tri- or multi-partition of the system. This is due to the fact that this partition cannot be decomposed further. Every other partition will be coarser than the MaxIP and will therefore have at least some of its parts as composites of the irreducible units in the MaxIP. As these composites integrate more information than its own irreducible units, subtracting the information of a composite (when treating the composite as a part) from the information of the whole system will always produce a smaller $\langle \Phi \rangle$ than that obtained by subtracting the information of each irreducible unit of the network from that of the whole network. Therefore $\langle \Phi \rangle$ computed using the MaxIP is the maximum possible integrated information of the system compared to $\langle \Phi \rangle$ computed using any other partition of the network. In that sense, unlike the MIP or MIB, the MaxIP in fact captures the complete information integrated by the network and is therefore a more natural choice for quantifying whole versus parts.

2.3   Analytic Solutions

Now that we have a rigorous analytic formulation of integrated information, let us first demonstrate examples of computations performed using artificial networks.

---

[1] For the case of asymmetric weights, the entries of the covariance matrix cannot be explicitly expressed as a matrix equation. However, they may still be solved by Jordan decomposition of both sides of the Lyapunov equation.

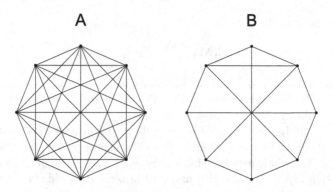

Fig. 1. Graphs of two artificial networks, (A) and (B).

In Fig. 1 we consider two artificial networks. For these cases, we want to compute the exact analytic solution for $\langle \Phi \rangle$. Each of these networks have 8 dimensional adjacency matrices with bi-directional weights (though our analysis does not depend on that and works as well with directed graphs). We want to compute $\langle \Phi \rangle$ as a function of network weights, which we keep as free parameters. However, in order to constrain the space of parameters, we shall set all weights to a single parameter, the global coupling strength g. This gives us $\langle \Phi \rangle$ as a function of g. The results for the two networks labeled A and B respectively are shown in Eqs. (17), (18) respectively. These are computed for a single time-step, when the dynamics of the system lies in the stable stationary regime.

$$\langle \Phi \rangle_A = \frac{1}{2} \log \frac{\left(1 - 43g^2\right)^8}{\left(1 - 50g^2 + 49g^4\right)^8} \tag{17}$$

$$\langle \Phi \rangle_B = \frac{1}{2} \log \frac{B_1 \cdot B_2 \cdot B_3 \cdot B_4 \cdot B_5}{\left(-1 + g^2\right)^4 \left(1 - 8g^2 + 4g^4\right)^6 \left(1 - 17g^2 + 72g^4 - 64g^6 + 16g^8\right)^8} \tag{18}$$

where

$$B_1 = \left(1 - 15g^2 + 56g^4 - 56g^6 + 16g^8\right)$$
$$B_2 = \left(1 - 15g^2 + 54g^4 - 54g^6 + 16g^8\right)$$
$$B_3 = \left(1 - 22g^2 + 159g^4 - 426g^6 + 336g^8 - 80g^{1}0\right)^2$$
$$B_4 = \left(1 - 21g^2 + 147g^4 - 401g^6 + 374g^8 - 136g^{1}0 + 16g^{1}2\right)^2$$
$$B_5 = \left(1 - 23g^2 + 183g^4 - 612g^6 + 835g^8 - 526g^{1}0 + 152g^{1}2 - 16g^{1}4\right)^2$$

Note that the mathematical framework described above is in no way limited by the size of the network and thus, in principle, can be applied to networks of any size, to yield exact results. The only practical difficulty would be in the form of available computing hardware resources. Hence, for very large data networks, such as those from brain imaging, numerical computations of $\langle \Phi \rangle$ would be more practical to perform.

2.4 Application to Brain Connectomics

The framework described above, provides us with the tools to compute how much information is integrated in bits in a single time-step, by a large network with linear stochastic dynamics. We now apply this to real structural connectivity data of white matter fiber tracts in the human cerebral cortex, obtained from diffusion spectrum imaging [13,14]. The data is shown as a 998 dimensional matrix on the left-hand side of Fig. 2. The 998 brain voxels represent the nodes of the network. Each node is physically a population of neurons. The edges are weighted fiber counts between populations. Additionally, we include a global coupling variable g, multiplying the entire matrix, that can be used to tune the overall strength of the weights.

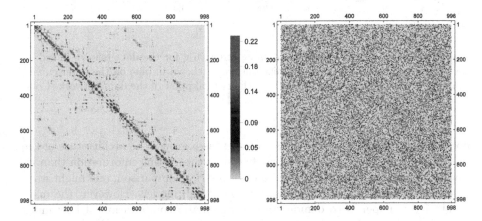

Fig. 2. *Left*: Connectivity matrix of human cerebral white matter. *Right*: Randomized version of the same matrix, preserving network weights.

To simulate brain dynamics, one may chose from among a variety of possible models, discussed in [1,3,5,12]. To run these simulations, one may use customizable tools such as those described in [9–11,16]. The simplest model among the ones mentioned above is the linear stochastic Wilson-Cowen model. In fact, it can be seen from [12] that Eq. (6) is precisely a special case of the discrete-time limit of the linear stochastic Wilson-Cowen model. That is what we use here. The brain's state of spontaneous activity or resting-state is usually identified as the attractor state of these models. This corresponds to finding stable stationary solutions of the system. This is precisely the regime in which we compute $\langle \Phi \rangle$ in bits as a function of the coupling g. The results are shown in the red profile in Fig. 3. Further, in order to contrast this result with a null model, we also rewired the edges of the connectome network randomly, while preserving the magnitude of the weights. This generates the randomized data matrix shown on the right-hand side of Fig. 2. We also compute $\langle \Phi \rangle$ for this matrix. The resulting profile is the blue curve in Fig. 3. For extremely small couplings, the two networks

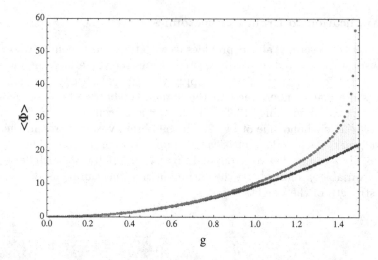

Fig. 3. $\langle \Phi \rangle$ as a function of global coupling strength g for the data (shown in red on the upper curve) and for the randomized network (shown in blue on the lower curve). Stationary solutions exist up to g = 1.49, the critical point of the data network (Color figure online).

are indistinguishable on $\langle \Phi \rangle$ scores, however, as g grows, the architecture of the brain's network turns out to perform better at integrating information than its randomized counterpart. It is true that for a strict comparison, one might want to check this against an entire distribution of null models. However, the main point of this paper is to demonstrate a systematic computation of how much information a realistic large network integrates. Functionally, what this corresponds to in terms of brain function or disease is another interesting question by itself.

3   Discussion

In this paper, we have demonstrated a computational framework, built on a rich body of earlier work on information-theoretic complexity measures and applied it to compute information integration of large networks endowed with linear stochastic dynamics. Earlier attempts to compute integrated information have so far been limited to much smaller networks (16 nodes and less in [6,15], and 8 nodes in [8]). This was mainly due to normalization ambiguities and explosive combinatorics associated with bi-partitions used therein. Instead, what we find is that the finest partitioning of the system solves all these problems and opens the window of applicability to large-scale networks. In particular, we apply our theoretical formulation to the human brain connectome network. This network is constructed from white matter tractography data from the human cerebral cortex and consists of 998 nodes with about 28,000 symmetric and weighted connections between them [13,14]. Using a discrete-time linear stochastic neuronal population model to generate the dynamics of neural activity on this network, we compute the integrated information of this dynamical system during a single time-step in the stationary regime corresponding to the network's resting state attractor point. The computed integrated information depends on both, the structural anatomy as well as the network's dynamical operating point (the value of the global coupling).

We see potentially useful applications of such information-based measures for other types of neuroimaging data as well, for example, tracing studies or detailed microscopic connectivity data. The clinical utility of this measure would be in identifying information-based differences between healthy subjects and patients of neurodegenerative diseases. Just as we identified a transitionary phase after which an anatomical network strongly differs in information integration and differentiation from a randomly rewired network, similar comparative analysis for patients compared to healthy controls might provide a quantification of the extent of the disorder and even provide an analytic way to suggest diagnostic surgical rewiring to restore network processing. As a next step, we also seek to extend our formalism to include non-stationary and meta-stable states. This would be particularly useful for task-based neuroimaging paradigms, in order to quantify complexity of specific cognitive functions.

Acknowledgments. This work has been supported by the European Research Council's CDAC project: "The Role of Consciousness in Adaptive Behavior: A Combined Empirical, Computational and Robot based Approach" (ERC-2013- ADG 341196).

References

1. Arsiwalla, X.D., Betella, A., Martínez, E., Omedas, P., Zucca, R., Verschure, P.: The dynamic connectome: a tool for large scale 3D reconstruction of brain activity in real time. In: Rekdalsbakken, W., Bye, R., Zhang, H., (eds.) 27th European Conference on Modeling and Simulation, ECMS, Alesund, Norway (2013)
2. Arsiwalla, X.D.: Entropy functions with 5D chern-simons terms. J. High Energy Phys. **2009**(09), 059 (2009)
3. Arsiwalla, X.D., Dalmazzo, D., Zucca, R., Betella, A., Brandi, S., Martinez, E., Omedas, P., Verschure, P.: Connectomics to semantomics: Addressing the brain's big data challenge. Procedia Comput. Sci. **53**, 48–55 (2015)
4. Arsiwalla, X.D., Verschure, P.F.: Integrated information for large complex networks. In: The 2013 International Joint Conference on Neural Networks (IJCNN), pp. 1–7. IEEE (2013)
5. Arsiwalla, X.D., Zucca, R., Betella, A., Martinez, E., Dalmazzo, D., Omedas, P., Deco, G., Verschure, P.: Network dynamics with brainx3: A large-scale simulation of the human brain network with real-time interaction. Front. Neuroinformatics 9(2) (2015). http://www.frontiersin.org/neuroinformatics/10.3389/fninf.2015.00002/abstract
6. Balduzzi, D., Tononi, G.: Integrated information in discrete dynamical systems: motivation and theoretical framework. PLoS Comput. Biol. 4(6), e1000091 (2008)
7. Barrett, A.B., Barnett, L., Seth, A.K.: Multivariate granger causality and generalized variance. Phys. Rev. E 81(4), 041907 (2010)

8. Barrett, A.B., Seth, A.K.: Practical measures of integrated information for time-series data. PLoS Comput. Biol. **7**(1), e1001052 (2011)

9. Betella, A., Bueno, E.M., Kongsantad, W., Zucca, R., Arsiwalla, X.D., Omedas, P., Verschure, P.F.: Understanding large network datasets through embodied interaction in virtual reality. In: Proceedings of the 2014 Virtual Reality International Conference, p. 23. ACM (2014)

10. Betella, A., Cetnarski, R., Zucca, R., Arsiwalla, X.D., Martinez, E., Omedas, P., Mura, A., Verschure, P.F.M.J.: BrainX3: embodied exploration of neural data. In: Virtual Reality International Conference (VRIC 2014), Laval, France (2014)

11. Betella, A., Martínez, E., Zucca, R., Arsiwalla, X.D., Omedas, P., Wierenga, S., Mura, A., Wagner, J., Lingenfelser, F., André, E., et al.: Advanced interfaces to stem the data deluge in mixed reality: placing human (un) consciousness in the loop. In: ACM SIGGRAPH 2013 Posters, p. 68. ACM (2013)

12. Galán, R.F., et al.: On how network architecture determines the dominant patterns of spontaneous neural activity. PLoS One **3**(5), e2148 (2008)

13. Hagmann, P., Cammoun, L., Gigandet, X., Meuli, R., Honey, C.J., Wedeen, V.J., Sporns, O.: Mapping the structural core of human cerebral cortex. PLoS Biol. **6**(7), 15(2008). http://www.ncbi.nlm.nih.gov/pubmed/18597554

14. Honey, C., Sporns, O., Cammoun, L., Gigandet, X., Thiran, J.P., Meuli, R., Hagmann, P.: Predicting human resting-state functional connectivity from structural connectivity. Proc. Natl. Acad. Sci. **106**(6), 2035–2040 (2009)

15. Oizumi, M., Albantakis, L., Tononi, G.: From the phenomenology to the mechanisms of consciousness: integrated information theory 3.0. PLoS Comput. Biol. **10**(5), e1003588 (2014)

16. Omedas, P., Betella, A., Zucca, R., Arsiwalla, X.D., Pacheco, D., Wagner, J., Lingenfelser, F., Andre, E., Mazzei, D., Lanatá, A., Tognetti, A., de Rossi, D., Grau, A., Goldhoorn, A., Guerra, E., Alquezar, R., Sanfeliu, A., Verschure, P.F.M.J.: XIM-engine: a software framework to support the development of interactive applications that uses conscious and unconscious reactions in immersive mixed reality. In: Proceedings of the 2014 Virtual Reality International Conference, VRIC 2014, pp. 26:1–26:4. ACM (2014). http://doi.acm.org/10.1145/2617841.2620714

17. Tononi, G.: An information integration theory of consciousness. BMC Neurosci. **5**(1), 42 (2004)

18. Tononi, G., Sporns, O.: Measuring information integration. BMC Neurosci. **4**(1), 31 (2003)

19. Tononi, G., Sporns, O., Edelman, G.M.: A measure for brain complexity: relating functional segregation and integration in the nervous system. Proc. Nat. Acad. Sci. **91**(11), 5033–5037 (1994)

Embracing n-ary Relations in Network Science

Jeffrey H. Johnson$^{(\boxtimes)}$

Topdrim Project, The Open University, Milton Keynes MK7 6AA, UK
jeff.johnson@open.ac.uk
http://www.topdrim.eu

Abstract. Most network scientists restrict their attention to relations between pairs of things, even though most complex systems have structures and dynamics determined by n-ary relation where n is greater than two. Various examples are given to illustrate this. The basic mathematical structures allowing more than two vertices have existed for more than half a century, including hypergraphs and simplicial complexes. To these can be added hypernetworks which, like multiplex networks, allow many relations to be defined on the vertices. Furthermore, hypersimplices provide an essential formalism for representing multilevel part-whole and taxonomic structures for integrating the dynamics of systems between levels. Graphs, hypergraphs, networks, simplicial complex, multiplex network and hypernetworks form a coherent whole from which, for any particular application, the scientist can select the most suitable.

Keywords: n-ary relation · Graph · Hypergraph · Network · Simplicial complex · Multiplex network · Hypernetwork

1 Introduction

Given the success of graph and network theory since computers became available to scientists in the nineteen sixties, it is remarkable that the majority of the research done in network science has remained focussed on edges representing binary relations between two vertices. If all relations were binary relations this would be understandable. However, the structure and dynamics of many systems depend on relations between many things.

For example, the participants in a dinner party do not just interact in pairs. Nor do the member of a team or a committee. The members of a choir are not singing pairwise with the others. A great part of the dynamics of social and biological systems involves interactions between many individuals and many things. Surely a science of multidimensional universe should not be constrained to representing it solely through one dimensional objects.

Supported by the European *Dynamics of Multi-Level Complex Systems* (DyM-CS) FP7 FET programme, http://cordis.europa.eu/fp7/ict/fet-proactive/dymcs_en. html.

© Springer International Publishing Switzerland 2016
A. Wierzbicki et al. (Eds.): NetSci-X 2016, LNCS 9564, pp. 147–160, 2016.
DOI: 10.1007/978-3-319-28361-6_12

This is not to criticise networks in any way. As will become clear, they are part of a wider story that extends to hypergraphs, simplicial complexes and hypernetworks. It begins with graphs.

In the literature the terminology for graph theory varies considerably. Here, let a *graph*, G, be defined to be a set, V with elements called *vertices* and a set, E, of pairs of vertices called edges. Write $G = (V, E)$. Let a and b be vertices and let $\{a, b\}$ be an edge Graphs are usually drawn with dots such as a and b representing vertices and, for example, a line joint a and b to represent the edge $\{a, b\}$. Usually the edges in graphs represent *binary relations* between the vertices. To go beyond binary relation something else is required.

2 Hypergraphs

Hypergraphs represent an early attempt to allow graph edges to have more than two vertices [7]. Berge writes 'The idea of looking at a family of sets from this standpoint took shape around 1960. In regarding each set as a "generalised edge" and in calling the family itself a "hypergraph", the initial idea was to try to extend certain classical results of Graph Theory. ... Next it was noticed that this generalisation often led to simplification; moreover, one single statement ... could unify several theorems on graphs" [8]. In his 1969 paper [7] he gives the following definition. 'Let $X = \{x_1, x_2, ..., x_n\}$ be a finite set. A *hypergraph* on X is a family $H = (E_1, E_2, ..., E_m)$ of subsets of X such that

(1) $E_i \neq \emptyset \qquad (i = 1, 2, ..., m)$
(2) $\bigcup_{i=1}^{m} = X$.

The elements $x_1, x_2, ..., x_m$ are called *vertices* and the sets $E_1, E_2, ..., E_m$ are the edges of the hypergraph.' Berge gives the example shown in Fig. 1 where the relationship between the vertices and edges is given as an incidence matrix.

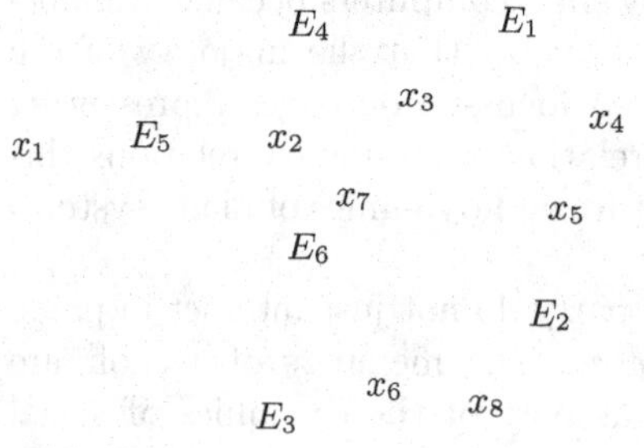

(a)

$$V = \begin{array}{c} \\ x_1 \\ x_2 \\ x_3 \\ x_4 \\ x_5 \\ x_6 \\ x_7 \\ x_8 \end{array} \begin{array}{c} \begin{array}{cccccc} E_1 & E_2 & E_3 & E_4 & E_5 & E_6 \end{array} \\ \begin{bmatrix} 0 & 0 & 0 & 0 & 1 & 0 \\ 0 & 0 & 0 & 1 & 1 & 0 \\ 1 & 0 & 0 & 1 & 0 & 0 \\ 1 & 0 & 0 & 0 & 0 & 0 \\ 1 & 1 & 0 & 0 & 0 & 0 \\ 0 & 0 & 1 & 0 & 0 & 0 \\ 0 & 0 & 1 & 1 & 0 & 1 \\ 0 & 1 & 1 & 0 & 0 & 0 \end{bmatrix} \end{array}$$

(b)

Fig. 1. The Berge hypergraph

Berge's method of drawing hypergraphs is a hybrid between graph-theoretic links and loops, and hypergraph-theoretic sets. Figure 2(a) shows the Berge hypergraph drawn entirely as sets. Here the edges corresponding to pairs of

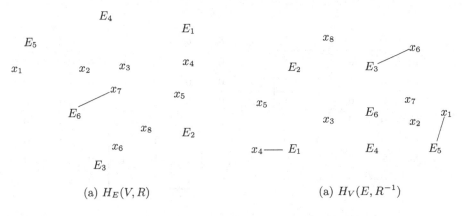

(a) $H_E(V, R)$ (a) $H_V(E, R^{-1})$

Fig. 2. The dual Berge hypergraphs

vertices are shown as sets, namely $\{x_1, x_2\}$ and $\{x_5, x_8\}$, and the loop from x_7 to itself is draw as a singleton set $\{x_7\}$ which is the edge E_6.

Figure 2(a) shows the hypergraph with the columns of the incidence matrix as the edges. The *dual hypergraph* has sets of edges corresponding to the vertices as shown in Fig. 2(c). Looking along the rows, each vertex is related to a set of edges, for example x_7 is related to the set of edges $\{E_3, E_4, E_6\}$ This is a 'dual' edge in the *dual hypergraph*, as shown in Fig. 2(b).

The Galois Lattice. Figure 3 shows a set of arches, $A = \{a_1, a_2, a_3, a_4, a_5, a_6, a_7\}$ with each arch made from a subset of the blocks $B = \{b_1, b_2, b_3, b_4, b_5, b_6, b_7, b_8, b_9, b_{10}, b_{11}, b_{12}\}$. Let arch a_i be R-related to block b_j if it contains that block. This bipartite relation can be represented by the incidence matrix shown in Fig. 4. The entry in the ith row and the jth column of the matrix is one if a_i is related to b_j, and it zero otherwise. Let $E(a_i)$ be the set of blocks related to arch a_i. Then:

a_1 a_2 a_3 a_4 a_5 a_6 a_7

Fig. 3. Arches related to the blocks used to construct them

$E(a_1) = \{b_1, b_3, b_4\}$ $E(a_2) = \{b_2, b_3, b_4\}$ $E(a_3) = \{b_3, b_4, b_5\}$
$E(a_4) = \{b_4, b_5, b_6, b_7\}$ $E(a_5) = \{b_7, b_8, b_9, b_{10}\}$ $E(a_6) = \{b_7, b_8, b_9, b_{11}\}$
$E(a_7) = \{b_7, b_8, b_9, b_{12}\}$.

Apart from these 'first order' edges it is interesting to generate 'higher order' edges from all their intersections:

$E(a_1) \cap E(a_2) \cap E(a_3) = \{b_3, b_4\}$ $E(a_1) \cap E(a_2) \cap E(a_3) \cap E(a_4) = \{b_4\}$
$E(a_3) \cap E(a_4) = \{b_4, b_5\}$ $E(a_4) \cap E(a_5) \cap E(a_6) \cap E(a_7) = \{b_7\}$
$E(a_5) \cap E(a_6) \cap E(a_7) = \{b_7, b_8, b_9\}$

	b_1	b_2	b_3	b_4	b_5	b_6	b_7	b_8	b_9	b_{10}	b_{11}	b_{12}
a_1	1	0	1	1	0	0	0	0	0	0	0	0
a_2	0	1	1	1	0	0	0	0	0	0	0	0
a_3	0	0	1	1	1	0	0	0	0	0	0	0
a_4	0	0	0	1	1	1	1	0	0	0	0	0
a_5	0	0	0	0	0	0	1	1	1	1	0	0
a_6	0	0	0	0	0	0	1	1	1	0	1	0
a_7	0	0	0	0	0	0	1	1	1	0	0	1

Fig. 4. Maximal rectangles in the arch-block structure

Let the set of first order and higher order edges be called the *augmented hypergraph* for the relation in Fig. 5. The edges of the augmented dual hypergraph can be found in a similar way:

$$E(b_1) = \{a_1\} \qquad E(b_2) = \{a_2\} \qquad E(b_3) = \{a_1, a_2, a_3\}$$
$$E(b_4) = \{a_1, a_2, a_3, a_4\} \quad E(b_5) = \{a_3, a_4\} \qquad E(b_6) = \{a_4\}$$
$$E(b_7) = \{a_4, a_5, a_6, a_7\} \quad E(b_8) = \{a_5, a_6, a_7\} \qquad E(b_9) = \{a_5, a_6, a_7\}$$
$$E(b_{10}) = \{a_5\} \qquad E(b_{11}) = \{a_6\} \qquad E(b_{12}) = \{a_7\}$$

$$E(b_1) \cap E(b_3) \cap E(b_4) = \{a_1\} \qquad E(b_2) \cap E(b_3) \cap E(b_4) = \{a_2\}$$
$$E(b_3) \cap E(b_4) = \{a_1, a_2, a_3\} \qquad E(b_3) \cap E(b_4) \cap E(b_5) = \{a_3\}$$
$$E(b_4) \cap E(b_5) = \{a_3, a_4\} \qquad E(b_4) \cap E(b_5) \cap E(b_6) \cap E(b_7) = \{a_4\}$$
$$E(b_7) \cap E(b_8) \cap E(b_9) = \{a_5, a_6, a_7\} \quad E(b_7) \cap E(b_8) \cap E(b_9) \cap E(b_{10}) = \{a_5\}$$
$$E(b_7) \cap E(b_8) \cap E(b_9) \cap E(b_{11}) = \{a_6\} \quad E(b_7) \cap E(b_8) \cap E(b_9) \cap E(b_{12}) = \{a_7\}$$

Bringing together the sets in the augmented hypergraphs shows that they can be put is one-to-one correspondence. This is known as the *Galois connection* and the *Galois pairs* can be listed as:

$$\{b_1, b_3, b_4\} \leftrightarrow \{a_1\} \qquad \{b_7, b_8, b_9, b_{10}\} \leftrightarrow \{a_5\} \qquad \{b_3, b_4\} \leftrightarrow \{a_1, a_2, a_3\}$$
$$\{b_2, b_3, b_4\} \leftrightarrow \{a_2\} \qquad \{b_7, b_8, b_9, b_{11}\} \leftrightarrow \{a_6\} \quad \{b_7, b_8, b_9\} \leftrightarrow \{a_5, a_6, a_7\}$$
$$\{b_3, b_4, b_5\} \leftrightarrow \{a_3\} \qquad \{b_7, b_8, b_9, b_{12}\} \leftrightarrow \{a_7\} \qquad \{b_4\} \leftrightarrow \{a_1, a_2, a_3, a_4\}$$
$$\{b_4, b_5, b_6, b_7\} \leftrightarrow \{a_4\} \qquad \{b_4, b_5\} \leftrightarrow \{a_3, a_4\} \qquad \{b_7\} \leftrightarrow \{a_4, a_5, a_6, a_7\}$$

In a Galois pair $A' \leftrightarrow B'$ every a in A' is R-related to every b in B'. Therefore the rows and columns of the matrix can be rearranged so that all the a_i in A' are contiguous and all the b_j in B' are contiguous, with the corresponding rectangle of entries in the matrix all ones. For example, let $A' = \{a_1, a_2, a_3\}$ and $B' = \{b_3, b_4\}$. Then as shown in Fig. 4 the corresponding rectangle is filled with ones because each of a_1, a_2 and a_3 is related to b_3 and b_4.

The rectangle corresponding to $A' = \{a_1, a_2, a_3\} \leftrightarrow B' = \{b_3, b_4\}$ is *maximal*. Two other maximal rectangles are shown in Fig. 4 corresponding to the Galois

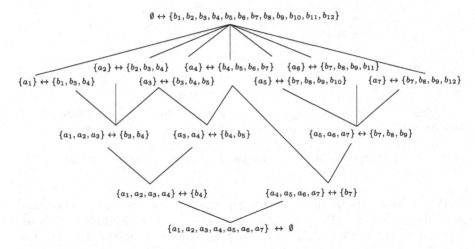

Fig. 5. The Galois Lattice for the arch-block relation of Fig. 4

pairs $\{a_3, a_4\} \leftrightarrow \{b_4, b_5\}$ and $\{a_5, a_6, a_7\} \leftrightarrow \{b_7, b_8, b_9\}$. The maximal rectangles $A' \leftrightarrow B'$ where A' has just one element or B' has just one element are not shown.

The Galois pairs can be arranged as a *Galois lattice* [13] with upwards set inclusion on the left and downward set inclusion on the right (Fig. 5).

Galois pairs are particularly interesting, since they are sites of relatively high connectivity. However for relations between large sets there can be a combinatorial explosion of Galois pairs making computation difficult. Nonetheless Galois pairs play an important role in hypernetwork theory [17].

Hypergraphs are an excellent first step towards mathematical structure able to represent n-ary relations. However they are essentially set-theoretic and have no orientation. Simplicial complexes provide this.

3   Simplicial Complexes

In the nineteen fifties C.H. Dowker published the paper *The homology groups of relations* [11] which showed that relations between n things could be represented by multidimensional polyhedra with n vertices, such as those shown in Fig. 6. This idea lay dormant for a quarter of a century until in the nineteen sixties R.H. Atkin introduced the revolutionary idea that social relations could be represented by polyhedra. For example, a business deal between three people can be represented by a triangle, written as $\langle a, b, c \rangle$, the relation of four people playing music together can be represented by a tetrahedron, $\langle a, b, c, d \rangle$, and the relationship between five people working together as a team can be represented by a 5-hedron, $\langle a, b, c, d, e \rangle$. This idea is entirely compatible with network theory since, for example, a relationship between two people having a conversation can be represented by a polyhedron with two vertices, namely a line or an edge, $\langle a, b \rangle$. These ideas first appeared in the article *A mathematical approach towards a social science*, published in the *Essex Review* in 1968 [1].

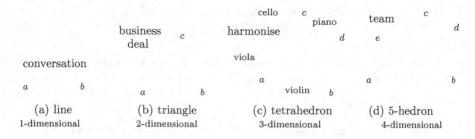

| (a) line | (b) triangle | (c) tetrahedron | (d) 5-hedron |
| 1-dimensional | 2-dimensional | 3-dimensional | 4-dimensional |

Fig. 6. Simplices can represent relations between two or more things

Polyhedra are the geometric realisation of more abstract objects called *simplices*. Let V be a set of vertices. An abstract *p-simplex* is determined by a set of $p+1$ vertices, written as $\langle v_0, v_1, ..., v_p \rangle$. Simplices are often represented by the symbol σ.

A simplex σ is a *face* of a simplex σ', $\sigma \lesssim \sigma'$, if every vertex of σ is also a vertex of σ'. For example the 2-dimensional simplex $\langle x_1, x_2, x_3 \rangle$ is a triangular face of the tetrahedron representing the 3-dimensional simplex $\langle x_1, x_2, x_3, x_4 \rangle$. A set of simplices with all its faces is called a *simplicial complex*.

Algebraic Topology. In algebraic topology simplices provide an algebraic way of calculating the topological invariants of spaces. The ideas will be briefly and informally sketched here. Figure 7 shows a complex made up of three triangles with all their faces (lines and vertices). This complex has the topological feature of a *hole* surrounded by the triangles.

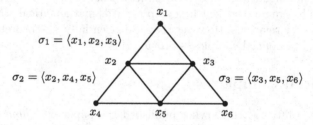

Fig. 7. A hole in a simplicial complex.

A q-dimension chain is an expression of the form $\Sigma_{i \in I} n \sigma_i$ where n is a number. The *boundary* operator, ∂, maps a simplex to its boundary according to the rule $\partial \langle x_0, ..., x_p \rangle = \Sigma_{i=0}^{p} (-1)^i \langle x_0, ..., \hat{x}_i, ..., x_p \rangle$, where $\hat{x}_i$ means omit the ith entry along, counting from zero. For example, $\partial \langle x_1, x_2, x_3 \rangle = \langle x_2, x_3 \rangle - \langle x_1, x_3 \rangle + \langle x_1, x_2 \rangle$. This chain of 1-simplices is called a *cycle*.

In algebraic topology switching a pair of vertices changes the sign (and orientation) of a simplex, so $-\langle x_1, x_3 \rangle = \langle x_3, x_1 \rangle$. Thus the cycle can be written as $\langle x_2, x_3 \rangle + \langle x_3, x_1 \rangle + \langle x_1, x_2 \rangle$. In this case it is a *bounding cycle* because it is a closed loop of 1-simplices that goes round the shaded 2-dimensional triangle. It starts at $\langle x_2 \rangle$ and goes to $\langle x_3 \rangle$ along the oriented edge $\langle x_2, x_3 \rangle$, goes to x_1 along the oriented edge $\langle x_3, x_1 \rangle$ and back to close the loop at x_2 along the oriented edge $\langle x_3, x_2 \rangle$.

The boundary operator is *nilpotent*, *i.e.* when applied twice it gives zero. For example, $\partial^2 \langle x_1, x_2, x_3 \rangle = \partial \langle x_2, x_3 \rangle - \partial \langle x_1, x_3 \rangle + \partial \langle x_1, x_2 \rangle = \langle x_3 \rangle - \langle x_2 \rangle - \langle x_3 \rangle + \langle x_1 \rangle + \langle x_2 \rangle - \langle x_1 \rangle = 0$.

Any chain c with $\partial c = 0$ is defined to be a *cycle*. Apart from bounding cycles as seen above, there can be *non-bounding cycles*. For example consider $c = \langle x_2, x_5 \rangle + \langle x_5, x_3 \rangle + \langle x_3, x_2 \rangle$. Then $\partial c = \langle x_5 \rangle - \langle x_2 \rangle + \langle x_3 \rangle - \langle x_5 \rangle + \langle x_2 \rangle - \langle x_3 \rangle = 0$ and c is a cycle. However there is no 2-dimensional chain c' with $\partial c' = c$ so c is a non-bounding cycle. In general, non-bounding cycles correspond to holes, in this case exactly the hole bounded by c.

Atkin's Q-analysis. In the early seventies Atkin and coworkers investigated the topological properties of relations in the context of town planning. Atkin suggested a new kind of connectivity based on the shared faces of social polyhedra [3–5].

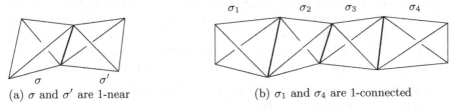

(a) σ and σ' are 1-near   (b) σ_1 and σ_4 are 1-connected

Fig. 8. q-connected polyhedra

Two simplices are q-*near* if they share a q-dimensional face. Two simplices are q-*connected* if there is a chain of pairwise q-near simplices between them. The tetrahedra σ and σ' are 1-near in Fig. 8(a) because they share an edge, or 1-dimensional face. In Fig. 8(b) the tetrahedra σ_1 and σ_4 are 1-connected, since σ_1 is 1-near σ_2, σ_2 is 1-near σ_3, and σ_3 is 1-near σ_4. A *Q-analysis determines* classes of q-*connected components*, sets of simplices that are all q-connected. An early application of Q-analysis studied land uses in Colchester [6].

Backcloth and Traffic. The vertices and edges of networks often have numbers associated with them. For example in a social network the vertices may be associated with the amount of money a person has and the edges may be associated with how much money passes between pairs of people. In electrical networks the vertices have voltage associated with them and the edges have current. Although the network's voltages and currents may change, the network itself does not. Similarly in a road network the daily traffic flows may vary but usually the network infrastructure does not. The same holds for simplicial complexes when there are patterns of numbers across the vertices and the simplices. The numbers may change when the underlying simplicial complex does not.

Atkin suggested that the relatively unchanging network or simplicial complex structure be called a *backcloth* and that the numbers be called the *traffic* of activity on the backcloth. As an example, the airline network acts as a backcloth to the traffic of airline passengers. The term backcloth comes from the scenery painted on large canvas sheets used in theatres as a static backdrop behind the actors.

Atkin first used simplicial complexes to characterise a wide variety of phenomena in physics by his *Cocycle Law* that the space-time backcloth supporting many physical phenomena has no holes. His conceptual leap "from cohomology in physics to q-connectivity in social science" was published in 1972 [2].

Flows and q-transmission as Multidimensional Percolation. Networks are excellent for representing and calculating the dynamics of flows, from electricity to oil to cars and sentiments. Simplicial complexes are multidimensional networks and they too can carry equally diverse traffic flows. Generally the q-connectivity of the underlying backcloth constraints the dynamics of the flows. This has been called *q-transmission* and has been described as a multidimensional analogue analogue to percolation in networks [17].

Example: Road Accidents. A study of road accidents illustrates the combinatorial nature of simplices [17]. Drivers who had been involved in accidents were interviewed to find out the possible causes. The telephone interviews were unstructured with the interviewer eliciting the causes from the interviewees, *e.g.* interviewees would often would volunteer that they were going too fast for the conditions. Some typical examples of the 57 reported accident simplices are:

⟨mechanical failure, need to stop, lack anticipation, stress; R_1⟩
⟨carelessness, unexpected manoeuvre; R_8⟩
⟨change in road layout, poor signposting, bad visibility; R_{16}⟩
⟨speed, lack of concentration; R_{23}⟩
⟨inexperienced driver, car in wrong position; R_{31}⟩
⟨poor visibility, lack of caution, road wet; R_{23}⟩
⟨not paying attention, to near/too fast, brakes poor, unexpected manoeuvre; R_{51}⟩
⟨narrow road, speed R_{53}⟩

These combinations of causes were expressed in everyday language. The data was analysed according to the classes:

D1–Stress	D2–carelessness	D3–Poor anticipation
D4–Too close	D5–Looking wrong way	D6–Alcohol
D7–Health/Tiredness	D8–Young male ego	D9–Inexperience
D10–Unfamiliarity with vehicle	D11–Cyclist blind	D12–In a hurry
D13–Unfamiliar with road	D14–Speed	D15–Mistaken priority
V1–Mechanical failure	R1–Difficult configuration	R2–Poor visibility
R3–Poor signposting	R4–Difficult surface	R6–Heavy traffic
A1–Unexpected event	A2–Slow vehicle in front	

Like hypergraphs, simplicial complex also have Galois pairs:

⟨D2–Carelessness, R1–Difficult configuration⟩	⟨2, 5, 9, 12, 35, 40, 42, 51, 57⟩
⟨D1–Stress, R1–Difficult configuration⟩	⟨1, 2, 20, 26, 34, 51, 52⟩
⟨D2–Carelessness, R2–Poor visibility⟩	⟨2, 3, 4, 35, 38, 40⟩
⟨D14–Speed, R1–Difficult configuration⟩	⟨10, 12, 22, 39, 43, 53⟩

⟨D1–Stress, R2–Poor visibility⟩   ⟨2, 3, 11, 13, 26⟩
⟨R1–Difficult configuration, R2–Poor visibility⟩   ⟨2, 26, 35, 40, 43⟩
⟨R2–Poor visibility, R4–Difficult road surface⟩   ⟨11, 13, 26, 36, 38⟩
⟨R2–Poor visibility, A1–Unexpected event⟩   ⟨11, 13, 16, 36, 54⟩
⟨R2–Poor visibility, R3–Poor signposting⟩   ⟨2, 16, 26, 56⟩
⟨D1–Stress, D13–Unfamiliar with road⟩   ⟨2, 3, 25, 52⟩
⟨D2–Carelessness, A1–Unexpected event⟩   ⟨1, 9, 10, 41⟩
⟨R2–Poor visibility, R4–Difficult road surface⟩   ⟨11, 13, 26⟩
⟨R2–Poor visibility, R4–Difficult road surface, A1–Unexpected event⟩   ⟨11, 13, 36⟩
⟨D2–Carelessnes, R1–Difficult configuration, R2–Poor visibility⟩   ⟨2, 35, 40⟩

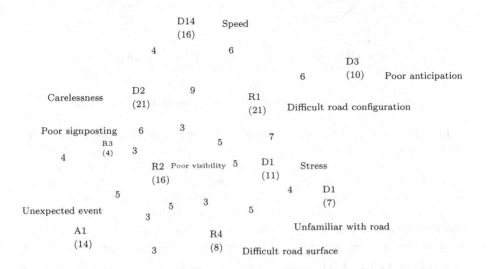

Fig. 9. Frequencies of occurrences of accident factors

Figure 9 gives a graphical summary of the Galois pairs and the numbers accidents associated with the simplices. The interviewees were asked to rate the
importance of the factors on a five-point low-high scale. For example, σ(Accident-
2) = ⟨D1–Stress(5), D2–Careless(3), D13–Unfamiliar road(5), D15–Mistaken prior-
ity(5), R1–Difficult config(5), R2–Poor visibility(3), R3–Poor signposting(5)⟩, and
σ(Accident–2) = ⟨D1–Stress(5), D2–Careless(4), D6–Alcohol(1), D7–Tired(5), D13–
Unfamiliar road(3), D15–Speed(3) R2–Poor visibility(2)⟩. Let $\mu(v_i)$ be the weighting
given to accident factor v_i, $\mu(v_i)$. A value on the whole simplex, the *fuzzy con-
junction*, can be defined as $\mu\sigma = \min\{\mu(v_i) \mid v_i \lesssim \sigma\}$. Then for a fuzzy value
of 3, σ(Accident-2) and σ(Accident-3) share the face ⟨D1-Stress, D2-Careless,
D13-Unfamiliar road⟩, and they are 3-fuzzy 2-near.

4   Hypernetworks

Figure 10(a) shows the lines $\ell_1, ..., \ell_{16}$ arranged in a circle by the relation R_1.
The resulting structure $\langle \ell_1, ..., \ell_{16}; R_1 \rangle$ has the emergent property that most
people see a white disk at the centre of the lines, the so-called *sun illusion*.

Figure 10(b) shows the same set of lines assembled under a different relation, R_2. Now there is no disk but a rectangle shape emerges. This example illustrates that the same ordered set of elements can be the subject of more than one relation, and that the simplex notation $\langle \ell_1, ..., \ell_{16} \rangle$ cannot discriminate these very different cases.

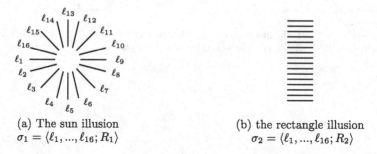

(a) The sun illusion
$\sigma_1 = \langle \ell_1, ..., \ell_{16}; R_1 \rangle$

(b) the rectangle illusion
$\sigma_2 = \langle \ell_1, ..., \ell_{16}; R_2 \rangle$

Fig. 10. The lines $\ell_1, ..., \ell_{16}$ organised by two different relations, R_1 and R_2

In order to do this another symbol is necessary to represent the relation. We write $R_1 : \langle \ell_1, ..., \ell_{16} \rangle \rightarrow \langle \ell_1, ..., \ell_{16}; R_1 \rangle$ and $R_2 : \langle \ell_1, ..., \ell_{16} \rangle \rightarrow \langle \ell_1, ..., \ell_{16}; R_2 \rangle$. Let σ_1 represent the sun configuration and σ_2 represent the rectangle configuration. Then σ_1 and σ_2 are examples of *relational simplices*, or *hypersimplices*. Now the notation enables σ_1 to be discriminated from σ_2, since $\sigma_1 \neq \sigma_2$.

In general a *hypernetwork* is defined to be any collection of hypersimplices. This definition is deliberately undemanding, so that almost anything can be a hypersimplex, and any collection of hypersimplices can be a hypernetwork.

Example: Chemical Molecules. Chemical molecules illustrate the idea of hypersimplices. For example, propanol assembles three carbon atoms with eight hydrogen atoms and one oxygen atom, written as C_3H_8O or C_3H_7OH. Figure 11 shows the atoms of propanol arranged in a variety of ways. The first two show the isomers *n*-propyl alcohol and isopropyl alcohol. The oxygen atom is attached to an end carbon in the first isomer and to the centre carbon in the second, but the C-O-H hydroxyl group substructure is common to both. The rightmost isomer of C_3H_8O, methoxyethane, has the oxygen atom connected to two carbon atoms and there is no C-O-H substructure. This makes it an ether, methyl-ethyl-ether, rather than an alcohol. Thus the relational simplices of the isomers have

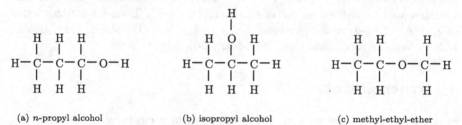

(a) *n*-propyl alcohol   (b) isopropyl alcohol   (c) methyl-ethyl-ether

Fig. 11. Chemical isomers as relational simplices

the same vertices, but the assembly relations are different. n-propyl alcohol and isopropyl alcohol share the hydroxyl group substructure C-O-H and are similar, but methyl-ethyl-ether does not and has different properties. Thus

$$\langle\, C, C, C, H, H, H, H, H, H, H, H, O\,;\, R_{n-\text{propylalcohol}}\,\rangle \quad \neq$$

]
$$\langle\, C, C, C, H, H, H, H, H, H, H, H, O\,;\, R_{\text{isopropylalcohol}}\,\rangle \quad \neq$$
$$\langle\, C, C, C, H, H, H, H, H, H, H, H, O\,;\, R_{\text{methyl}-\text{ethyl}-\text{ether}}\,\rangle$$

The Vertex Removal Test for n-ary Relations. The essential feature of a polyhedron is that it ceases to exist if any of the vertices are removed. For example, consider a cyclist represented as the combination $\langle$rider, bicycle; $R_{\text{riding}}\rangle$. Remove either the man or the bicycle and what is left ceases to be a cyclist. Removing a vertex is like sticking a pin in a balloon, causing the structure to collapse and whatever is left is not the whole simplex. Remove any vertex from $\langle$gin, tonic, ice, lemon; $R_{\text{mixed}}\rangle$ and it ceases to be the perfect gin and tonic. Generalising edges to polyhedra allows a distinction to be made between the *parts* of things represented by vertices, and *wholes* represented by hypersimplices. Using this test it is easy to find many examples of n-ary relations, *e.g.* a path with n edges in a network forms a hypersimplex - remove an edge and the path ceases to exist; four bridge players form a hypersimplex - remove one and the game collapses; and a car and its wheels are 5-ary related - without any of them it won't work.

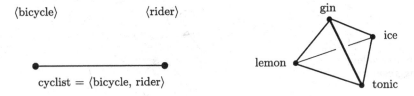

(a) Remove a vertex and the cyclist simplex ceases to exist

(b) Remove a vertex and the perfect gin and tonic ceases to exist

Fig. 12. Remove a vertex and the simplex ceases to exist.

5   Hypernetworks and Multilevel Structure

Hypersimplices enable the definition of multilevel part-whole structures, *e.g.* the four blocks assembled by the 4-ary relation R to form an arch in Fig. 13. Here the whole has the emergent property of a gap not possessed by any of its parts. If the parts exist in the system at an arbitrary *Level N* then the whole exists at a higher level, here shown as *Level N+1*. Thus assembly relations provide an immutable upwards arrow for the definition of multilevel structure.

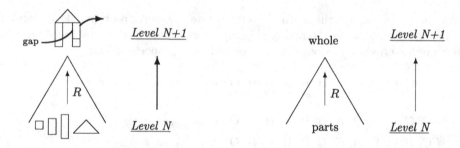

Fig. 13. The fundamental part-whole diagram of multilevel aggregation

Part-whole aggregations are interleaved with taxonomic aggregations, as shown in Fig. 14. The aggregation between *Level N* and *Level N+1* combines graphical parts to form faces. The aggregation between *Level N+1* and *Level N+2* establishes classes of faces in a taxonomy. Such aggregations depend on the purpose of the taxonomy. For example, there is no class of 'frowny' faces because, for the purpose here, it is not required. Note that part-whole aggregation require *all* the parts. In contrast taxonomic aggregations require just one example to aggregate. For example, the round smiley face is sufficient for there to be a smiley face, irrespective of whether or not there is a square smiley face.

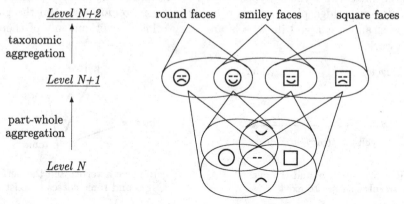

Fig. 14. Part-whole and taxonomic aggregation

6 Embracing *n*-ary Relations in Network Science

Despite the mathematics literature on multi-vertex relational structure dating back at least to the 1950s, and despite the efforts of visionaries such as Berge and Atkin in the 1960s, today many scientists still shy away from relations between more than two things. It is all the more remarkable because graph theorists have known about this mathematics but not adopted it, *e.g.* in his classic book on graph theory, Harary [14] quotes Veblen's 1922 book [19] as a source for his definition of simplicial complex but, frustratingly, notes in passing that a graph is a one-dimensional simplicial complex, even though Veblen explicitly considers two-dimensional simplicies in the second chapter of his book. In contrast, computer science recognises the importance of *n*-ary relations, *e.g.* Codd [9] uses them in his seminal paper on relational data structures, and the WC3 consortium defines their use in the semantic web [15].

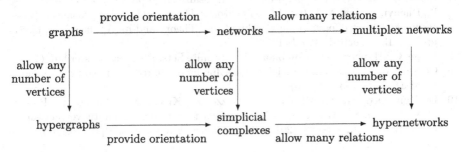

Fig. 15. The natural family of network structures embraces *n*-ary relations

It is unfortunate that network scientists should neglect *n*-ary relations since they are part of a natural family of network structures (Fig. 15). Assuming appropriate definitions, providing orientation makes a non-oriented graph into a network, and allowing pairs of vertices to support many relations makes multiplex networks. Vertically, allowing edges to have many vertices generalises graphs to hypergraphs, allowing oriented edges to have many vertices generalises networks to simplicial complexes, and allowing oriented edges supporting many relations to have many vertices generalises multiplex networks to hypernetworks. Horizontally, orienting the edges of hypergraphs creates simplicial families and complexes, and allowing a simplex to support many relations creates hypernetworks. Thus the diagram in Fig. 15 commutes and these structures form a natural family by adding structure from top left to bottom right.

Hopefully this paper will stimulate more interest in *n*-ary relations in network science:

- many systems involve *n*-ary relations – ignoring this misrepresents them
- *n*-ary relations are essential for representing part-whole structures and related dynamics in multilevel systems
- there is a rich and coherent mathematical theory for *n*-ary relations - with many remaining challenges and opportunities for the network community.

References

1. Atkin, R.H., Bray, R., Cook, I.: 'A mathematical approach towards a social science', The Essex Review, University of Essex, Autumn 1968, no. 2, 3–5 (1968)
2. Atkin, R.H.: From cohomology in physics to Q-connectivity in social science. Int. J. Man-Mach. Stud. **4**(2), 139–167 (1972)
3. Atkin, R.H.: Mathematical Structure in Human Affairs. Heinemann Educational Books, London (1974)

4. Atkin, R.H.: Combinatorial Connectivities in Social Systems. Birkhäuser (Basel), Basel (1974)
5. Atkin, R.H.: Multidimensional Man. Penguin Books, Harmondsworth (1981)
6. Atkin, R.H., Johnson, J.H., Mancini, V.: An analysis of urban structure using concepts of algebraic topology. Urban Stud. **8**, 221–242 (1971)
7. Berge, C.: Sur certains hypergraphes généralisant les graphes bipartites. In: Erdös, P., Rhényi, A., Sós, V.T. (eds.) Combinatorial Theory and its Applications I, (Proceedings of the Colloquium on Combinatorial Theory and its Applications, 1969), pp. 119–133, North-Holland (1970)
8. Berge, C.: Hypergraphs: Combinatorics of Finite Sets. Elseiver, Amsterdam (1989)
9. Codd, E.F.: A relational model of data for large shared data banks. Commun. ACM **16**(6), 377–387 (1970)
10. De Domenico, M., Solé-Ribalta, A., Cozzo, E., Kivela, M., Moreno, Y., Porter, M.A., Gómez, S., Arenas, A.: Mathematical formulation of multilayer networks. Phys. Rev. X **3**, 041022 (2013). http://journals.aps.org/prx/pdf/10.1103/Phys RevX.3.041022
11. Dowker, C.H.: The homology groups of relations. Ann. Math. **56**(1), 84–95 (1952)
12. Freeman, L.C., White, D.R., Romney, A.K.: Research Methods in Social Network Analysis. Transaction Publishers, New Brunswick (1991)
13. Freeman, L.C., White, D.R.: Using Galois lattices to represent network data. Sociol. Methodol. **23** (1993). ISBN 1-55786-464-0, ISSN 0081-1750, http://eclectic.ss.uci. edu/~drwhite/pw/Galois.pdf
14. Harary, F.: Graph Theory, (third printing 1972). Addison-Wesley, Reading (1969)
15. Hayes, P., Welty, C.,: Defining N-ary relations on the semantic web. W3C Working Group Note (12 April 2006). http://www.w3.org/TR/swbp-n-aryRelations
16. Johnson, J.H.: Hypernetworks for reconstructing the dynamics of multilevel systems. In: European Conference on Complex Systems 2006 (25–29 September 2006), Oxford. http://oro.open.ac.uk/4628/1/ECCS06-Johnson-R.pdf
17. Johnson, J.H.: Hypernetworks in the Science of Complex Systems. Imperial College Press, London (2014)
18. Lee, K.-M., Mina, B., Gohb, K.-I.: Towards real-world complexity: an introduction to multiplex networks. Eur. Phys. J. B **88**, 48 (2015). doi:10.1140/epjb/ e2015-50742-1
19. Veblen, O.: Analysis Situs. American Mathematical Society Colloquium Lectures, Volume 5, The Cambridge Colloquium, 1916. Part II. Reprinted facsimile, Leopold Classic Library. http://www.leopoldclassiclibrary.com

Studying Successful Public *Plazas* in the City of Murcia (Spain) Using a Ranking Nodes Algorithm and Foursquare Data

Taras Agryzkov[1], Pablo Martí[2], Almudena Nolasco-Cirugeda[2],
Leticia Serrano-Estrada[2], Leandro Tortosa[1(✉)], and José F. Vicent[1]

[1] Departamento de Ciencia de la Computación e Inteligencia Artificial,
Universidad de Alicante, Ap. Correos 99, E-03080 Alicante, Spain
{taras.agryzkov,tortosa,jvicent}@ua.es
[2] Departamento de Edificación y Urbanismo,
Universidad de Alicante, Ap. Correos 99, E-03080 Alicante, Spain
{pablo.marti,almudena.nolasco,leticia.serrano}@ua.es

Abstract. In this paper we study the success of public spaces (exactly, *plazas*) existing in the urban fabric of the city of Murcia, Spain, from two points of view. On the one hand, we apply an algorithm to classify the nodes of a graph in order of importance, from the data obtained through a fieldwork developed on the city itself. On the other hand, we use the data that gives us the social network Foursquare in this city to extract the preferences of its users, related to the different *plazas* present in the public space in the city. These two perspectives or views allows us to establish two rankings of *plazas* places in the city, which is the subject of comparative study to determine potential differences or similarities in the results.

Keywords: Networks · Primal graph · Urban networks · Public spaces · PageRank vector · Foursquare

1 Introduction

The city is a complex system where a large information and data is generated and this is used as an essential part of the characteristics of the system itself. The origin of this vast information can be very diverse; developed from field work in person until Web services supported by social networks and existing databases (open or protected). Social networks such as Facebook, Foursquare and Twitter have been considered as the newest new data sources [1,6] as a consequence of the relatively new phenomenon associated to the digital world: "a growing shift in internet browsing from PCs to mobile devices -tablets and smartphones:" [9]. Thus, as an activity that happens in the real world is shared

---

Partially supported by Spanish Govern, Ministerio de Economía y Competividad, grant number TIN2014-53855-P.

© Springer International Publishing Switzerland 2016
A. Wierzbicki et al. (Eds.): NetSci-X 2016, LNCS 9564, pp. 161–168, 2016.
DOI: 10.1007/978-3-319-28361-6_13

on line, its location -latitude and longitude values- gets shared as well as part of the physical place's digital overlay [8].

The main objective of this paper is the analysis of successful public spaces in a particular urban network, as it is the city of Murcia, from two points of view. On the one hand the APA algorithm [2] is applied to determine, from the data collected through fieldwork, the importance of public places studied, specifically existing *plazas* in the city. In other words, with the application of the APA algorithm, we obtain a classification of the public spaces according to their importance in the network; so, we can say that a ranking is established. On the other hand, we extract and analyze the results that the social network Foursquare provides us, specially those related to the category outdoors and recreations where the word *plaza* appears. This way, taking both analysis we can make comparisons between them looking for possible similarities.

2   The City of Murcia and Data Obtained from Different Sources

To study an urban layout, we first need to represent it by an abstraction model. To represent the abstract model we use a primal graph [4,5], whereas to analyze the network we need some mathematical model or algorithm. For this, we create the network (primal graph) from a connected graph where the streets become undirected edges. Nodes usually represent the intersections of the streets, but we can also assign nodes to some points of interest in long streets. The primal graph allows us either to represent the topology of an urban fabric as well as to organize the geolocated data.

In this paper we will work only with a part of the city, the historical center (Fig. 1(a)) and the neighborhoods that are placed around it. The reason that motivates this limitation lies, on the one hand, in reducing the amount of data to work with and, on the other hand, because the historical center is the most active area of the city and where most activity takes place.

The selected area of study (in Fig. 1(a)) occupies an area of 40 hectares and it is characterized by a dense concentration of commercial venues and facilities.

2.1   Foursquare Data in the City of Murcia

Foursquare (foursquare.com) is, as categorised by Sui and Goodchild [13], a social check-in site that enables users to share their whereabouts with their friends [11] and, in most cases, with any on line user. The "basis of the platform consists of user-generated venues for business and points of interests" [11] from where Foursquare users can check-in. Currently, the number of registered individuals and businesses that are part of the Foursquare community surpasses the 50 million and 1.9 million businesses respectively (Foursquare, 2014). Moreover, the enormous amount of the geographic information generated overtime on Foursquare is accessible to the public through Application Programming Interfaces (API) [12].

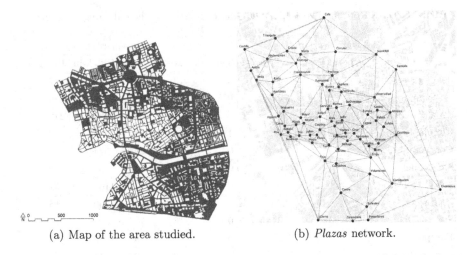

(a) Map of the area studied.   (b) *Plazas* network.

Fig. 1. The area of the city of Murcia object of this study and the *Plazas* that we detect from the map.

The reason to choose Murcia in this work as a case study is based on the fact that Murcia is Spain's fourth city in terms of amount of activity on Foursquare (www.puromarketing.com/16/15391/comousan-espanoles-foursquare.html). This is a reliable reflection of the importance of this city in the whole country if we talk in terms of network users. Therefore, we analyze the data that we can obtain from the web service. According to the data downloaded for the purpose of this study, Foursquare categorizes each venue into five predefined categories: Outdoors & Recreation, Shops and Services, Food, Nightlife, Arts & Entertainment. In turn, each category is divided into a number of subcategories.

Since we are interested in the public spaces and, in particular, in the *plazas* of the city, we focus at the data extracted for the category Outdoors-recreation and for the subcategory *Plaza*. In Table 1 we summarize the data obtained from Foursquare Web service for the city of Murcia in the area studied related to the subcategory *plaza*.

In Table 1 we show data concerning Foursquare 20 *plazas* that most visits have registered in the geographical area under study. Note that 37 venues have been identified in the Foursquare data with the word *Plaza* in its subcategory. The table shows the number of visits, the number of check-in as well as photos associated with that place. The data reflected here do not correspond to a particular time period, the data represent historical since the place has been registered in the social network. Thus, both the number of visits as the check-in refers to the accumulated by users since the venue exists on the network.

2.2 A Fieldwork in the City of Murcia

The data collection process is a field study that consists of collecting the data or information we want to analyze or visualize. Subsequently, these data must

Table 1. Data from fieldwork and Foursquare related to the subcategory *Plaza*.

Plaza	Fieldwork data					Foursquare data		
	Type I	Type II	Type III	Type IV	Total	Visits	Check-in	Pictures
de las Flores	8	4	1	0	13	1219	2669	187
St. Domingo	12	6	0	0	13	788	2756	146
de la Catedral	5	2	1	0	8	650	1436	242
Circular	4	16	7	1	28	329	1589	46
Condestable	3	3	6	0	12	294	574	38
Sta. Isabel	4	15	6	0	25	233	787	22
Julian Romea	5	4	0	0	9	224	1169	52
Mayor	6	3	0	0	9	140	460	15
Sta Catalina	7	3	0	0	10	100	308	15
Europa	4	9	2	0	15	94	229	3
Dez de Revenga	3	15	5	0	23	90	644	16
Camachos	6	10	0	0	16	75	514	17
de la Merced	1	3	1	0	5	75	167	4
Cetina	3	10	1	0	14	63	451	11
San Juan	4	2	0	0	6	43	103	2
Juan XXIII	4	8	0	1	13	36	208	2
de la Cruz	0	0	0	0	0	36	60	12
Castilla	1	6	1	0	8	35	323	14
de los Apostoles	5	4	0	0	9	32	49	10
De la Seda	0	8	0	0	8	32	134	17

be assigned to the nodes of the network so that each node has a set of numerical values associated with the information that is being studied. We want to study the city from the point of view of the facilities and commercial activity. In this analysis, we distinguish the following types of facilities: Type I (Bars, restaurants, coffee, snack bar, ...), Type II (small shops), Type III (Sales and bank offices), Type IV (Big shops).

The number of tertiary endowments that have been collected through fieldwork are: 552 venues (Type I), 2216 venues (Type II), 285 venues (Type III) and 33 venues (Type IV). Note the large number of endowments of Type II (small shops) that have been collected and geolocated.

3   The Adapted PageRank Algorithm as a Centrality Measure

The *PageRank* method [3,10] was proposed to compute a ranking for every Web page based on the graph of the Web (see [7]). In [2], the authors propose an adaptation of the PageRank model to establish a ranking of nodes in an urban network, taking into account the influence of external activities or information. In the following, we refer to this algorithm as the *Adapted PageRank Algorithm* (APA algorithm).

The central idea behind the APA algorithm for ranking the nodes is the construction of a data matrix D, which summarizes the numerical value of the data that we are measuring. This matrix allows us to represent numerically the information of the network that we are going to analyze and measure. This information is placed by columns, where each column represents a specific characteristic or type of information that we want to evaluate or analyze. The result of applying this algorithm to a network is a ranking vector with N components, where the i-th component represents the ranking of the i-th node within the overall network.

4 Numerical Results

The first objective of the paper is to apply the APA algorithm to the network generated by the plazas of the city. First, we proceed by determining all the squares, circus (*plazas*) that are in the urban network. We have identified a total of 72 *plazas* in the city area under study. These venues are shown in Fig. 1(b), where we locate the different *plazas* over the map of the city and construct a graph taking these venues as nodes and edges connecting neighbor *plazas*.

The first part of our study is the APA algorithm launch to the network made up by these 72 *plazas* that were identified on the map of the city (see Fig. 1). The data used for the algorithm launch are the data obtained from fieldwork (see Sect. 2.2), according to the four categories listed related to the commercial activity, where each of them is associated to a different business sector.

Note that the data collected by fieldwork are located in the entire urban network, i.e. do not distinguish any specific part of the network; therefore, they are not referred to the *plazas* that we are studying. Consequently, it was necessary to conduct a preliminary extraction process of the data corresponding to the nodes forming the network of *plazas* we want to study.

Therefore, in Table 1 it is reflected in a detailed manner the data concerning the venues identified in the urban fabric as *plazas*. The data shown in Table 1 correspond to the data of fieldwork in four categories (type I to IV), respect to the venues *plazas* that have received more visits in the social network Foursquare. This table only includes data from the 20 *plazas* in the urban area studied that have received more visits from the social network users.

We apply the APA Algorithm to the data collected for all the *plazas* that we have detected in the map of the city (there were 72). After running the APA Algorithm we obtain a classification of the nodes (*plazas*, in this case) according to their importance in the network. So, we have a ranking of the plazas of the city, according to the information studied. In this example, the data are related to the commercial activity developed in the city, classified by different sectors. To see the details of the model used to perform the visualization of the ranking in the network, see [2].

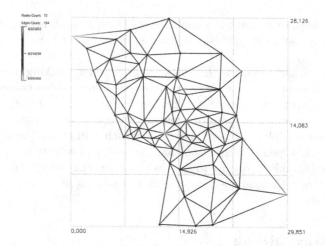

Fig. 2. Visualization of the APA theoretical scheme over the graph of the *plazas*.

(a) *Plazas* over the geolocated facilities.   (b) *Plazas* over the food-service facilities.

Fig. 3. Visualization of the twenty first *plazas* in the ranking of the Foursquare users over the geolocated facilities obtained by the fieldwork.

Consequently, we have two distinct scales: first, the scale of the domain of values that provides quantification of information and, on the other hand, the scale that provides us with the graphic scale. It is necessary to enhance a linear interpolation to set the color that is assigned to each of the nodes, according to the amount of information associated with it. Once we have this color range in the nodes, a graphical representation of the edges follows the same format representation. Using this visualization model by means of a chromatic scale in the graph, the result obtained for the graph where the nodes are the plazas in the area studied is shown in Fig. 2. We note that the most important nodes in the *plazas* network are located not only in the downtown of the city but in the historic center of it, where the network of streets has a classic ancient layout with narrow streets and irregular polygons.

Now, we have two different rankings of importance; one is the classification given by the APA Algorithm taking the commercial data of a fieldwork. The other one is given by the preferences of Foursquare users. It is interesting that some of the places that occupy very high positions in the ranking given by the visitors of Foursquare, also occupy high positions in the ranking offered by the APA algorithm. It is important to note that within the various types of data that Foursquare offers, we focus to establish a classification according to the tastes of network users in the visits to each venue and not the check-in that accumulates. The reason is that one user can make various check-in of a venue.

Thus, in particular, the node *Plaza de las Flores*, occupying the first position in the social network ranking, also ranks first in the classification given by APA algorithm. This coincidence is a remarkable circumstance, the absolute coincidence in the importance given to this venue (plaza), from the point of view of the interests of users of social network and within the framework of the network topology and commercial facilities. Figure 3(a) shows a map of the historical center of the city of Murcia where you have geolocated all facilities and business that have been obtained in fieldwork. Red allocations have been drawn regarding the commercial food-service sector. In green color are shown shops or small business, while in blue color we have represented bank offices; finally, in orange color the large department stores and supermarkets are displayed. Overlying this information the 20 most visited places by users have shown Foursquare. The circles have a size proportional to its importance. We notice the coincidence between the most visited *plazas* and the existence of trade provisions or facilities. From Fig. 3(a) we highlight the correlation between the *plazas* that were most commonly visited by social network users and areas with a high density of commercial allocations or facilities. Especially significant is this coincidence in the three most visited places in Foursquare, where we found a remarkable concentration of commercial activity in both the place itself and its surroundings. Figure 3(a) shows us all the allocations of fieldwork relating to the four categories studied, i.e., the food-service sector (type I), small shops (Type II), bank offices and businesses (type III) and malls and supermarkets (type IV). More significant is this correlation if we only look at the food-service sector, where we have restaurants, bars, coffees, and so on. We clearly see this fact in Fig. 3(b). In Fig. 3(b) can be seen as the *plazas* that succeed in accordance with the tastes or preferences of the social network users is directly related to a significant presence of facilities or endowments in the food-service commercial sector.

5   Conclusions

We have studied the set of places that exist in the city center of Murcia from two perspectives. The first is based on applying a classification algorithm of complex networks to determine the most important nodes. The second, using the data that the users of social network Foursquare provide us about their tastes and preferences in the city. The experimental results show that the venues (*plazas*) most visited by the network users are *plazas* with a remarkable importance within the network, especially those who are at the top in the ranking given by the number of visits. Furthermore, it is given the fact that data from the preferences of social network users suggest us some fundamental characteristics or features of the city that can be confirmed by the theoretical study based on the classification algorithm. This feature is related to the fact that the most characteristic activity taking place in the downtown of the city is highly related to the food-service sector and to a lesser extent, of small shops. This is clearly verified by comparing rankings given by the algorithm applied to the *plazas* network to display the classification of network nodes and the location of the most visited *plazas* by Foursquare users.

References

1. Adnan, M., Leak, A., Longley, P.: A geocomputational analysis of Twitter activity around different world cities. Geo-spatial Inf. Sci. **17**(3), 145–152 (2014)
2. Agryzkov, T., Oliver, J.L., Tortosa, L., Vicent, J.F.: An algorithm for ranking the nodes of an urban network based on concept of PageRank vector. Appl. Math. Comput. **219**, 2186–2193 (2012)
3. Berkhin, P.: A survey on PageRank computing. Internet Math. **2**(1), 73–120 (2005)
4. Crucitti, P., Latora, V., Porta, S.: The network analysis of urban streets: a primal approach. Plan. Des. **33**(5), 705–725 (2006)
5. Crucitti, P., Latora, V., Porta, S.: The network analysis of urban streets: a dual approach. Phys. A: Stat. Mech. Appl. **369**(2), 853–866 (2006)
6. Gantz, J., Reinsel, D.: Extracting value from chaos. IDC iView, International Data Corporation (IDC), Massachusetts (2011)
7. Langville, A.N., Mayer, C.D.: Deeper inside PageRank. Internet Math. **1**(3), 335–380 (2005)
8. López, G.B.: Geolocalización y redes sociales. Un mundo social, local y móvil. (In Spanish) Bubok, Spain (2012)
9. Mazzoccola, G.: The internet goes mobile: Nielsen and Audiweb respond with "Total Digital Audience" (2014). http://www.nielseninsights.eu/articles/the-internet-goes-mobile-nielsen-and-audiweb-respond-with-total-digital-audience
10. Page, L., Brin, S., Motwani, R., Winogrand, T.: The pagerank citation ranking: bringing order to the web. Technical report 1999–66, Stanford InfoLab (1999)
11. Reed, R.: The SoLoMo Manifesto or just about everything marketers need to know about the convergence of social, local and mobile. In: MOMENTFEED (ed.) (2014)
12. Roick, O., Heuser, S.: Location based social networks - definition, current state of the art and research agenda. Trans. GIS **17**, 763–784 (2013)
13. Sui, D., Goodchild, M.: The convergence of GIS and social media: challenges for GIScience. Int. J. Geogr. Inf. Sci. **25**(11), 1737–1748 (2011)

A Comparison of Fundamental Network Formation Principles Between Offline and Online Friends on Twitter

Felicia Natali[(⊠)] and Feida Zhu

School of Information Systems, Singapore Management University,
80 Stamford Rd, 178902 Singapore, Singapore
{felician.2013,fdzhu}@smu.edu.sg

Abstract. We investigate the differences between how some of the fundamental principles of network formation apply among offline friends and how they apply among online friends on Twitter. We consider three fundamental principles of network formation proposed by Schaefer et al.: reciprocity, popularity, and triadic closure. Overall, we discover that these principles mainly apply to offline friends on Twitter. Based on how these principles apply to offline versus online friends, we formulate rules to predict offline friendship on Twitter. We compare our algorithm with popular machine learning algorithms and Xiewei's random walk algorithm. Our algorithm beats the machine learning algorithms on average by 15 % in terms of f-score. Although our algorithm loses 6 % to Xiewei's random walk algorithm in terms of f-score, it still performs well (f-score above 70 %), and it reduces prediction time complexity from $O(n^2)$ to $O(n)$.

Keywords: Network formation · Offline friends · Online friends · Twitter · Social network · Offline friends prediction · Machine learning · Offline online

1 Introduction

Network formation has been studied in both the offline social network and the online social network. Before the emergence of the online social network, researchers investigated the offline social network. They discovered that the formation of the offline social network was characterized by a number of *dependencies* [16], also called *principles* [14]. These principles were by no means arbitrarily generated but were empirically discovered or theoretically formulated in previous studies on social networks [16]. When the online social network emerged, it was seen as a solution to the inconsistency and the high cost of procuring a large real life social networks data [12]. The principles of network formation that were previously discovered in the offline social network are now studied in the online social network. Most of these studies reveal that the principles that apply to the offline social network – such as reciprocity, mutuality, preferential attachment,

© Springer International Publishing Switzerland 2016
A. Wierzbicki et al. (Eds.): NetSci-X 2016, LNCS 9564, pp. 169–177, 2016.
DOI: 10.1007/978-3-319-28361-6_14

and homophily – also apply to the online social network [7,9,11]. A provoking question then arises as to whether these similarities between the principles of offline and online network formation happen because "online social networks primarily support pre-existing social relations [3]", particularly the existing offline contacts [5].

To answer the question, we investigate how three fundamental principles of network formation proposed by Schaefer et al. [14] apply among offline pre-existing social relations — referred to as *offline friends* — versus non pre-existing social relations — referred to as *online friends* — on Twitter. In this study, *offline friends* comprises of followers or followees on Twitter whom a user knows in the real world, whereas *online friends* comprises of followers and followees on Twitter whom a user does not know in the real world. As such, the set of offline friends and the set of online friends are mutually exclusive.

Since we only have the ground-truth data of a user's offline and online friends, we are making an assumption that all offline friends are pre-existing social relations, and all online friends are non pre-existing social relations. We believe this is a reasonable assumption to make because people maintain an online social network mainly to keep in touch with existing social relations that they have offline and meet new people online [5].

2   Fundamental Principles of Network Formation Among Offline Versus Online Friends

Social networks are formed through multiple principles. Snijders listed some of the important ones in his work [16], they are: reciprocity, homophily, transitivity, degree differentials (popularity), and hierarchies. Schaefer et al. particularly picked up three principles — reciprocity, popularity, and triadic closure — to study the process of network formation among preschool children [14]. They proposed that these principles were general. Through longitudinal study using the SIENA modeling framework [15], they discovered that reciprocity, popularity and triadic closure shaped the formation of pre-school children's networks. As most children regularly interact with their peers for the first time in preschool, and they do not have prior social experience that might contaminate their motivation in creating social ties with their friends, the principles that govern their network formation are considered fundamental. Therefore, we choose these three principles to investigate in this study.

For our analysis, we use the dataset by Xie et al. [17]. This dataset contains the data of 98 Twitter users that includes his ego network in 2011 and the list of his Twitter friends (followers or followees) whom he knows in real life. Overall, the dataset has 20030 Twitter users (ego users and their alters) and 23225 edges labeled as an offline or an online friend. We only use 49 ego networks (9380 users and 10153 labeled edges) for our observation. Based on our observation, we formulate rules to predict offline friendship and use the rest 49 ego networks for our prediction task.

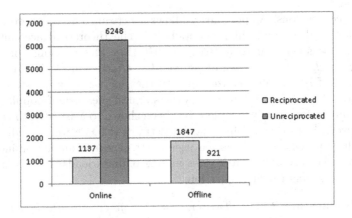

Fig. 1. Reciprocated links among offline and online friends.

2.1 Reciprocity

Reciprocity means requiting a benefit received [8]. Since friends enjoy equality in right, privileges, and obligations [10], reciprocity becomes the basis of friendship. On Twitter, reciprocity can happen when two users reply each other, mention each other, follow each other, etc. In this study, we focus on reciprocity that has a direct impact on a Twitter follow network dependency, that is, reciprocity when two users follow each other. Although reciprocity is one of the basic principles of moral codes in a society which enables social stability [8], it may not necessarily assume such a fundamental role when it comes to online friends in an online society. Therefore, in this study, we answer the following research question:

Research Question 1. *Does reciprocity as the basis of Twitter follow network formation happen as often among online friends as among offline friends?*

Figure 1 shows the distribution of reciprocated links among offline and online friends. To answer the research question, we perform chi-square test of independence to check whether reciprocity depends on the type of friendship (offline or online). Our result shows that reciprocity depends on the type of friendship with odds ratio 11.02 ($\chi^2 = 2553.8$, p-value < 0.001). Offline friends are 11 times more likely to reciprocate on Twitter.

Based on this observation, we create our first rule to predict offline friendship. Given two online friends, A and B, on Twitter,

Rule 1. *IF A and B reciprocate on Twitter THEN A and B are offline friends.*

2.2 Popularity

Popularity means the state of having many connections. An individual's popularity increases as the idealized qualities imposed by society increase, e.g. wealth, beauty, and social skill [1]. These idealized qualities increase one's attractiveness and invite connections. As popularity allows a person to access more resources [4], popularity also entails higher popularity. The theoretical account of this phenomenon was elaborated by Price in 1976 [13]. This phenomenon is called *the-rich-get-richer phenomenon*, or *preferential attachment* [2]. Therefore, popularity in itself is also an idealized quality that increases one's attractiveness. On Twitter, the number of followers is the simplest measure of popularity.

Although preferential attachment has been shown to exist in both the online social network [11] and the offline social network [13], we wonder whether the rate at which popularity increases a user's attractiveness among online friends differs from the rate at which it does among offline friends. In this study, we answer the following research question:

Research Question 2. *On Twitter, does preferential attachment happen among online friends at the same rate as it does among offline friends?*

We plot the distributions of the number of followers of offline friends and online friends. Although in general they follow the power law, there is too much fluctuation in the distributions, thus making it impossible to find the parameters that fit a power law curve closely. Therefore, we try several folds of number of followers and discover that the distributions of the number of followers (in 70-fold) of both offline friends and online friends fit the power law closely ($N = cx^{-\alpha}$ where N is the frequency of users with a specific number of followers, and x is the number of followers in 70-fold), but at different parameters c and α (c is 1482.16 and α is 1.70 among offline friends, c is 769.13 and α is 0.92 among online friends. See Fig. 2a). The power law distributions show that preferential attachment exists [13], and it happens at a faster attachment rate among offline friends judging by the larger α.

A stranger (online friend) has a thicker tail, meaning he has a greater tendency to have a higher number of followers. The next question is, whether there

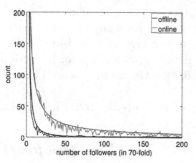

(a) Distributions of the number of followers of offline and online friends follow the power law.

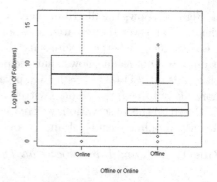

(b) Boxplot of the number of followers of offline friends and online friends.

Fig. 2. The number of followers of offline and online friends

is a number of followers at which a user is likely to be an online friend to anyone. According to previous studies, there may be. Kwak et al. discovered that homophily was not observed between a user who had more than 1000 followers and his reciprocal friends [9]. Moreover, another study showed that 71 % of top link farmers (users who try to acquire large numbers of follower links to amass influence) on Twitter had more than 1000 followers [6]. Link farmers usually reciprocate even those whom they do not know to amass social capital and promote their Twitter content. As a result, many of the users in their network are strangers. Our boxplot in Fig. 2b also shows that a user who has more than 1000 followers (log $1000 = 6.9$) is at around the 87th percentile of all offline friends. Meanwhile, such a user is only at around the 25th percentile of all online friends. Thus, we formulate our second rule to predict offline friendship. Given two online friends A and B on Twitter,

Rule 2. *IF B has more than 1000 followers THEN A and B are not offline friends.*

2.3   Triadic Closure

Triadic closure happens between offline friends because of the increased propinquity and the psychological need for balance between two individuals who share mutual friends [14]. If we assume that a triadic closure in real life translates into a triadic closure online, it is likely that triadic closure happens between offline friends on Twitter. On the other hand, as the pressure towards closure may not be as strong among online friends due to the lack of propinquity, we ask the following research question:

Research Question 3. *Are triadic closures on Twitter as likely to happen among online friends as they are among offline friends?*

We answer the research question by the following logit function:

$$Pr(triadicclosure = 1|I_1, I_2) = F(\beta_0 + \beta_1 I_1 + \beta_2 I_2) \qquad (1)$$

I_1 is 1 if there is 1 offline friendship between any two users in a triad, I_2 is 1 if there are 2 offline friendships between any two users in a triad, and I_1 and I_2 are 0 if there is no offline friendship in a triad. F is the cumulative standard logistic distribution function.

The result shows that when offline friendship does not exist, a triadic closure is unlikely to happen (β_0 -3.36, p-value < 0.0001). When an offline friendship exists, the probability of a triadic closure increases ($\beta_1 = 0.60$, p-value < 0.0001). When two offline friendships exist, the probability increases further ($\beta_2 = 1.41$, p-value < 0.0001). From the result, we expect that when three offline friendships exist in a triad, an online triadic closure is even more likely to happen even though the ground-truth data that we have does not allow us to validate our expectation. In summary, when offline friendships exist in a triad, a triadic closure online is more likely to happen.

From this observation, we formulate the following rule to predict offline friendship. Given A-B-C, an online closed triad on Twitter,

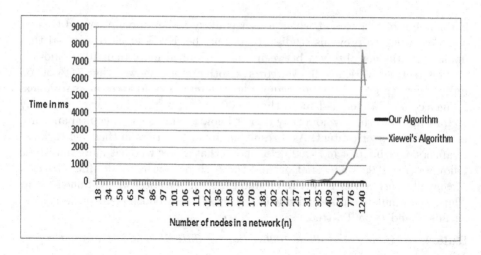

Fig. 3. Milliseconds required to perform prediction

Table 1. Prediction Results

Algorithm		Precision	Recall	F-score
Our algorithm		0.78	0.74	0.76
Machine learning	Logistic regression	0.73	0.52	0.61
	Naive bayes	0.47	0.81	0.60
	Support vector machine	0.78	0.36	0.50
	Artificial neural network	0.72	0.72	0.72
Xiewei's random walk algorithm		0.77	0.88	0.82

Rule 3. *IF A and B are offline friends AND B and C are offline friends, THEN A and C are offline friends.*

3   Practical Application: Predicting Offline Friendship on a Twitter Network

A hands-on practical application from the above observation is the formulation of rules for offline friendship prediction on a Twitter network which we will investigate in this work. We predict a user's offline friends on Twitter based on the three rules we formulate above (Algorithm 1). We compare the results with Xiewei's random walk algorithm and several popular machine learning algorithms. Xiewei's algorithm [17] creates a matrix of a user's ego network and assigns a probability of walk from a user to his Twitter followers that decreases polynomially as a user's number of followers increases. Therefore, a user who has 1000 followers has a lower probability of walk to anyone than a user who has 100 followers. When the probability of walk to a friend is higher than the probability of walk to another friend who has the median number of followers, the friend is regarded as an offline friend. The process is performed iteratively to include offline friends of offline friends as offline friends. For the machine learning algorithms, we extract various features on Twitter as predictors such as tweets LDA-topic similarity, the number of replies, the number of mentions, various centrality measures, follower overlap, followee overlap, the type of following link, etc.

The prediction result is shown in Table 1. Overall, our algorithm performs well and beats the machine learning algorithms. Although its predictive accuracy loses to Xiewei's, our algorithm reduces the time complexity from $O(n^2)$ to $O(n)$ (See Fig. 3).

Data: a Twitter user, u_i
Result: u_i's offline friends, C_i
u_i has a set of friends on Twitter S_i where $S_i = \{f_1, f_2, f_3...\}$;
Let C_i be the set of u_i's offline friends;
for *each friend $f_j \in S_i$* **do**
    Apply *Rule 1*: If u_i and f_j reciprocates on Twitter then $f_j \in C_i$;
    for *each friend $f_j \in C_i$* **do**
        Apply *Rule 2*: If f_j has a number of followers larger than 1000
        then $f_j \notin C_i$
    end
end
Apply *Rule 3*: Offline friends of an offline friend are offline friends;
$temp = \{u_i\}$;
while *temp.size != 0* **do**
    for *each friend $f_j \in C_i$* **do**
        Let S_j be the set of f_j's friends on Twitter where $S_j \subset S_i$;
        Let C_j be the set of f_j's offline friends where $C_j \subset S_i$;
        for *each friend $f_g \in S_j$* **do**
            Apply *Rule 1*: If f_j and f_g reciprocates on Twitter then
            $f_g \in C_j$;
            for *each friend $f_g \in C_j$* **do**
                Apply *Rule 2*: If f_g has a number of followers larger than
                1000 then $f_g \notin C_j$
            end
        end
        $temp = \{temp \cup C_j\}$;
    end
    $temp = temp \setminus \{C_i, u_i\}$;
    $C_i = \{C_i \cup temp\}$;
end

Algorithm 1. Offline friendship prediction

4 Conclusion

We have shown that some of the fundamental principles of social network formation, namely reciprocity, popularity, and triadic closure apply mainly to offline friends on Twitter. The results suggest that using an online social network as a substitute for a real life social network requires careful consideration as the dynamics that apply to the offline social network does not necessarily apply to the online friends in the online social network. We also use the results of our observation to create an efficient algorithm for offline friendship prediction. Future work can be directed to assess the applicability of the algorithm across various social networks in a larger dataset.

Acknowledgment. This research is supported by the Singapore National Research Foundation under its International Research Centre @ Singapore Funding Initiative and administered by the IDM Programme Office, Media Development Authority(MDA). It is also partly supported by Pinnacle Lab at Singapore Management University(SMU).

References

1. Adler, P.A., Kless, S.J., Adler, P.: Socialization to gender roles: popularity among elementary school boys and girls. Sociol. Educ. **65**(3), 169–187 (1992)
2. Barabási, A.-L., Albert, R.: Emergence of scaling in random networks. Science **286**(5439), 509–512 (1999)
3. Boyd, D.M., Ellison, N.B.: Social network sites: definition, history, and scholarship. J. Comput. Mediated Commun. **13**(1), 210–230 (2007)
4. Coie, J.D., Dodge, K.A.: Continuities and changes in children's social status: a five-year longitudinal study. Merrill-Palmer Q. **29**, 261–282 (1983)
5. Ellison, N.B., Steinfield, C., Lampe, C.: The benefits of Facebook friends: social capital and college students use of online social network sites. J. Comput. Mediated Commun. **12**(4), 1143–1168 (2007)
6. Ghosh, S., Viswanath, B., Kooti, F., Sharma, N.K., Korlam, G., Benevenuto, F., Ganguly, N., Gummad, K.P.: Understanding and combating link farming in the twitter social network. In: WWW 2012 Proceedings of the 21st international conference on World Wide Web, pp. 61–70. ACM (2012)
7. Golder, S., Yardi, S.: Structural predictors of tie formation in twitter: transitivity and mutuality. In: 2010 IEEE Second International Conference on Social Computing (SocialCom), pp. 88–95. IEEE (2010)
8. Gouldner, A.W.: The norm of reciprocity: a preliminary statement. Am. Sociol. Rev. **25**(2), 161–178 (1960)
9. Kwak, H., Lee, C., Park, H., Moon, S.: What is twitter, a social network or a news media? In: WWW 2010 Proceedings of the 19th International Conference on World Wide Web, pp. 591–600. ACM (2010)
10. Laursen, B., Hartup, W.W.: The origins of reciprocity and social exchange in friendships. New Dir. Child Adolesc. Dev. **2002**(95), 27–40 (2002)
11. Leskovec, J., Backstrom, L., Kumar, R., Tomkins, A.: Microscopic evolution of social networks. In: KDD 2008 Proceedings of the 14th ACM SIGKDD International Conference on Knowledge Discovery and Data Mining, pp. 462–470. ACM (2008)

12. Newman, M.E.J.: The structure and function of complex networks. Soc. Ind. Appl. Math. (SIAM) Rev. **45**(2), 167–256 (2003)
13. Price, D.D.S.: A general theory of bibliometric and other cumulative advantage processes. J. Am. Soc. Inf. Sci. **27**(5), 292–306 (1976)
14. Schaefer, D.R., Light, J.M., Fabes, R.A., Hanish, L.D., Martin, C.L.: Fundamental principles of network formation among preschool children. Soc. Netw. **32**, 61–71 (2010)
15. Snijders, T.A.B.: The statistical evaluation of social network dynamics. Sociol. Methodol. **31**(1), 361–395 (2001)
16. Snijders, T.A.: Statistical models for social networks. Ann. Rev. Sociol. **37**, 131–153, 469 (2011)
17. Xie, W., Li, C., Zhu, F., Lim, E., Gong, X.: When a friend in twitter is a friend in life. In: WebSci 2012 Proceedings of the 4th Annual ACM Web Science Conference, pp. 344–347. ACM (2012)

Social Ties as Predictors of Economic Development

Buster O. Holzbauer[1]([⊠]), Boleslaw K. Szymanski[1], Tommy Nguyen[1],
and Alex Pentland[2]

[1] Social Cognitive Network Academic Research Center (SCNARC),
Rensselaer Polytechnic Institute, Troy, NY 12180, USA
holzbh@rpi.edu
[2] Massachusetts Institute of Technology, Cambridge, MA 02139, USA

Abstract. A social network is not only a system of connections or relationships, but pathways along which ideas from various communities may
flow. Here we show that the economic development of U.S. states may
be predicted by using quantitative measures of their social tie network
structure derived from location-based social media. We find that long
ties, defined here as ties between people in different states, are strongly
correlated with economic development in the US states from 2009–2012
in terms of GDP, patents, and number of startups. In contrast, within-
state ties are much less predictive of economic development. Our results
suggest that such long ties support innovation by enabling more effective
idea flow.

1 Introduction and Related Work

Studies in economic sociology suggest that peer-to-peer human relationships
affect economic opportunities because information about these opportunities
often spread most effectively between people [7,9,10,15,16,23,24]. Information
spreading via interpersonal relationships is often richer than traditional broad-
cast media such as television, newspaper, radio, etc. because acquaintances can
interact face-to-face, provide relevant information when needed, and influence
one another with respect to adopting new behavior and ideas [22].

It has been argued that information coming from weak ties is often richer
than information arriving via strong ties because "those to whom we are weakly
tied are more likely to move in circles different from our own ... and have access
to information different from what we [usually] receive [16]." Weak ties have been
shown to be valuable sources of information because individuals can use them
to find jobs [7,15], solicit feedback on starting new ventures [24], and search for

Research was partially sponsored by the Army Research Laboratory and was accomplished under Cooperative Agreement Number W911NF-09-2-0053 (the ARL Network Science CTA) and by the Office of Naval Research Contract N00014-15-1-2640.
The content of this paper does not necessarily reflect the position or policy of the U.S.
Government, ARL or ONR, no official endorsement should be inferred or implied.

© Springer International Publishing Switzerland 2016
A. Wierzbicki et al. (Eds.): NetSci-X 2016, LNCS 9564, pp. 178–185, 2016.
DOI: 10.1007/978-3-319-28361-6_15

people like in the small-world experiment [4,17,18,25]. In other settings such as examining workplaces, social network structure can affect productivity and innovation of employees and could lead to higher compensation, more promotion opportunities, and better performance evaluations [9,10,23,24]. Therefore, the effect of weak ties on economic opportunities suggests that perhaps the number and distribution of social ties might also be used for measuring economic development on a larger scale.

Contemporary research on urban characteristics and growth has demonstrated scaling laws for innovation and wealth creation as a power function of the population size as expressed by the equation: $y(t) = cx(t)^m$ where $x(t)$ is the population size and $y(t)$ is the metric of innovation at time t [5,6]. These results show that as the population size increases, GDP, wages, patents, private research employment and development increase at superlinear rates where $1.03 \leq m \leq 1.46$ [6]. Perhaps the best explanation for the superlinear scaling of wealth creation is that as the population size increases, the density of social relationships between people increases because there are more choices for establishing relationships [21]; therefore, increasing the connectivity between people decreases the time for ideas to spread.

Following this line of thinking, recent results in [21] suggest that a generative model for tie formation as a function of social tie density yields somewhat better results than purely descriptive models based only on population size, and in addition offers a simple causal theory of these scaling phenomena. Results obtained under modest assumptions (nodes distributed uniformly on a Euclidean space, connections established following the rank friendship model [18]) show that algorithmically generated social ties based on social tie density can be used to model urban characteristics of cities such as GDP, number of patents, research employment, etc.

Here we extend this line of thinking by focusing on characteristics of economic development as a function of idea flow based on peer-to-peer social relationships and find that "long ties" (defined below) are a main component enabling such flow. This was accomplished by using data containing geographical locations and friendship information of hundreds of thousands of people from location-based social media, namely Gowalla [20]. Also, these datasets allow us to infer face-to-face interactions [19] and measure the strength of ties in terms of not only interactions but also geographical and "administrative" distances (i.e., short or long ties [11,14]).

Other approaches for measuring economic development of large geographical areas include examining the diversity of social contacts (i.e., call detail records as a proxy for social relationships) since more contacts imply more channels for receiving information [13]. Yet using calling patterns to infer social contacts is biased towards those that are more likely to be connected via strong ties since weak ties are by definition those that are used infrequently. While these approaches [13,21] can vary in their methodologies, ranging from mathematically oriented to data-driven, what they share in common is using social network analysis to predict innovation, wealth creation, and other patterns of complex human behavior. In this paper, the novelty of our approach lies at the intersection of economic sociology (i.e., the interplay of long ties and economic opportunities) and simple contagion models (i.e., the spread of ideas from one place to another). Results show that the speed of access to ideas is a strongly correlated with social diversity and also a signature of the economic development of US states without needing to tune parameters or incorporate secondary factors such as the level of educational attainment and internal transportation infrastructure.

2 Data

Our primary focus in this paper is the Gowalla dataset detailed in previous publication [20]. The reasoning behind using Gowalla is that a location-based social network allowed us to analyze both social interactions and geographic interactions separately (through friendships and check-ins respectively). In this paper we considered specifically applying the network towards modeling U.S. GDP [1], patents [3], and small startups (20 or less employees) [2], so we removed any users and corresponding friendship links that were not internal to the United States. This left us with 75,803 users, 464,556 "long ties" (defined as friendships where the two users were in different physical U.S. states), and 222,072 "short ties" (friendships where users were in the same state).

In this paper we do not discuss our model for idea flow, but note that by examining correlations between GDP, patents, startups, and idea flow, we found a near-perfect match between correlations using long ties and simulated idea flow. For this reason, we elected to do the rest of our analysis and discussion here using long ties as a proxy for idea flow. This is advantageous since long ties can be observed directly from the network structure, so there is less uncertainty in the accuracy of analysis based on long ties. For a given state i, we define its census population as P_i, the number of long ties L_i as the number of ties with one end in another state, and the number of short ties (edges) entirely within the state as S_i.

In addition we also considered a community-detection (network clustering) approach, however due to the space limitations and their much lower correlations, we chose to exclude the results based on "bridges" between communities from this paper. The correlations we found for community bridges were very similar to those of the short ties discussed here, though the reasons that both bridges and short ties poorly match our economic metrics of interest may be unrelated. In contrast, idea flow could be formally calculated based on long ties, and this is why we are comfortable claiming that long ties can be used as a simple and accurate substitute for more direct but difficult methods of representing flow of ideas.

3 Methods and Results

The first thing we examined was how indicators P_i, L_i, and S_i correlate with metrics GDP_i, $Patents_i$, and $Startups_i$. The results shown in Table 1 indicate that population is better correlated with the metrics then either type of ties, and short ties correlations are particularly low.

Table 1. Correlations between indicators and economic metrics

Feature	GDP	Patents	Startups
Population	.985	.865	.982
Long ties	.921	.788	.892
Short ties	.692	.531	.599

Such high correlations of total population can arise because either each additional person adds a similar increment to the network of social relationships and idea flow, or their individual cognitive processes are generating innovations independent of their social context. Thus, it is interesting that short ties (within the same state) are relatively less correlated with the metrics, while long ties (between states) have correlations that are significantly stronger.

We therefore examined P_i, L_i, and S_i in the context of distributions over each indicator and computed the probability that state data are drawn from them. Moreover, we looked how this probability changes as we enrich models by adding successively more indicators. For the sake of space we omit here details of the models, but based on a linear model we estimated Gaussian distributions for each economic metric against single variables (P,L,S models), pairs (PL,PS,LS models), and a three-variable model (PLS) using Maximum Likelihood Estimation [12]. This estimation was computed by approximating the likelihood function derivative solution to zero and then following the highest gradient descent to the nearest maximum, so we cannot guarantee that we found the global extrema. The logs of maximum likelihoods of fitting state data by each model are shown in Table 2.

From examining the likelihood ratios, we can find the probability that the two models are not the same via the Likelihood Ratio Test (LRT) [12]. This method works when the compared models are nested (one model's parameters are a

Table 2. MLE of indicators fit to economic metrics

Feature	GDP	Patents	Startups
S	−691.53	−451.31	−667.43
L	−665.86	−435.15	−641.84
LS	−660.96	−434.82	−641.02
P	−632.15	−425.11	−576.98
PS	−632.15	−417.08	−575.24
PL	−609.46	−425.16	−576.62
PLS	−604.33	−417.08	−575.24

subset of the other model's parameters). In this case, a Chi-Square distribution with the degree of freedom equal to the difference in the number of parameters between the models can be used to find confidence level with which we can conclude if the models are different.

For cases where the models are not nested, we instead apply the Akaike information criterion (AIC) [8], in which case we require a difference in AIC of around 3.0-4.0 (depending on the number of parameters), which can be derived from standard log-normal distribution tables. The AIC of the model is defined as $-ln(L) + 2(p + 1)$ where L is the likelihood of fitting the state data with the model and p is its number of parameters, as shown in Table 3.

Table 3. MLE differences for confidence levels using LRT

Confidence level	0.95	0.99	0.999
ΔDegrees of freedom $= 1$	1.92	3.32	5.5
ΔDegrees of freedom $= 2$	3.00	4.61	6.9

Using this methodology, we find that the joint PL model noticeably benefits from information provided by long ties for GDP. The improvement is so significant that it is likely to result from information contributed by the long ties and not captured by the population alone. In contrast, the difference of likelihoods between PS model which includes short ties and population-only P model is not statistically significant for GDP and Startups. The same is true for the LS and L models for Patents and Startups, and since L is statistically significantly better than S model, this means that long ties alone capture all features that make LS superior to the S model. Moreover in all cases of independent variables, long ties alone are significantly better than short ties for all three independent variables. Because of the nearly exact match of long ties and our simulation of idea flow, the same should be true of other measurements of idea flow. As a summary, the list of models for which the differences in likelihoods are not statistically significant is: P and PS models for GDP, L and LS for Patents and Startups, P and PL as well as PS and PLS for Patents and finally P, PS, PL, and PLS for Startups.

4   Discussion

From our observations, it appears that productivity and innovation at the state level within the US are more about connecting different states than bridging across different local communities operating in the same state. When taken together with the fact that idea flow accounts for the super-linear scaling of cities, and that long ties are nearly perfectly correlated with simulations of idea flow across the entire US, these results support the hypothesis that idea flow between states is a major source of state level innovation and productivity.

This conjecture that it is idea flow between separated communities that accounts for state-level economic variations is supported by the significant increase in model matches to data for both GDP and patents that are obtained when network structure is added to population information. The fact that adding long ties to population model increases the probability of the extended model fitness suggests that the correlation between long ties and the economic metrics is due to a different phenomenon than that associated with simple variation in population.

In the Granovetter paper cited earlier, the authors discussed that there are many criteria one can use to define strength of a tie. Even within community detection there are many decisions to be made, for example depending on the algorithm, there may be room for overlapping communities, thresholds that can be changed, or different methods of weighting ties. We find it telling that there is a disparity in the fraction of long ties that are weak and the fraction of short ties that are weak, and believe that this explains why long ties improved our economic predictions more than short ties. It is a particularly attractive idea since it encodes idea flow across borders, which a social network could contribute, but raw population values would not.

It is also important to note that our subject sample were users of Gowalla, both because users of Gowalla must have more than average disposable income in order to be able to possess a smartphone and be innovative enough to embrace technology that was at that time quite new and make use of such a location-based social network. We believe that economic performance such as GDP or having startups is furthered by the advancement and utilization of technology, and so the Gowalla userbase may be a more appropriate sample than the U.S. population as a whole. We do not, of course, believe that the Gowalla population is a representative sample of the entire population, but rather a sample that is well suited to predicting the economic factors we examined.

Communities were still useful as one way to measure strength of ties. While long ties and short ties are not directly analogous to the concept of strong and weak ties, our thought process was that long and short ties might some of the same properties as strong and weak ties. To test this intuition, we ran community detection using GANXiS [26], and defined a pair of users as having a strong tie if they were in the same community, and otherwise we considered the pair to have a weak tie. We summarize information about ties in the Gowalla component that we use in Table 4; clearly, nearly the same fractions of short and long ties are weak and close to the fraction of weak ties among all ties. Since, as we show

Table 4. Summary of geographic ties and strength-based ties

Total short	444144	Total short and weak	308132
Total long	929112	Total long and weak	723900
% of Short ties that are weak	69.38	% of Ties that are weak	75.15
% of Long ties that are weak	77.91	% of Ties that are long	67.86

later, long ties perform better than short ones, we expect that long ties will also outperform weak ties as predictors of economic metrics.

5   Conclusion

GDP, patents, and startups are three economic measurements that can be used to quantify productivity and innovation. By modeling these measurements using location-based social network data, we find that not only do we get a linear relationship with high correlation, but also that the long tie network produces this correlation through different means than the population-only model. While correlation is not causation, there is intuition to support a conjecture that the long tie network features are connections that allow diverse ideas to be shared among individuals. Since ideas may be readily shared among individuals in a particular geographic region due to shared culture and higher probability of regular interaction, long ties are an especially good candidate for measuring the speed of sharing of novel ideas because they connect people acting in separate innovation support infrastructures of different states.

Our results indicate that while we see improvements by combining long ties and population for GDP and patent prediction, we do not see the same behavior for predicting startups. One plausible explanation why startups behave differently is that only a small percentage of startups are innovation-based, while the majority are self-employed individuals providing standard personal services. We plan to verify this hypothesis in future work. In the future we also intend to expand on the other probability distributions we looked at, additional network features and measurements derived from network features, and provide the rigorous mathematical derivations that lead to our parameter estimation and MLE bounding.

References

1. U.S. Bureau of Economic Analysis. http://www.bea.gov/newsreleases/regional/gdp_state/2015/xls/gsp0615.xlsx. Accessed 28 September 2015
2. U.S. Census Bureau, Statistics of U.S. Businesses (SUSB). http://www2.census.gov/econ/susb/data/2012/us_state_totals_2012.xls. Accessed 28 September 2015
3. U.S. patent and trademark office, patent technology monitoring team. http://www.uspto.gov/web/offices/ac/ido/oeip/taf/cst_utl.htm. Accessed 28 September 2015
4. Adamic, L., Adar, E.: How to search a social network. Soc. Netw. **27**(3), 187–203 (2005)
5. Bettencourt, L., West, G.: A unified theory of urban living. Nature **467**(7318), 912–913 (2010)
6. Bettencourt, L.M., Lobo, J., Helbing, D., Kühnert, C., West, G.B.: Growth, innovation, scaling, and the pace of life in cities. Proc. Nat. Acad. Sci. **104**(17), 7301–7306 (2007)
7. Boxman, E.A., De Graaf, P.M., Flap, H.D.: The impact of social and human capital on the income attainment of dutch managers. Soc. Netw. **13**(1), 51–73 (1991)

8. Burnham, K.P., Anderson, D.R.: Model Selection and Inference. Springer, New York (1998)
9. Burt, R.S.: Structural holes and good ideas. Am. J. Sociol. **110**(2), 349–399 (2004)
10. Burt, R.S.: Structural Holes: The Social Structure of Competition. Harvard University Press, Cambridge (2009)
11. Centola, D., Macy, M.: Complex contagions and the weakness of long ties1. Am. J. Sociol. **113**(3), 702–734 (2007)
12. Dempster, A.P., Laird, N.M., Rubin, D.B.: Maximum likelihood from incomplete data via the em algorithm. J. Roy. Stat. Soc.: Ser. B (Methodol.) **39**, 1–38 (1977)
13. Eagle, N., Macy, M., Claxton, R.: Network diversity and economic development. Science **328**(5981), 1029–1031 (2010)
14. Ghasemiesfeh, G., Ebrahimi, R., Gao, J.: Complex contagion and the weakness of long ties in social networks: revisited. In: Proceedings of the Fourteenth ACM Conference on Electronic Commerce, pp. 507–524. ACM (2013)
15. Granovetter, M.: Getting a Job: A Study of Contacts and Careers. University of Chicago Press, Chicago (1995)
16. Granovetter, M.: The impact of social structure on economic outcomes. J. Econ. Perspect. **19**, 33–50 (2005)
17. Kleinberg, J.: The small-world phenomenon: an algorithmic perspective. In: Proceedings of the Thirty-Second Annual ACM Symposium on Theory of Computing, pp. 163–170. ACM (2000)
18. Liben-Nowell, D., Novak, J., Kumar, R., Raghavan, P., Tomkins, A.: Geographic routing in social networks. Proc. Nat. Acad. Sci. U.S.A. **102**(33), 11623–11628 (2005)
19. Nguyen, T., Chen, M., Szymanski, B.K.: Analyzing the proximity and interactions of friends in communities in gowalla. In: 2013 IEEE 13th International Conference on Data Mining Workshops (ICDMW), pp. 1036–1044. IEEE (2013)
20. Nguyen, T., Szymanski, B.K.: Using location-based social networks to validate human mobility and relationships models. In: 2012 IEEE/ACM International Conference on Advances in Social Networks Analysis and Mining (ASONAM), pp. 1215–1221. IEEE (2012)
21. Pan, W., Ghoshal, G., Krumme, C., Cebrian, M., Pentland, A.: Urban characteristics attributable to density-driven tie formation. Nat. Commun. **4** (2013). http://www.nature.com/ncomms/2013/130604/ncomms2961/full/ncomms2961.html
22. Pentland, A.: Social Physics: How Good Ideas Spread-The Lessons From A New Science. Penguin Press, Harmondsworth (2014)
23. Reagans, R., Zuckerman, E.W.: Networks, diversity, and productivity: the social capital of corporate r&d teams. Organ. Sci. **12**(4), 502–517 (2001)
24. Ruef, M.: Strong ties, weak ties and islands: structural and cultural predictors of organizational innovation. Ind. Corp. Change **11**(3), 427–449 (2002)
25. Watts, D.J., Dodds, P.S., Newman, M.E.: Identity and search in social networks. Science **296**(5571), 1302–1305 (2002)
26. Xie, J., Szymanski, B.: Labelrank: a stabilized label propagation algorithm for community detection in networks. In: 2013 IEEE 2nd Proceedings of Network Science Workshop (NSW), pp. 138–143, April 2013

Large Scale Graph Representations
for Subgraph Census

Pedro Paredes[(⊠)] and Pedro Ribeiro

CRACS & INESC-TEC DCC-FCUP, Universidade Do Porto, Porto, Portugal
{pparedes,pribeiro}@dcc.fc.up.pt

Abstract. A Subgraph Census (determining the frequency of smaller
subgraphs in a network) is an important computational task at the heart
of several graph mining algorithms. Here we focus on the g-tries, an efficient state-of-the art data structure. Its algorithm makes extensive use
of the graph primitive that checks if a certain edge exists. The original
implementation used adjacency matrices in order to make this operation
as fast as possible, as is the case with most past approaches. This representation is very expensive in memory usage, limiting the applicability.
In this paper we study a number of possible approaches that scale lin-
early with the number of edges. We make an extensive empirical study
of these alternatives in order to find an efficient hybrid approach that
combines the best representations. We achieve a performance that is less
than 50 % slower than the adjacency matrix on average (almost 3 times
more efficient than a naive binary search implementation), while being
memory efficient and tunable for different memory restrictions.

Keywords: Complex networks · Motifs · Large scale graphs · G-tries

1 Introduction

The use of complex networks to model real-life systems and problems has been
more than established in the past few years. To characterize and compare these
networks, numerous metrics have been proposed and studied. One important
example are network motifs [10]. These are over-represented substructures of a
network, that is, subgraphs that appear in a higher number than expected in
random networks with similar topological traits. Network motif analysis has been
successfully applied in several domains such as brain networks [17] or protein-
protein interactions [1].

To perform a network motif analysis, one needs to compute one or potentially more subgraph census. A subgraph census is an operation that finds the
frequencies of all or a subset of subgraphs of a network. This is a computationally hard task since it is related to the subgraph isomorphism problem, a
known NP-Complete problem [3] and consequently the main bottleneck in the
calculation of network motifs and similar metrics.

In this paper we address a more specific question, namely large scale representations of networks that can be quickly queried for information by subgraph

© Springer International Publishing Switzerland 2016
A. Wierzbicki et al. (Eds.): NetSci-X 2016, LNCS 9564, pp. 186–194, 2016.
DOI: 10.1007/978-3-319-28361-6_16

census algorithms. We will expand on a previous work of ours, specifically the g-tries [15] in order to study the effect of different representations.

The remainder of the paper is organized as follows. In Sect. 2 we discuss the problem the paper addresses and also briefly go through some of the existing techniques that tackle the problem. Section 3 describes the g-trie data structure and its subgraph counting algorithm. Section 4 starts by describing our definition of large scale in this context, we then pinpoint the bottleneck primitives of the representation, followed by presenting several possible alternatives and concludes with a discussion of different optimizations. We follow this with Sect. 5 by presenting the detailed experimental analysis. Finally, we close with Sect. 6.

2   Preliminaries

2.1   Problem Definition

The base problem we are addressing in this paper is the Subgraph Census Problem (also known as Subgraph Counting Problem). Here we define it precisely.

Definition 1. *Given an integer k and a graph G, determine the frequency of a set S of connected induced k-subgraphs of G. Two occurrences of a subgraph are considered different if they have at least one node that they do not share.*

Where a k-subgraph is a subgraph with k vertices and a subgraph is said to be *induced* when all vertices connected on the original graph are also connected on the subgraph and vice-versa.

Our goal is to find an efficient scalable graph representation that is applicable to large scale networks, in order to increase the applicability of Subgraph Census algorithms to larger networks. We note that it is important that the representation is efficient in the context of Subgraph Census algorithms, which means that we are not concerned with the complexity or efficiency of any one operation in a particular graph, but the full weight it induces on the subgraph census algorithm execution.

Finally, another important aspect to note is that our representation is static, besides some pre computing, it is not necessary to account for insertion or removal of edges or vertices.

2.2   Current Work on Subgraph Census

As far as we know, there are no current works on large scale representations for subgraph census algorithms. Some papers describing established approaches briefly mention this issue, but none goes into detail or performs any studies on different representations. Thus in this subsection we briefly present some of the previous works on the area.

Previous approaches range in the way they tackle the problem. Methods like FaSE [13] and QuateXelero [7] aim at enumerating and classifying all subgraph occurrences. The work by Grochow and Kellis [6], on the other hand, computes a single subgraph frequency. Finally, g-tries [15], the work we focus on, determines the frequency of a set of subgraphs.

3   G-Trie Based Subgraph Census

3.1   The G-Trie Data Structure

The g-trie data structure is an application of the concept of prefix-trees to graphs. By identifying common topologies and substructures, a g-trie represents a set of graphs, much like a classic string prefix-tree does with string prefixes. It is a multiway tree where each node represents a single subgraph and each descendant node represents a node that shares a common topology with its parent.

The goal of the g-trie data structure is to efficiently compress a set of subgraphs in order to guide the enumeration to only consider the given subgraphs.

An important issue is the symmetries exhibited by the subgraphs, caused by automorphisms, which could lead to redundant paths and repeated occurrence finding. To solve this problem, symmetry breaking conditions of the form $X < Y$ (where X and Y are labels of two vertices) are inserted in order to only consider each symmetry once. Due to space constraints, we direct the reader to works like [15] that further explain these topics.

3.2   Subgraph Counting with G-Tries

Algorithm 1 details how to use an already built g-trie to count subgraphs. It uses the information stored in the g-trie to guide the search by constraining it. Initially all vertices are considered potential occurrences, since they all match the g-trie root. Afterwards, all vertices that match the current g-trie node are found and for each of them, if we are at a g-trie leaf (which means we have just found an occurrence of a desired subgraph) we increment its frequency, otherwise

---

Algorithm 1. The g-trie subgraph counting algorithm

Input: A graph G and a set of subgraphs S (described by a g-trie T)
Result: Frequencies of all elements of S

```
1:  procedure COUNTALL(T, G)
2:      for all vertex v in G do
3:          for all children c in T.root do
4:              Count(c, {v})
5:  procedure COUNT(T, V_used)
6:      V ← MatchVertices(T, V_used)
7:      for all vertex v in V do
8:          if T.isLeaf then
9:              T.frequency += 1
10:         else
11:             for all children c in T do
12:                 Count(c, V_used ∪ {v})
13: procedure MATCHVERTICES(T, V_used)
14:     V_conn ← vertices in V_used connected to the vertex being added
15:     m ← vertex of V_conn with smallest neighborhood
16:     V_cand ← neighbors of m that respect connections to ancestors
                   and symmetry breaking conditions
17:     return V_cand
```

---

we continue recursively to match the next g-trie node. Again, we refer to [15] for more information.

4   Graph Representations

4.1   Large Scale Representations

In the context of this paper, we define a large scale representation as a representation which has a memory usage that scales with the number of edges or the number of nodes of the network. This forbids classic representations like adjacency matrices that, as we shall see in the next subsection, allow for more efficient primitives required by the base algorithm.

The reason for this restriction is based on the applicability of Subgraph Census algorithms. All of the state of the art algorithms have a complexity that is super exponential, which is based on the natural combinatoric explosion of the number of subgraphs, even of the smallest sizes, as the networks grow larger. Thus, for most networks with a number of nodes in the order of 100 thousand, the calculations start to last several hours or days, even for a $k = 3$ computation. These numbers are based on the results obtained by several established algorithms like [7,13,15], which are omitted for briefness.

Also, with the development of different techniques, like efficient parallel algorithms [11] or approximated algorithms [14], it is possible to increase the applicability and run calculations on networks with up to a million or 10 million nodes in feasible time.

4.2   Role of Edge Verification

Having described the base algorithm, it is possible to observe that the main primitive the graph representation needs to handle is determining if two given nodes are connected, which is needed in order to do match the partially enumerated subgraph with the current g-trie node.

This operation is obvious if we have an adjacency matrix, but since the goal of this paper is to be able to scale to larger networks, that is not feasible. So a representation like an adjacency list is required. However, the question then arises: how much weight does this operation have on the full computation?

To answer it, we performed a series of tests. We first profiled the original g-tries code from [15] and ran it with some datasets described in Sect. 5. The results showed that on average the percentage of time spent in the edge verification primitive is between 30 % to 40 % of the total runtime, thus they showed it has a relevant weight.

However, the previous results did not exclude the possibility that a naive approach would only have negligible effect. Thus we ran the original code against a modified code that used an adjacency list with sorted lists in order to perform simple binary searches. The results obtained showed that a naive representation can be much slower than the base adjacency matrix one, ranging from a factor of 3 to 4.5 slowdown. This can be further observed in the results of Sect. 5.

4.3   Proposed Representations

We describe a set of possible representations that we study and compare on different data sets. The goal of each method is to perform an operation of checking if two nodes are connected. The following list details all the studied representations and labels them with simple three letter names (like BNS). These labels will be used in further discussions and on the results section. All of these methods are built on top of an augmented simple adjacency list representation. We denote the set of edges as E and the set of nodes as V.

Binary Search [BNS]. The classic divide and conquer approach to finding elements in sets ($\mathcal{O}(\log |V|)$). It requires the neighbor list of each node to be sorted in the pre computation step.

Hash Table Node Based [HSN]. Each node has a simple hash table with size $\frac{|E|}{|V|}$, where the hash table is simply the *mod* of its size ($\mathcal{O}(1)$). To sort out collisions it uses a simple linked list. Requires a pre computation step of creating and filling the hash tables.

Hash Table Edge Based [HSE]. A different hash table setup where each node has a hash table of a constant number times its original neighbor list size ($\mathcal{O}(1)$). The constant used in the implementation was 2.5, where this value was fined tuned after several manual experiments in order to balance time and memory efficiency.

Trie [TRI]. A prefix-tree of digits of the individual elements of the original adjacency list ($\mathcal{O}(\log |V|)$). Requires a pre computation step of creating the prefix-tree.

Hybrid [HBR]. A hybrid approach that combines three of the previously mentioned approaches to apply them in the best possible way. For an adjacency list of size less than 2, a simple linear search is used; for the $\frac{|E|}{|V|}$ nodes with highest degree, a line from the adjacency matrix is stored; finally for the rest, the edge based hash table method is used. It requires the pre computation of the hash table.

4.4   Optimizations

To complement the methods described in the previous subsection, several optimizations where tried, some with success and others without.

Based on the tests performed in the beginning of this section and on some of the results of Sect. 5, it is noticeable that small changes in one method lead to a large impact on the overall run time. For example, if one method only requires doing a couple of sums, but another has to perform one or two division operations, the latter is usually a lot slower. This is due to the large number of times the primitive of edge verification is called.

Thus, in all methods (like HSN, HSE and TRI) where an operation of a mod b (where a, b are arbitrary integers) was required, instead the closest power of two of b was determined, that is $\min(p : 2^p \geq b)$, and the modular operation was

Table 1. Datasets used in the experiments

Network	Directed	Nodes	Edges	Avg. Degree	Type	Source
Jazz	No	198	2,742	13.85	Social	Arenas [5]
Facebook	No	4,039	88,234	21.85	Social	SNAP [9]
Wordnet	No	146,005	656,999	9.00	Semantic	KONECT [4]
Enron	No	36,692	367,662	10.02	Social	SNAP [8]
Foldoc	Yes	13,356	120,700	9.04	Semantic	Pajek [2]
Metabolic	Yes	453	2,025	4.47	Biological	Arenas [5]
Flights	Yes	2,939	30,501	20.76	Geometric	KONECT [12]
Epinions	Yes	75,879	508,837	13.41	Social	KONECT [16]

performed as a more efficient `bitwise and` operation (`&`in C++) with $2^p - 1$ (which is equivalent to a a mod $(2^p - 1)$ operation).

Additionally, we also experimented with a simple node cache, which stored the most recent queries per node, and different data structures, like a bloom filter and a quotient filter. The former had some improvements on specific cases, but we failed to tune the latter in order to have satisfactory results.

5 Experimental Results

We now turn to the experimental evaluation. We implemented [1] these approaches in C++ on top of the already existing code of the g-tries [15]. We ran all tests on a Linux machine with an AMD Opteron 6376 (2.3GHz) and 4GB of memory.

In order to compare with the adjacency matrix approach (which we will denote as AMT in a similar fashion to what was done in the previous section), we ran our implementations on data sets feasible for that approach. We list the data sets used in Table 1. Note that we included a wide range of networks, directed and undirected, ranging from social to biological to geographic networks in source, with different orders of magnitude. This is important to establish the generalness of the results.

We started by testing all the methods on all the data sets. Table 2 lists these results. The highlighted cells indicate the fastest time for each dataset.

Note first that there is a lot of fluctuation in the relative results between the various methods, for example, the BNS is mostly outperformed by HSN, but it outperformed it in one case, the same happens with TRI and HSN. This indicates that different types of graphs prefer different representations, which means there is space for hybrid methods to use the best methods for different graph sources.

The most important conclusion to take from Table 2 is that HSE and HBR consistently outperform the rest. The HBR seems to capture the best of HSE since

---

[1] Available at https://github.com/ComplexNetworks-DCC-FCUP/gtrieScanner/tree/DynamicGraph.

Table 2. Detailed experimental results for the 8 datasets used (times in seconds)

Method (k)	Jazz (6)	Facebook (4)	Wordnet (4)	Enron (4)	Foldoc (4)	Metabolic (5)	Flights (4)	Epinions (3)
AMT	198.03	68.39	-	-	28.12	21.20	20.74	-
BNS	1,129.39	320.08	767.09	1,034.71	88.40	107.02	109.25	36.51
HSN	488.22	159.46	522.81	877.59	65.67	80.77	63.88	50.09
TRI	691.49	223.43	658.89	749.46	65.19	60.91	54.45	28.19
HSE	461.08	135.14	**438.78**	**557.50**	51.39	49.98	43.91	**18.58**
HBR	**289.31**	**125.83**	480.83	586.49	**50.67**	**45.80**	**39.34**	20.77

(-) For these networks the adjacency matrix method requires too much memory

Table 3. Experimental results for the final implementation (times in seconds)

Method (k)	Jazz (6)	Facebook (4)	Wordnet (4)	Enron (4)	Foldoc (4)	Metabolic (5)	Flights (4)	Epinions (3)
AMT	198.03	68.39	-	-	28.12	21.20	20.74	-
Runtime	235.02	102.33	397.68	495.56	35.02	30.19	27.78	15.76
Slow down	1.19	1.50	-	-	1.25	1.42	1.34	-

(-) For these networks the adjacency matrix method requires too much memory

it has similar results for most networks, outperforming it on most, indicating that there are some graph types where bypassing the hash map pays off.

Overall, we seem to achieve a method that ranges from almost one to two times slower than the base AMT method. Further tests indicate that reducing the constant for HSE (saving more memory) can yield similar results in most networks (due to cache and similar effects, using more memory does not yield a linear time benefit, it has more of a threshold effect).

We conclude this section by trying to select the best possible approach. Our results and analysis clearly show that the HBR[2] worked the best on our datasets. Intuitively, this makes sense since it only uses very light operations and can mimic fairly well the behavior of an adjacency matrix. We stripped the previous implementation of all other methods and kept only HBR and ran it with the same datasets. These results are described in Table 3 and show a slow down factor improvement from about 4 of the initial naive binary search, to a factor of less than 1.5 on average.

6   Conclusion

In this paper we studied a number of alternative graph representations that scale with the number of edges or the number of nodes of the network memory-wise, in order to extend the applicability of current algorithms to larger networks. The goal was to find an efficient representation to be used by subgraph census algorithms, more specifically, our study was tailored to a previous work of ours, a state-of-the-art data structure called g-tries.

---

[2] Available at https://github.com/ComplexNetworks-DCC-FCUP/gtrieScanner/tree/finalGraph.

We studied different methods with several optimizations and additional improvement strategies. In the end, they converged in a hybrid method that tries to apply some of the best methods in their preferred situations. The described method is easily tuned to be used with different memory restricted environments. In the end, it improved the slow down factor of the naive binary search method in relation to the adjacency matrix from 4 to around 1.5.

This work did not have any parallel considerations, but a possible further work would be to do this type of analysis in parallel versions of the subgraph census algorithms, considering different effects that can harm the computation (like cache hierarchies) and even distributing the graph by different machines. Another different progression would be applying the methods to different datasets and obtaining relevant results on those.

Acknowledgements. This work is partially funded by FCT, within project UID/EEA/50014/2013.

References

1. Albert, I., Albert, R.: Conserved network motifs allow protein-protein interaction prediction. Bioinformatics **20**(18), 3346–3352 (2004)
2. Batagelj, V., Mrvar, A.: Pajek datasets (2006). http://vlado.fmf.uni-lj.si/pub/networks/data/
3. Cook, S.A.: The complexity of theorem-proving procedures. In: ACM Symposium on Theory of computing STOC, pp. 151–158. ACM, New York, USA (1971)
4. Fellbaum, C.: WordNet. Wiley Online Library (1998)
5. Gleiser, P.M., Danon, L.: Community structure in jazz. Adv. Complex Syst. **06**(04), 565–573 (2003)
6. Grochow, J.A., Kellis, M.: Network motif discovery using subgraph enumeration and symmetry-breaking. In: Speed, T., Huang, H. (eds.) RECOMB 2007. LNCS (LNBI), vol. 4453, pp. 92–106. Springer, Heidelberg (2007)
7. Khakabimamaghani, S., Sharafuddin, I., Dichter, N., Koch, I., Masoudi-Nejad, A.: Quatexelero: an accelerated exact network motif detection algorithm. PLoS ONE **8**(7), e68073 (2013)
8. Klimt, B., Yang, Y.: Introducing the enron corpus. In: CEAS (2004)
9. Leskovec, J., Mcauley, J.J.: Learning to discover social circles in ego networks. In: Advances in Neural Information Processing Systems, pp. 539–547 (2012)
10. Milo, R., Shen-Orr, S., Itzkovitz, S., Kashtan, N., Chklovskii, D., Alon, U.: Network motifs: simple building blocks of complex networks. Science **298**(5594), 824–827 (2002)
11. Oliveira Aparicio, D., Pinto Ribeiro, P.M., Da Silva, F.M.A.: Parallel subgraph counting for multicore architectures. In: 2014 IEEE International Symposium on Parallel and Distributed Processing with Applications (ISPA), pp. 34–41. IEEE (2014)
12. Opsahl, T., Agneessens, F., Skvoretz, J.: Node centrality in weighted networks: Generalizing degree and shortest paths. Soc. Netw. **32**(3), 245–251 (2010)
13. Paredes, P., Ribeiro, P.: Towards a faster network-centric subgraph census. In: 2013 IEEE/ACM International Conference on Advances in Social Networks Analysis and Mining (ASONAM), pp. 264–271. IEEE (2013)

14. Ribeiro, P., Silva, F.: Efficient subgraph frequency estimation with G-tries. In: Moulton, V., Singh, M. (eds.) WABI 2010. LNCS, vol. 6293, pp. 238–249. Springer, Heidelberg (2010)
15. Ribeiro, P., Silva, F.: G-tries: a data structure for storing and finding subgraphs. Data Min. Knowl. Disc. **28**(2), 337–377 (2014)
16. Richardson, M., Agrawal, R., Domingos, P.: Trust management for the semantic web. In: Fensel, D., Sycara, K., Mylopoulos, J. (eds.) ISWC 2003. LNCS, vol. 2870, pp. 351–368. Springer, Heidelberg (2003)
17. Sporns, O., Kötter, R.: Motifs in brain networks. PLoS Biol. **2**(11), e369 (2004)

An Exploration of Fetish Social Networks and Communities

Damien Fay[1,2,3,4,5]([⊠]), Hamed Haddadi[1,2,3,4,5], Michael C. Seto[1,2,3,4,5],
Han Wang[1,2,3,4,5], and Christoph Kling[1,2,3,4,5]

[1] Department of Computing, Bournemouth, UK
dfay@bournemouth.ac.uk
[2] School of Electronic Engineering and Computer Science,
Queen Mary University, London, UK
[3] The Royal's Institute of Mental Health Research, Ottawa, Canada
[4] National University of Ireland, Galway, Ireland
[5] GESIS - Leibniz Institute for the Social Sciences, Cologne, Germany

Abstract. Online Social Networks (OSNs) provide a venue for virtual interactions and relationships between individuals. In some communities, OSNs also facilitate arranging offline meetings and relationships. FetLife, the world's largest anonymous social network for the BDSM, fetish and kink communities, provides a unique example of an OSN that serves as an interaction space, community organizing tool, and sexual market. In this paper, we present a first look at the characteristics of European members of Fetlife, comprising 504,416 individual nodes with 1,912,196 connections. We looked at user characteristics in terms of gender, sexual orientation, and preferred role. We further examined the homophilic communities and find that women in particular are far more platonically involved on the site than straight males. Our results suggest there are important differences between the FetLife community and conventional OSNs.

Keywords: Social network properties · Sexuality · Topic modelling

1 Introduction

Social interaction is motivated at the individual level in need for power, prestige and approval [22] which are expressed in modern life in activities such as business, friendship/emotional learning exchange, and knowledge exchange; and from an evolutionary perspective the need to seek a mate. This latter function of a social network is known as the *sexual market* and every social network has a secondary function as a sexual market, although disaggregating this function from others can be challenging [12]. In the last decade, Online Social Networks (OSNs) have become a focal point of the web and the most popular activity of individuals online. There are a large number of popular OSNs and a large body of research focuses on a variety of OSNs. Despite a large number of papers on analysis of large scale OSNs [2,14], and a large number of social science papers

© Springer International Publishing Switzerland 2016
A. Wierzbicki et al. (Eds.): NetSci-X 2016, LNCS 9564, pp. 195–204, 2016.
DOI: 10.1007/978-3-319-28361-6_17

on social relationships, sexuality and orientations [10,15], there have not been any academic papers which have examined online social networks focused on variations in sexual orientations and interests.

In this paper, we take a first look at the anonymised profiles of the European users of the most popular fetish website, and ask if the characteristics of the network are different from those of a conventional OSN. This is a rich dataset of over half a million users and captures patterns of traditionally secret interests and behaviours. We choose this online fetish network as it is oriented towards friendships, social groups, and arranging events, where the social is primary and sexual market is secondary but explicitly included (unlike, say, Facebook or other non-dating OSNs). It is important to social scientists and psychologists to understand whether a social network is also present or not required. As FetLife reveals sexuality in a social context it allows us to understand sexual networks in a way that dating sites such as Tinder, Grindr etc. might not allow; this is also vital for creating models for the spread of sexually transmitted infections [17].

We use our large dataset to assess the properties of these multi-relationship networks, where a user can have a number of different types of relationships with others.[1] Understanding the nature of the interactions is also important for real and cyber crime investigations, as the privacy and safety of users could also be compromised by malicious users of such websites.[2]

2   Online Fetish Networks

We collected our data from FetLife,[3] the most popular Social Network for the BDSM, Fetish, and kink communities, with millions of users worldwide. The fetish community has grown rapidly in recent years and now consists of a diverse collection of people whose interests cover a broad spectrum including, fashion, burlesque, a nightclub scene, particular types of music and of course a focus on sexual experimentation. As in Facebook, the interaction of the community is both real-world and virtual with a large collection of real-world events attended by members; contrary to expectations, FetLife it is not a paid dating website. For example, there is no "search" functionality within the website for specific types of members. However, the site is used for social events, workshops, and parties which are organised regionally. Members create a personal profile, similar to most OSNs, specify their gender, age, role, orientation, and list the fetishes they are interested in or are curious about. The users are organised into tens of thousands of groups, and thousands of events are arranged annually through the website. Users pay particular attention to the experience of the group members and event organisers and hence these individuals play a central role in the community. In essence, FetLife is a niche OSN. BDSM is a sexual interest or subculture attractive to a minority [18]. What makes FetLife unique particularly interesting

---

[1] In the interest of space and scientific focus, we encourage the readers to see [13,16] for a description of different types of fetish relationships.

[2] http://sexandthe405.com/fetlife-is-not-safe-for-users/.

[3] https://fetlife.com/.

for OSN analysts is that this website observes sexual interaction (present in dating websites, absent in typical social networks such as Facebook) but in the presence of a social context (absent in dating websites).

We collected our data from the European members of FetLife during the early months of 2014. The data includes anonymized (at the time of collection) user IDs, relationship types, and number of friends. In order to comply with the website policy and ethics approval requirements, we did not crawl any names, details of friends, pictures, posts, or other personally identifiable information available on the site. Overall, there are 506 K individual nodes in our dataset, with 1.9 M connections. The main connected component is comprised of just over 156 K nodes, and the rest of the users are mainly isolated or small groups of maximum size 20. Although this is a sample of the population and only captures the individuals who chose to be on a fetish OSN, this data is more inclusive and less biased than the offline club members or those who self-identify for sample surveys in existing literature [4,18]. The perceived anonymity online and low (essentially zero) cost of entry into Fetlife means more individuals might be active online than joining actual clubs, going to local BDSM themed parties or self-identifying to researchers at universities.

3   Demographic Analysis

In this section we document the demographics of the fetish network such as gender, sexual preference, and connections. The identity acronyms are defined as follows: M = cis male; F = cis female; TV = transvestite; TS = transsexual, which can be further distinguished into male-to-female transsexuals (MtF or trans females) and female-to-male transsexuals (FtM or trans males); Kajira/Kajiru are slave girl/boy; I = intersex, B = butch, Fem = Femme. If not otherwise stated, Trans = trans females and TVs. GF = gender fluid and GQ = gender queer, referring to persons who do not identify as male or female or see themselves as having aspects of both genders. We first look at the gender demographics of the users as a whole. As mentioned previously, there are larger number of users with no friends than would otherwise be expected. Figure 1 shows the distribution of user gender for all users. When the singletons have been removed, the gender distribution changes drastically; most of those with few or no friends are male (Fig. 3 shows that in addition they tend to be heterosexual males). When we have taken out those with fewer than 5 friends then the gender distribution is quite even with (cis) 54 % male, 40.5 % female and other (non-cis) genders making up the remainder. Figure 2 diagrammatically is a graph indicative of the potential partners of different genders taking orientations into account. The graph is quite complicated with heterosexual relationships being reciprocal, gay relationships being homophilic (manifesting as graph loops), several unidirectional links (ex: a lesbian may consider a straight girl as a potential partner but this may not be reciprocated). In essence the sexual market which presents itself is neither bipartite nor undirected and so defies OSN analysis such as that in [11]. In Table 1 we examine the congruence of users with respect to gender and orientation. The network congruence is defined in [20] as the probability of one's friends having the same attributes or related attributes. That is, we wish to ask if people of a particular gender and orientation have preference for another gender. The results here show a strong preference in accordance with the graph shown in Fig. 2. For example, gay men have on average 32 % of their friends composed of gay men, far exceeding the population average of 1.5 %. A straight female will have 57 % of her friends as straight males, higher than the population average (39 %), slightly higher than the bisexual female average (53.4 %) and significantly higher than the gay female average (42 %). Overall the platonic relationships (in blue) are mostly lower than the population averages (exceptions are gay females who have a slightly higher than population average friendship with straight males; and gay trans to gay females). For straight females 73 % of their friends are straight/bisexual males. For straight males, 61.2 % of their friends are (straight/bisexual) females. This would strongly suggest a sexual market (for hetero- and bi-sexual people) as it implies not only a bias towards the opposite sex but also competition (see [1] for an excellent discussion). It implies that a male is less likely to be friends with the *male friends of his female friends* than he would with a person from the population as a whole. That is, there would appear to be evidence of competition between males (and vice versa; also between females). This behaviour online complements existing research in the literature that shows atypical sexual interests are more common in men than in women [4].

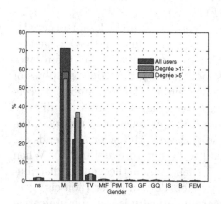

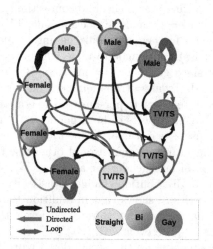

Fig. 1. Distribution of genders for all users, users with >1 friends, and >5 friends.

Fig. 2. Graph of potential partners. Note that some links are directed, and the graph is not complete.

We compared our results with that of Pokec, a large European OSN of over 1.6 million subscribers with gender specifications [21]. In Pokec, male members

Table 1. Congruency of gender and orientation: $\{Male, Female, Trans\}$ × $\{Straight, Bisexual, Gay\}$. Potential partners in black, platonic in grey, and conventional partners in **bold**.

	M-S	M-Bi	M-G	F-S	F-Bi	F-G	Tr-S	Tr-Bi	Tr-G
M-S	27.1	7.1	0.7	**17.1**	44.1	1.5	0.3	1.9	0.3
M-Bi	26.8	12.9	3.0	12.7	36.4	1.4	0.6	5.6	0.6
M-G	23.8	27.6	**32.9**	2.7	8.4	0.8	0.2	3.1	0.5
F-S	**57.0**	16.3	0.4	6.5	14.9	0.9	0.6	3.2	0.3
F-Bi	53.4	16.8	0.4	5.4	18.7	1.4	0.5	3.1	0.3
F-G	42.9	12.9	0.8	6.2	26.8	**6.1**	0.5	3.0	0.8
Tr-S	25.6	12.2	0.6	9.4	22.8	1.1	3.5	22.9	1.8
Tr-Bi	23.9	15.7	1.0	7.0	18.7	0.9	3.0	27.6	2.3
Tr-G	29.9	16.1	1.5	5.8	17.8	2.3	2.2	21.4	**3.0**
All	39.1	13.2	1.5	10.3	28.8	1.4	0.6	4.7	0.5

are 49 % and 51 % likely to connect to males and females respectively, (55 % and 45 % for females). This is a rather balanced ratio and in a rather significant contrast with the fetish network's data which has a strong bias towards the opposite sex, further supporting the sexual market social network hypotheses. It is worth noting that, although men are more active users of cybersex channels, significantly more women than men state that their online sexual activities had led to real-life sexual encounters [19]. For the TV, MtF, FtM, and TG users there appears to be a strong preference towards friends of the same gender. For example, a TV will tend to have 29.5 % friends, far above the population average of 4.7 %. However, it is interesting to note that while there is a strong bias towards people of the same gender the majority of friends still come from other genders; there is no evidence to support the idea of closed minority gender communities. Figure 3 shows the distribution of sexual orientations of users. Of the users, 45 % describe themselves as heterosexual while less than 5 % describe themselves as exclusively gay or lesbian. Large survey-based studies show that BDSM activities are more common among non-heterosexual individuals (gay, lesbian or bisexual) [18].

For comparison we examined the fetish network structure with those of standard OSNs (YouTube, Flickr, LiveJournal and Orkut) following the analysis, and using results, of [14]. We then look into more complex measures such as the average path length, Joint Degree Distribution (JDD, a measure of connectivity of one's neighbours), clustering coefficient (measure of density of triangular ties between adjacent nodes), and assortativity, which indicate the relations between the nodes on a local basis. We also explore the hierarchical structure of the network using k-cores and Kernel density estimation.[4] The degree distribution is unremarkable except that there is a larger than expected number of users with

---

[4] A complete explanation of the theoretical definitions and implications of these measures is available in [7,9].

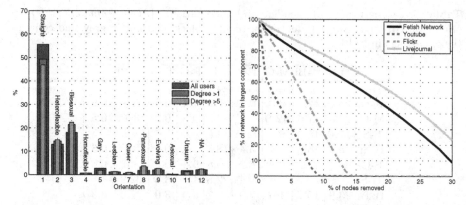

Fig. 3. Distribution of orientations for all users, users with >1 friends, and >5 friends.

Fig. 4. Percentage of main component remaining after removal of the highest degree users.

Table 2. Network measures from the fetish and ordinary OSNs.

	α	Avg path length	Radius— Diameter	Assortativity	Scale free metric	Clustering coefficient
Fetish	2.98	4.05	7—11	−0.01	0.0031	0.15
Flickr	1.74	5.67	13—27	0.202	0.49	0.313
Livejournal	1.59	5.88	12—20	0.179	0.34	0.330
Orkut	1.50	4.25	6—9	0.072	0.36	0.171
Youtube	1.63	5.10	13—21	−0.033	0.19	0.136
Web	2.57	16.12	475—905	−0.067	−	0.081

low degree. These are removed when we examine the main component of the graph (as previously mentioned these users would appear to be *lurkers*; mostly heterosexual males who do not participate in the social network). Finally, Table 2 gives a summary of common network measures.[5] The main conclusion is that FetLife has a very similar structure to most OSN's.

Figure 4 shows the k-core of removal rate and that the network is highly resilient to removal of high degree nodes. In fact we could remove the top 10 % of the nodes and only lose 30 % off the largest connected component. This indicates that the network consists of lots of small connections between people ignoring the core. The large number of small groups and local clusters, as opposed to large inter-mixed nodes, is the main reason behind this effect, which has also recently been observed in the Internet topology [8]. In FetLife, the events and connections are centred around local events, meetings, and workshops. Although a direct search function is not available, many users of the website use the network as

---

[5] We assume that the reader is familiar with standard network measures (a good overview may be found in [6,7,9]).

a portal to bootstrap their fetish sex life. Hence the *global* connectivity is not as important as traditional OSNs such as Twitter and Facebook, and far from *content*-centric OSNs such as Flickr and YouTube.

4   Homophilic Community Detection

From the analysis above (Table 1 in particular) we see a network where there are connections for many reasons. Some connections are created for sexual attraction, others are purely social. Within the sexual attractions there is homophilic and heterophilic factors and in addition there are heterophilic sexual connections to do with a persons role (a dominant person would in particular like a submissive person). It is possible to detect and separate homophilic communities from heterophilic communities to gain insights into the nature of homophilic relations in the network while factoring out heterophilic relations. Homophilic community detection is a complicated task requiring not just knowledge of the links in the network but also the attributes associated with those links. A recent paper by Yang et al. [23] proposed the CESNA model (Community Detection in Networks with Node Attributes). This model is generative and based on the assumption that a link is created between two users if they share membership of a particular community. Users within a community share similar attributes. Therefore, the model is able to extract homophilic communities from the link network. Vertices may be members of several *independent* communities such that the probability of creating an edge is 1 minus the probability that no edge is created in any of their common communities:

$$P_{u \to v} = 1 - \prod_{c \in C} \exp(-F_{uc} \cdot F_{vc}) \tag{1}$$

where F_{uc} is the potential of vertex u to community c and C is the set of all communities. In addition, it assumed that the attributes of a vertex are also generated from the communities they are members of and so the graph and the attributes are generated *jointly* by some underlying unknown community structure. Specifically the attributes are assumed to be binary (present or not present) and are generated according to a Bernoulli process:

$$X_{uk} \sim \mathcal{B}\left(Q_k\right) \tag{2}$$

where $Q_k = 1/\left(1 + \prod_{c \in C} \exp(-W_{kc}F_{uc})\right)$, W_{kc} is a weight matrix $\in \mathbb{R}^{N \times |C|}$,[6] which defines the strength of connection between the N attributes and the $|C|$ communities. W_{kc} is central to the model and is a set of logistic model parameters which – together with the number of communities, $|C|$ – forms the set of unknown parameters for the model. Parameter estimation is achieved by maximising the likelihood of the observed graph (i.e. the observed connections) and the observed attribute values given the membership potentials and weight matrix. An inference algorithm is given in [23].

---

[6] There is also a bias term W_0 which has an important role. We set this to –10; otherwise if someone has a community affiliation of zero, $F_u = 0$, Q_k has probability $\frac{1}{2}$.

Table 3. Q_K for 12 (combined) communities and the percentage of the classed population in the community using 10 attributes (X marks both attributes valid).

Attribute	M	F	Tr	GQ	Str8	Bi	Gay	Dom	Sub	Switch	%
SC1	0.0	0.0	0.0	1.0	1.0	1.0	0.0	0.0	1.0	1.0	2.90
SC2	1.0	0.0	0.0	X	0.0	X	X	0.0	1.0	0.0	2.70
SC3	0.0	1.0	0.0	0.0	1.0	1.0	0.0	X	X	X	21.00
SC4	0.0	1.0	0.0	0.0	1.0	1.0	1.0	0.0	0.0	X	16.42
SC5	0.0	1.0	0.0	0.0	0.0	0.0	1.0	1.0	1.0	1.0	6.36
SC6	0.0	1.0	0.0	1.0	1.0	0.0	0.0	X	X	X	48.10
SC7	0.0	1.0	0.0	1.0	1.0	X	X	0.0	0.0	X	10.16
SC8	0.0	0.0	1.0	1.0	1.0	1.0	0.0	0.0	0.0	1.0	3.61
SC9	1.0	1.0	0.0	0.0	0.0	X	X	X	X	X	11.24
SC10	1.0	1.0	0.0	1.0	X	X	0.0	0.0	0.0	X	3.59
SC11	0.0	1.0	1.0	0.0	1.0	1.0	1.0	0.0	0.0	0.0	8.02
SC12	0.0	1.0	1.0	1.0	1.0	X	0.0	0.0	0.0	X	8.25

The data used for homophilic community detection consists of the main component of the network together with the attributes {*Male, Female, Trans, GQ*} together with orientations {*Straight, Bisexual, Gay*} and roles {*submissive, dominant, switch*} for a total of 10 binary attributes. We found that, due to large imbalance in the size of communities, we needed to generate a large number of communities before observing the niche communities (e.g. trans and gay). Generating communities varying $|C|$ from 1 to 50, we observed the detected communities persist as $|C|$ grows or split into two communities (i.e. as $|C|$ increases we uncover a natural hierarchy). Table 3 shows the attribute probabilities for each community, specifically: $Q_k|_{F_u=10}$. For analysis we have grouped these communities into *Super-Communities* (SC's) based on common attributes.

The first five SC's are for a single gender alone (GQ, cis male, and cis female; SC3 and SC4, SC5). SC2 consists of only bi or gay males, mostly gay males, and the absence of any straight male (alone) group is very apparent. SC3 consists of straight and bi (cis) females, SC4; all cis females, and SC5; only gay females (i.e. lesbian). SC6 consists mainly of cis females (GQ account for only 1% of the population.). There is therefore very strong evidence of many communities of (i.e. complex) female to female interaction that is largely platonic. In SC8 the transgender community appears clearly. SC10 is the only community to contain straight (cis) males and straight females together and accounts for only 3.6% of those classified. SC11 and SC12 shows interaction between cis females and trans members which accounts for at least 8% of those classified. The above shows complex interactions between the members, some are expected (trans and gay specific communities) while the absence of straight males from all but a small community is stark (see Conclusion).

5 Conclusion

We conducted the first in-depth study of a large fetish community, exploring not only the attributes of users but also analysing the rich structures behind the social network of community members.

The importance of the diversity of online sexual contacts is of growing importance [3] and several studies have looked at how it effecting our sexuality [5]. The studied fetish network is a valuable source of information as it is neither a dating website nor a standard OSN. Rather, it is an OSN where the sexual market aspects of the network have been amplified. The picture that emerges is one of complex hetero and homo-philic interacting communities and in addition, people that form friendships which are purely platonic. We successfully extracted and analysed homophilic relations and communities from the network employing the CESNA community detection algorithm, paving the way for further studies on homophilic and heterophilic communities. The dearth of straight males in homophilic communities is an interesting phenomenon and might indicate that straight women in particular are on the site for platonic social reasons more than other groups. Note this does not mean that *all* straight men are not interested in platonic relationships; rather every straight man interested in *only* sexual connections is a counter-example to the others and there is no extra information (one could imagine for example "*platonic* straight male") to discriminate the two groups. In future work we will further investigate and stochastically model the complex community structures behind the social network, including additional profile information such as freely chosen tags by the users.

References

1. Buss, D.M.: The Evolution of Desire: Strategies of Human Mating. Basic Books, New York (2003)
2. Cha, M., Benevenuto, F., Haddadi, H., Gummadi, K.: The world of connections and information flow in Twitter. IEEE Trans. Syst. Man Cybern. Part A: Syst. Hum. **42**(4), 991–998 (2012)
3. Cooper, A., Morahan-Martin, J., Mathy, R.M., Maheu, M.: Toward an increased understanding of user demographics in online sexual activities. J. Sex Marital Ther. **28**(2), 105–129 (2002). pMID: 11894795
4. Dawson, S.J., Bannerman, B.A., Lalumière, M.L.: Paraphilic interests: an examination of sex differences in a nonclinical sample. Sex. Abuse: J. Res. Treat. (2014)
5. Dring, N.M.: The internets impact on sexuality: a critical review of 15 years of research. Comput. Hum. Behav. **25**(5), 1089–1101 (2009). Including the special issue: design patterns for augmenting e-learning experiences
6. Easley, D., Kleinberg, J.: Networks, Crowds, and Markets: Reasoning About a Highly Connected World. Cambridge University Press, Cambridge (2010). http://www.cs.cornell.edu/home/kleinber/networks-book/
7. Fay, D., Haddadi, H., Thomason, A., Moore, A.W., Mortier, R., Jamakovic, A., Uhlig, S., Rio, M.: Weighted spectral distribution for internet topology analysis: theory and applications. IEEE/ACM Trans. Networking **18**(1), 164–176 (2010)

8. Haddadi, H., Fay, D., Uhlig, S., Moore, A., Mortier, R., Jamakovic, A.: Mixing biases: structural changes in the AS topology evolution. In: Ricciato, F., Mellia, M., Biersack, E. (eds.) TMA 2010. LNCS, vol. 6003, pp. 32–45. Springer, Heidelberg (2010)

9. Haddadi, H., Fay, D., Uhlig, S., Moore, A., Mortier, R., Jamakovic, A., Rio, M.: Tuning topology generators using spectral distributions. In: Kounev, S., Gorton, I., Sachs, K. (eds.) SIPEW 2008. LNCS, vol. 5119, pp. 154–173. Springer, Heidelberg (2008)

10. Joyal, C.C., Cossette, A., Lapierre, V.: What exactly is an unusual sexual fantasy? J. Sex. Med. **12**(2), 328–340 (2015)

11. Kunegis, J., Gröner, G., Gottron, T.: Online dating recommender systems: the split-complex number approach. In: Proceedings of Workshop on Recommender Systems and the Social Web, pp. 37–44 (2012)

12. Laumann, E.: The Sexual Organization of the City. Studies in Communication, Media, and Public Opinion. University of Chicago Press, Chicago (2004). http://books.google.com.qa/books?id=Lsg86vinpakC

13. Lewis, A.: Just your average Joe: getting to know a lifestyle kinkster. Counselling Aust. **11**(2) (2012)

14. Mislove, A., Marcon, M., Gummadi, K.P., Druschel, P., Bhattacharjee, B.: Measurement and analysis of online social networks. In: Proceedings of the 7th ACM SIGCOMM Conference on Internet Measurement, IMC 2007, pp. 29–42. ACM, New York (2007). http://doi.acm.org/10.1145/1298306.1298311

15. Mollenhorst, G., Vlker, B., Flap, H.: Social contexts and personal relationships: the effect of meeting opportunities on similarity for relationships of different strength. Soc. Netw. **30**(1), 60–68 (2008)

16. Mrozewski, T.: How do kinky people know what they know? The information behaviour of BDSM practitioners (2013). http://fims-grc.fims.uwo.ca/wp-content/uploads/2013/06/LIS9411-9412_Mrozewski.pdf

17. Niekamp, A.M., Mercken, L.A., Hoebe, C.J., Dukers-Muijrers, N.H.: A sexual affiliation network of swingers, heterosexuals practicing risk behaviours that potentiate the spread of sexually transmitted infections: a two-mode approach. Soc. Netw. **35**(2), 223–236 (2013). Special issue on advances in Two-mode social networks

18. Richters, J., de Visser, R.O., Rissel, C., Grulich, A., Smith, A.: Demographic and psychosocial features of participants in Bondage and Discipline, Sadomasochism or Dominance and Submission (BDSM): data from a national survey. J. Sex. Med. **5**(7), 1660–1668 (2008)

19. Schneider, J.P.: A qualitative study of cybersex participants: gender differences, recovery issues, and implications for therapists. Sex. Addict. Compulsivity: J. Treat. Prev. **7**(4), 249–278 (2000)

20. Singla, A., Weber, I.: Camera brand congruence in the flickr social graph. In: Proceedings of the Second ACM International Conference on Web Search and Data Mining, WSDM 2009, pp. 252–261. ACM, New York (2009). http://doi.acm.org/10.1145/1498759.1498834

21. Takac, L., Zabovsky, M.: Data analysis in public social networks. In: International Scientific Conference and International Workshop Present Day Trends of Innovations, May 2012

22. Turner, J.: A Theory of Social Interaction. Polity Press, Oxford (1988). http://books.google.ie/books?id=LB4EJwAACAAJ

23. Yang, J., McAuley, J.J., Leskovec, J.: Community detection in networks with node attributes. In: International Conference on Data Mining (2013)

Synergy Landscapes: A Multilayer Network for Collaboration in Biological Research

Konstantin Kuzmin[1]([✉]), Christopher Gaiteri[2],
and Boleslaw K. Szymanski[1,3]

[1] Network Science and Engineering Center, Rensselaer Polytechnic Institute,
Troy, NY 12180, USA
{kuzmik,szymab}@rpi.edu
[2] Rush University Medical Center, Rush University, Chicago, IL 60612, USA
gaiteri@gmail.com
[3] Społeczna Akademia Nauk, Lodz, Poland

Abstract. Physical interactions among molecules, cells, and tissues influence research in biology. While conferences and departments are created to study these interactions, previous attempts to understand the large-scale organization of science have only focused on social relationships among scientists. Here, we combine the structure of molecular interaction networks with other science networks, such as coauthorship networks, for a more complete representation of the interests and relationships that determine the direction and impact of research. This multilayer network that we call *Synergy Landscapes* will allow us to identify broad patterns of scientific research, and in particular factors that predict innovative and high-impact research. Synergy Landscapes also will dynamically track research trends in a customized framework that informs scientists of research on molecules which are relevant to their core research areas. This will facilitate collaborations that would otherwise be difficult to produce and which mirror the natural organization of biological systems.

Keywords: Multilayer networks · Collaboration networks · Molecular networks

1 Introduction

Biologists frequently have a deep understanding of the experimental and disease relevance of specific molecules. In contrast to the historical emphasis on developing highly specific knowledge, omics technologies, which can measure several thousands molecular features simultaneously, have increased the breadth of knowledge about the molecular interactions that carry out biological functions. It is challenging to simultaneously perform detailed research on a core topic of interest and also understand the relevance of hundreds of molecules that are connected to this core via molecular networks. Collaboration enables combining expertise among researchers and conducting experiments that are both

© Springer International Publishing Switzerland 2016
A. Wierzbicki et al. (Eds.): NetSci-X 2016, LNCS 9564, pp. 205–212, 2016.
DOI: 10.1007/978-3-319-28361-6_18

highly detailed and reflect the new information in omics data. Yet, finding relevant researchers to create synergistic effects is challenging when a single molecule may be relevant to many biological processes, each of which has its own complexity and nomenclature. Furthermore, the omics technologies that assess these interactions are evolving and growing, creating complex molecular networks that link researcher interests, but are rarely used in guiding researchers to beneficial collaborations.

We introduce a novel multilayer network approach to fostering innovation and collaboration among bio-medical researchers. The initial components of our multilayer networks are: (i) collaboration networks of bio-medical coauthors, (ii) networks of molecules interacting in bio-processes and papers describing them, and (iii) networks of bio-processes involved in different diseases.

The Synergy Landscapes project aims to combine those networks to establish new collaborative links between researchers, molecules, and diseases. This will enable, for example, identifying researchers that may collaborate in previously unknown ways to address complex diseases and tremendously impacting medical innovation and efficient disease research. The total effect will be synergistic, beyond a simple sum of the components.

2   Related Work

The idea of combining several different but related datasets into a single multilayer network is widely used in complex systems. The applications are mostly found in sociology and social information systems. A comprehensive review by Boccaletti et al. [1] contains a detailed description of the properties and structural and dynamic organization of networks that represent different relationships as layers. Such networks have shown utility in economics, technical systems, ecology, biology and psychology. We include molecular interaction networks as a novel layer in Synergy Landscapes. These networks originate from many experimental sources and model organisms. In many omics analyses it is now standard to project results into these networks structures, to identify the overall functional role of the results or additional related molecules. Many free and commercial online tools are available for this purpose (e.g., [3,4]). At the same time, methodologically related studies of coauthorship and human social networks have emphasized the relevance of network structure in determining patterns of collaboration [5]. Despite similar goals of understanding the scientific relevance of groups in molecular and social networks, the two approaches have never been fused to combine molecules and people in an integrated network space as shown in Fig. 1.

3   Synergy Landscape Concept and Use

Here, we introduce a unified solution to the dual problem of diverse causes of complex diseases and barriers in scientific collaboration. Our idea is that if molecules A and B interact, the researchers who study molecule A could benefit from interacting with those who study molecule B. The combined effect is achieved by

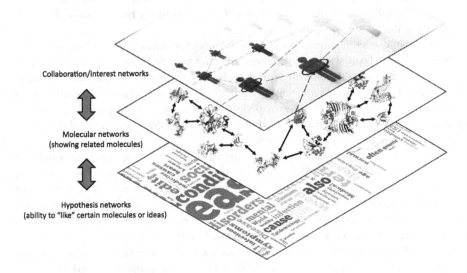

Fig. 1. Multilayer synergy network illustrating types of networks merged to form the basis of Synergy Landscapes. Network is prepopulated with molecular interests of specific scientists based on published papers in Scopus. Molecular interactions are determined from multiple sources. Specific molecular networks that are most relevant to the field of study of particular researchers can be selected as the basis for calculating researcher–researcher distances.

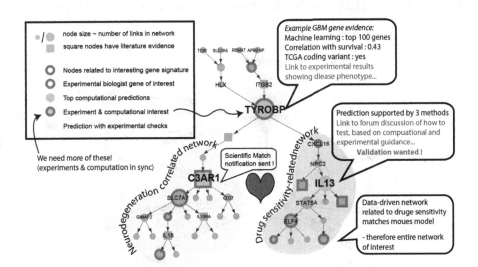

Fig. 2. An example of how molecular entities are annotated with human interests in Synergy Landscapes.

connecting researchers and resources through the structure of molecular interactions. Figure 2 shows how a synergy network combines relationships between
molecules, ideas, and people.

The first use we consider is designed around the ways a typical scientist can
utilize Synergy Landscapes to increase funding and publications. The ultimate
objective is to suggest customized, optimal research directions and collaborators
for users. The Synergy Landscapes multilayer network will be accessible as a
website searchable for molecules or people based on a user supplied list of query
terms. The output will resemble a personalized newsfeed based on the specific
interests of the user, as shown in Fig. 3.

The search engine will traverse edges in all three component networks in
paths that enable discovery of "neighboring" scientists, ideas, and resources.
Multiple molecular networks can be used to individually or collectively compute
researcher–researcher distances and to predict research synergy. As new omics
resources become available they will facilitate customized research landscapes
and updated distances between researchers. For instance, researchers who primarily utilize *drosophila* will find molecular interactions in that system most relevant to guiding them to collaborators by selecting a *drosophila*-based molecular
network and then surveying the landscape around them. Adding new interaction
knowledge to Synergy Landscapes acts like a molecular wormhole — bringing
some researchers who were previously distant into close contact.

To detect less obvious potential collaborators who could contribute to highly
innovative research we will classify adjacent researchers into those who are within
the user's community (defined by co-authorship clusters or location) vs. those
who link to other research communities. The latter, which can be highlighted in
the user interface (UI), may be ideal partners for interdisciplinary projects.

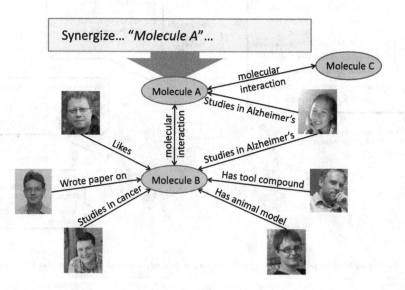

Fig. 3. Example of search functionality on Synergy Landscapes. The graphical output
emphasizes underlying molecular networks.

The Synergy Landscapes will also provide data to thoroughly study patterns of innovation and significance in research, and then to facilitate high-impact findings. Thanks to the availability of date-stamped and cross-referenced publications, it is possible to track the origin of influential trends in terms of how they are positioned in the molecular and coauthorship networks. This enables predicting topics and pairs or groups of researchers who are likely to collaboratively produce valuable findings. When such a matching is predicted, users can receive notifications whenever a "nearby" publication appears meaning that potential collaboration can result in a high-impact paper.

Institutions can utilize the hybrid network of researchers and molecules to improve efficiency and to organize collaborations across thousands of researchers. Synergy Landscapes creates an expansive definition of the molecules and humans that are relevant to a particular topic. In practice, by identifying their core molecules of interest, conference organizers can identify a radius of related researchers, even when those researchers do not formally belong to the field nor study molecules that are traditionally associated with the field. In this way conference organizers can recruit a diverse yet appropriate set of conference presenters. Using Synergy Landscapes, the participants will be able to meet other people who are likely to collaborate on future projects.

Another use of Synergy Landscapes is ranking job applicants based on their average distance in the molecular landscapes from all researchers currently on the team. Similarly, the connectivity of potential hires to two teams can be calculated in Synergy Landscapes. This provides a quantitative measure of the likelihood of future collaboration patterns that fulfill team objectives.

4   Architecture

Synergy Landscapes is designed to follow a multi-tier architecture model in order to separate presentation (UI), application processing, and data manipulation from each other. Moreover, each layer communicates with other layers using well-defined standardized protocols. Therefore, the internal implementation of each layer can be changed without affecting any other layers or requiring any changes in other parts of the system. Such an approach provides excellent scalability and enables easy expansion through the modular structure of its components.

The Synergy Landscapes architecture is discussed in the context of a typical expected query. One example is searching for authors working on molecule m who also worked on diseases d_i and d_j and another is finding diseases that were studied by researchers who considered molecule m in their publications. The architecture should also enable more complex queries. For example, one can start with some molecule m_i and find all diseases with which m_i has been associated in past publications. Then it would be possible to find if some other molecules m_j and m_k have ever been studied with those diseases and if so what authors and publications were involved. Finally, it can be determined if a pair of molecules m_i and m_j is associated with different diseases and who were the experts who described those reactions in their publications. The basic molecular network should be extensible — for instance by introducing additional layers associated with medications and their relationships with molecules and diseases. Similarly, the architecture should support user-selected subsets of networks that reflect the relationships most relevant to their research interests. The architecture described below supports these expected queries in a scalable extensible framework.

Synergy Landscapes obtains its data from the Scopus database. According to the study by Falagas et al. [2] which compares PubMed, Scopus, Web of Science, and Google Scholar, Scopus offers about 20 % more citation coverage than Web of Science and more consistent search results than Google Scholar. In addition, Scopus provides a convenient API in a form of RESTful services which can be queried by user code.

User queries are executed against the multilayer network which is gradually built layer by layer. First, a network of molecules is created. The initial list of names and aliases of molecules is processed into a network where each unique molecule is represented as a node, and edges correspond to relations between molecules. Although some edge information can be inferred from the initial list of molecules, the major part of the connectivity information corresponds to the relations which are not described by the initial data and which we would like to discover through our synergistic process. Following the same procedure that was used to create the network of molecules, additional layers can be added (e.g., based on the list of diseases) to enrich our multilayer network and provide greater flexibility in our ability to generate subsequent layers. For instance, we might consider not only publications related to certain molecules but also those which mention specific diseases.

Publication data are used as the source for the second group of layers in our multilayer network. The source publication data are extracted from an existing source or sources based on a list of search terms which are already available from layers of molecules, diseases, etc. As a result, several network layers can be generated from this data.

First, the publication layer of the network is generated with nodes representing publications and edges connecting publications which are related in a certain way (e.g., which are dedicated to the same molecule or disease). At this point there are no edges in this layer as relations are to be determined after processing subsequent layers and discovering associations between different parts of the network. Similarly to the publications layer, a layer of grants is also created. Since the publication layer is created from the molecule layer and the disease layer, the publication–molecule and publication–disease cross-layers are easy to build.

For instance, in a publication–molecule cross-layer, an edge connects a certain molecule to the publications which are known to refer to this molecule. Likewise, a publication–disease layer links diseases with publications dedicated to them. Such cross-layers represent layers consisting entirely of edges. Moreover, instead of connecting nodes of a single underlying node set, the edges in cross-layers go "vertically" across any two different layers, effectively "stitching" them together. Therefore, cross-layers are fundamental entities in the multilayer network since they facilitate "vertical" connectivity between layers and allow network analysis tools to traverse the whole stack of layers rather than being trapped in any single one of them. In a wider context, a cross-layer with two corresponding node sets can be regarded as a separate bipartite network linking two different entities (publications and molecules, authors and diseases, etc.)

An additional dimension to the publication layer is created by utilizing the publication–topic association. This layer is another example of a layer using the same node set as some other layer or layers (in this case, it is the set of publications) but constructs a completely different edge set. In the topic layer, two publications are connected if they share the same subject area classification as declared by the authors and recorded in the underlying publication database. For instance, Scopus provides a codified subject area classification; therefore, publications classification is consistent throughout the database. Each publication can be marked as related to zero or more subject areas. The weight on an edge is determined by the *overlap coefficient* according to the number of common subject area classifications that two publications share. Given the publication node set P, the overlapping coefficient (also known as the Szymkiewicz–Simpson coefficient [6]) is defined by (1) as follows:

$$w(p_i, p_j) = \frac{\left| SA_{p_i} \cap SA_{p_j} \right|}{min(\left| SA_{p_i} \right|, \left| SA_{p_j} \right|)} \tag{1}$$

where $p_i \in P$ and $p_j \in P$ are two publication nodes, and SA_{p_i} and SA_{p_j} are the sets of subject area classifications of the corresponding publications. A layer which links publications with index terms (index terms layer) is created following the same approach as for the topic layer.

Then, since each publication or grant also lists authors, the author and collaboration networks are naturally created from the same data used for the publication layer. For this layer, nodes represent authors and weighted edges connect authors who have collaborated on at least one publication or grant proposal. A publication–author cross-layer is also created. It consists of unweighted undirected edges linking publications with their authors.

Finally, a citations dataset is the third network layer extracted from the publication data. A citation layer contains only directed edges which connect nodes from the underlying publications. An edge from publication i to publication j is added to the layer if publication i cites publication j. Thus, the layer represents a "cites" relationship.

Using nodes from the publication layer, the author layer, the citation layer, and the publication–author cross-layer, an author citation layer is created. Although derived, this layer provides a convenient way of establishing links between different authors who cite the work of others. The author citation layer is comprised of edges only, using nodes from the author layer as its nodes. There is an edge from person i to another person j if and only if author i has ever cited any publication which was authored by j. Given the sets of nodes of authors A and publications P, the weight of an edge in the author citation layer is determined by the fraction of the number of times author i cited author j in their publications to the total number of times author i cited other authors' work, as given by (2):

$$w(a_i, a_j) = \frac{|\{p \in \mathcal{PC}_{a_i} | a_j \in \mathcal{A}_p\}|}{\sum_{p \in \mathcal{PC}_{a_i}} |\mathcal{A}_p|} \tag{2}$$

where $a_i \in A$ and $a_j \in A$ are two author nodes, $\mathcal{PC}_{a_i} \subseteq P$ is the set of all publications cited by a_i, $\mathcal{A}_p \subseteq A$ is the set of authors of publication p.

Once all the layers have been created, we can start querying our multilayer network to provide useful information about authors, molecules, diseases, and publications. The result of each query can be saved as a set which, in turn, can be used for subsequent queries. Thus, Synergy Landscapes can provide meaningful answers to complicated questions by combining the data from network layers with additional filtering and grouping capabilities of reusable queries.

5   Conclusions and Future Directions

Molecular networks play an increasing role in disease research. They are also central to Synergy Landscapes which uses them to facilitate scientific results, accelerate research, and foster interdisciplinary collaborations. These capabilities are directly useful to scientists but also essential for understanding consistent social and molecular features of the most innovative and cited scientific projects. Because Synergy Landscapes is the first hybrid human–molecular network, it opens the doors to improved higher-level management and distribution of scientific resources. For instance, granting institutions may use Synergy Landscapes to study the impact of their funds and their distribution across the community structure around their topics of interest. In this way, not only can scientists respond to incentives, but the incentives themselves can be created to achieve certain objectives in light of the current distribution of scientific interest and resources.

References

1. Boccaletti, S., Bianconi, G., Criado, R., Del Genio, C.I., Gómez-Gardeñes, J., Romance, M., Sendina-Nadal, I., Wang, Z., Zanin, M.: The structure and dynamics of multilayer networks. Phys. Rep. **544**(1), 1–122 (2014)
2. Falagas, M.E., Pitsouni, E.I., Malietzis, G.A., Pappas, G.: Comparison of PubMed, Scopus, Web of Science, and Google Scholar: strengths and weaknesses. FASEB J. **22**(2), 338–342 (2008)
3. Krämer, A., Green, J., Pollard, J., Tugendreich, S.: Causal analysis approaches in ingenuity pathway analysis. Bioinformatics **30**(4), 523–530 (2014)
4. Mostafavi, S., Ray, D., Warde-Farley, D., Grouios, C., Morris, Q., et al.: Genemania: a real-time multiple association network integration algorithm for predicting gene function. Genome Biol. **9**(Suppl 1), S4 (2008)
5. Newman, M.E.: Coauthorship networks and patterns of scientific collaboration. Proc. Nat. Acad. Sci. **101**(suppl 1), 5200–5205 (2004)
6. Simpson, G.G.: Notes on the measurement of faunal resemblance. Am. J. Sci. **258**(2), 300–311 (1960)

Author Index

Printed in the United States
by Baker & Taylor

Printed in the United States
By Bookmasters